BRJN

2

Royal Fe
on the

Overlord, Books 3 – 6

The Triumph of Light
1944 – 45

An Epic Poem

NICHOLAS HAGGER

ELEMENT
Shaftesbury, Dorset ● Rockport, Massachusetts
Brisbane, Queensland

First published in Great Britain in 1996 by
Element Books Limited
Shaftesbury, Dorset SP7 8BP

Published in the USA in 1996 by
Element Books, Inc.
PO Box 830, Rockport, MA 01966

Published in Australia in 1996 by
Element Books Limited
for Jacaranda Wiley Limited
33 Park Road, Milton, Brisbane 4064

Cover illustration by David Woodroffe
Cover design by Max Fairbrother
Design by Alison Goldsmith
Typeset by Wendy Murdoch
Printed and bound in Great Britain by
Hartnolls Limited, Bodmin, Cornwall

British Library Cataloguing in Publication
data available

Library of Congress Cataloging in Publication
data available

ISBN 1–85230–787–0

By the same author

The Fire and the Stones
A Mystic Way
Overlord
Selected Poems
A Smell of Leaves and Summer
A Spade Fresh With Mud
The Warlords
The Universe and the Light
A White Radiance

SUMMARY AND INDEX OF LINE NUMBERS

BOOK 3: THE GERMAN ARMY IS ENCIRCLED AND ROUTED

BOOK 4: THE ALLIES ARE REPULSED

BOOK 5: THE JEWS REVOLT AND STOP THE HOLOCAUST

PREFACE
TO OVERLORD, BOOKS 3-6

Books 3-6 of *Overlord* carry the story of Eisenhower's conflict with Hitler forward through Falaise, Arnhem, Auschwitz and the Ardennes. I visited each of these places and areas, and all the places in the invocations, in 1994 or 1995, and as my interpretation of events is distinctive, it is important that I should draw attention to some of the corroborating sources, particularly those I have not mentioned in my *Preface to Overlord, books 1 and 2*.

My sources for the occult roots of Nazism (books 3 and 5) include some books that are now hard to find. The suggestion that Hitler sold his soul to the Devil in a Faustian pact in 1942 nearly twenty-five years after Eckart's Satanic Annunciation can be found in a number of books, for example Nigel Pennick's *Hitler's Secret Sciences, His Quest for the Hidden Knowledge of the Ancients*, p175. Pennick also sees the SS's genocide as a State act of black magic, as does Gerald Suster in *Hitler, Black Magician*. Nazi links to the Fehme can be found in Paul Winkler's *The Thousand-Year Conspiracy: Secret Germany Behind the Mask*. Details of Hitler's Rosicrucianism (and Stalin's) and information on Rosicrucianism's Satanic aspects (for example, that the rose round the cross represents the serpent, Lucifer) can be found in Volume 1 of John Daniel's *Scarlet and the Beast, a History of the War between English and French Freemasonry*, which chronicles the eight hundred year old war between the Priory of Sion and its English Rosicrucian and Illuminati descendants associated with the Grand Lodge on the one hand, and (its creation) the French Knights Templar and their descendants associated with the Grand Orient on the other hand. Daniel's book sees Hitler as a product of the Priory of Sion and English Freemasonry, which financed him to destroy French Freemasonry. Hitler was originally a member of his teacher Lanz's Rosicrucian Order of the New Temple, and his interest in Templar-related Catharism can be corroborated in Jean-Michel Angebert's *The Occult and the Third Reich, The Mystical Origins of Nazism and the Search for the Holy Grail*.

Hitler's interest in the Grail and Himmler's search for the Grail in Montségur on his behalf (which is referred to in an epic digression in book 5) can be found in Col. Buechner's *Emerald Cup, The Quest of SS Lt Otto Rahn of the Third Reich*. Himmler's fascination with the Holy Lance and details of the rituals of the Knights of the Holy Lance at Wewelsburg can be found in Col. Buechner and Capt. Bernhart's *Adolf Hitler and the Secrets of the Holy Lance*. Details of Himmler's SS Headquarters at Schloss Wewelsburg can be found in the German *Wewelsburg, Kult-und Terrorstätte der SS*.

I have drawn on many sources for the passages involving Eisenhower, Montgomery and SHAEF (books 3-6). While I have been at pains to ground all their conversations in the correct historical time and place, I have used poetic licence in setting Christ's approach to Eisenhower on Mont-St.-Michel (book 3). Shortly after this imaginary episode Eisenhower *did* have a room overlooking Mont-St.-Michel, although I have again used poetic licence in giving him alternative visions of the future there (book 4). By contrast, Patton's prayer (book 6) is almost exactly as recorded. Some of the more minute details of the Arnhem operation (book 4) can be found in Urquhart's *Arnhem*, and some vivid details of the battle round Bastogne (book 6) can be found in Guy Franz Arend's *The Battle for Bastogne*.

The bare facts of Dorebus's October 7th revolt of the Jews in Auschwitz (book 5) are in Danuta Czech's *Auschwitz Chronicle 1939-45*, pp 724-9 and p775 (the final hangings), and in Martin Gilbert's *The Holocaust, The Jewish Tragedy*. An eye-witness view, which is not reliable as regards dates and times, is in Dr Miklos Nyiszli's *Auschwitz, A Doctor's Eye-Witness Account*. I have also drawn on Höss, Broad and Kremer's *KL Auschwitz Seen by the SS* (State Museum in Oswiecim), Swiebocka, Webber and Wibach's *Auschwitz, A History in Photographs* and Swiebocki (sic) and Bujak's *Auschwitz, Voices from the Ground*. There is a picture of Roza Robota in Michael Berenbaum's *The World Must Know, The History of the Holocaust as Told in the United States Holocaust Memorial Museum*. Evidence for Himmler's ending of the Holocaust soon after the October 7th revolt can be found in Martin Gilbert's *Auschwitz and the Allies,* ch 33 and Heinz Höhne's *The Order of the Death's Head, The Story of Hitler's SS*, ch 18.

My strict blank verse allows for certain two-syllable words to be scanned as one syllable where contemporary pronunciation usage permits ("fuel", "seventh", "iron", "given", "power"), and for certain three-syllable words to be scanned as two syllables ("conference", "personal", "senior", "Frederick", "serious", "travelling", "Hungary", "dangerous", "victory", "prisoners"); and for some five-syllable words to be scanned as four syllables ("crematoria"). Elision is allowed ("the offensive", "the Americans").

As with all epic, despite the grounding of the story in historical fact the poem is essentially a work of imagination. My imagination has taken known characters and recreated and presented them in a form that seeks to make sense of the worst horror of our time and locate its origins in the Satanic outlook and influence of certain occult secret societies within the neo-Illuminatist ambience of Rosicrucianism, to which both Hitler and Himmler belonged. I am now half-way through my epic, and am still in the process of resolving the long quarrel with myself between the nightmare of the worst evil and a vision of the highest order and good, and explaining how if all is One there can be a force of evil that can be reconciled with the underlying unity. I know that the horror of the Holocaust will be justified and transcended in the final Paradisal vision of the poem.

5th January 1996

~ BOOK 3 ~

THE GERMAN ARMY IS ENCIRCLED
AND ROUTED

O Goethe, whose *Werther*, penned in Frankfurt,
Brought in the dawn of the Romantic Age,
Who came to Weimar, to this Garden House
(Two down, four up), still under Weishaupt's spell,
Rejecting monarchy and religion
For Lucifer; then to this cobbled square
Where you received Schiller, Hegel and Fichte
In the Juno Room, satyrs over doors,
And in your study, elbows on table,
Cheeks in your hands, your library nearby,
Your quill before you, feet on wooden boards,
Your rocks and stones proclaiming your science,
Gazed out at grass and rejected your past,
Turned your back on storm und drang, and quietly
Wrote of Faust (your young self), who sold his soul
To Mephistopheles (Weishaupt), and made
A personal statement from Marlowe's theme,
Mindful how Weishaupt named you Abaris
After the Hyperborean Druid-priest
Apollo sent to seek Pythagoras,
And in your defence of Faust's inquiring
Quest for knowledge (Angels saying "He who
Exerts himself in constant striving, him
Can we save") justified Faust – and yourself;
An ex-Illuminatus wiser now
And though still an initiate who used
The Gnostic system of Basilides
(Of intermediate worlds, evil angels,
Spirits of spheres, stars, winds, separating
Man from God, Who can only intervene
In the cosmos from without by sending
Divine Spirit, the Logos; of Gnosis)
And though your German Romanticism
Inspired a Gnostic, Cathar revival,
Not interested in the two Schegels,
Not aware in seventeen ninety-seven
That Wordsworth was in Breide Street, Goslar,
The Holy Roman Empire's treasure-chest
With more old houses than any other

5

10

15

20

25

30

35

1

German town, in a medieval dream,
Snowed up the other side of Mount Brocken
(Which you climbed), writing of skaters, seeing
The Harz mountains imposed upon his lakes;
Not aware either that in Göttingen
Your side of Brocken, which he climbed three times,
Coleridge lived in Weender Street and walked
To the University and studied
German metaphysics and literature
And influenced Carlyle, whom Hitler read;
Not aware English Romanticism
Had come to learn from Germany, and you;
Who quietly worked on *Faust* until you died
In this bedroom next to your study, so
Faust II was not found till after your death,
Locked up in the light poplar cabinet,
Showing you wrote it for yourself, not cash –
O Goethe, help my Faustian theme and show
How Hitler, who had sold his soul to rule
The world and sacrificed a race's blood,
Found he was a Faustian hero who
Was cheated by his Mephistopheles
And, though promised the earth, received nothing
Like a penniless nephew who has worked
To look after a sick landed uncle
And was left out of his will when he died
And faces a life of debt and defeat.

Tell, Muse, of Hitler's esoteric roots,
Of his Gnostic Manichaean beliefs,
How he looked back to the Cathar "Pure Ones",
And how he came to Lucifer, his Lord,
How he was possessed by the Devil and
Believed he had sided with Light and good.
Tell how Gnosis, from hidden Aryan source,
Flowed into the Egyptians and the Greeks,
And, like a stream that runs underground, is
Gone and rises again, entered the Church
And then was laid under an interdict
With the pagan Neo-Platonist schools,
And in the Middle Ages resurfaced
In Catharism, was confluent with
Templarism (which looked east and followed
Satanism, the goat head Baphomet,
Rejecting Sion's Merovingian

Worship of Christ), and was again suppressed,
85 And trickled through Rosicrucianism
And through Weishaupt's Illuminated Ones,
And resurfaced yet again at the end
Of the nineteenth century in many groups,
When its renewal dimpled through Nazism.
90 The gnosis of Aryan Zoroaster
And of Mani – taken from missing stone
Tablets, the Aryan Grail of the lost First
Masters and the Central Asian Essenes –
Thus came down as conflict between good blond
95 Aryan sun-worshippers and evil
Dark-haired Semitic moon-worshippers to
The dualist Cathars of Languedoc.
Montségur castle perched high on a crag,
An eyrie on the Albigensian
100 Mount Tabor, eagle's nest, was not a fort
But a pentagonal Manichaean
Temple aligned to pagan sun-worship
With underground passages and altar.
Here the "Pure Ones" lived with initiates
105 And the masses. The Nazi structure was
Cathar: Pure Ones or lordly caste at top;
Members of the Nazi Party beneath;
And below them the masses. The Gnostic
Inspiration attributed to man
110 Three known natures: body, soul and spirit;
Body, the abode of the soul; and soul
The abode of spirit. Now the Cathars
Broadened the tradition of Mani and
Rejected sacraments, the cross, the Church
115 And had contempt for the *Old Testament*,
The work of Jews, and held that Jesus was
A Messenger sent directly from God,
A pure spirit, not human; and that there
Is eternal conflict between matter,
120 Which is of the Devil, and pure spirit,
Which is of God. As the earthly realm is
Possessed by Satan, the fallen angel,
The material world will be destroyed
As forecast in St. John's *Apocalypse*,
125 The spirit imprisoned in our earthly
Bodies will return to the Realm of Light,
And the Holy Spirit or Cosmic Christ
Will reign, which Hitler saw as energy

Of Vril. Opposed to the material world,
130 The Cathars were opposed to marriage and
To the eating of meat, as was Hitler.
Their Perfecti, Pure Ones, were robed in black,
And so the SS was a Black Order.
Hitler chose a black swastika or cross
135 As a universal symbol to link
With all the world's religions and magics
As the Thule held, to stress the Cathars' black.
They carried *The Gospel According to
St. John* and held their ceremonies in
140 Fields, woods or houses as at Sachsenhain
Or Externsteine. Hitler saw himself as
A Cathar, pure and chaste; eating no meat,
Unmarried, robed in black, in a cult of
Light, not of magic, in a movement of
145 Nazi Cathars who were taking revenge
Against the Crusaders' evil crusades
Of Simon de Montfort and Eisenhower.
Cathar gnosis flowed to the Templars and
Degenerated into black magic
150 And subversion in the Rosicrucians
And Bavarian Illuminati –
A group formed by the Priory of Sion
And Templars with help from Rosicrucians
Who were controlled by Charles of Lorraine, Grand
155 Master of Sion, who, disguised as (or
Through his agent) Kolmer, on Malta met
Cagliostro (alias Joseph Balsamo),
A Rosicrucian Sionist double-
Agent who joined the Templars, controller
160 Of Weishaupt when he joined the Grand Orient;
Illuminaten Orden of Weishaupt
(Which Goethe misguidedly flirted with,
And, torn, wrote *Faust* out of part retraction),
Who avenged the Templar Grand Master Jacques
165 De Molay, ally of the Cathars. He,
At the stake due to collusion between
Pope Clement the Fifth and Philip the Fair,
Cursed the Papal and Capetian heirs,
And the next day Aumont and seven Templars
170 Disguised as Masons, gathered the ashes,
And the lodges of Naples, Edinburgh,
Paris and Stockholm swore to extinguish
The Capetian line and kill the king,

4

Destroy the Popes' power, preach liberty
175 And found a universal religion.
Many years on, in seventeen eighty-five,
Weishaupt plotted with the Rosicrucians
To kill the Capetian King, Louis
The Sixteenth and was found out when lightning
180 Struck and strewed a lone horseman's documents
And the Court of Bavaria banned his
Illuminati. He posthumously
Fulfilled the oath and achieved revenge when
Freemasons, created as a front for
185 Rosicrucians and Illuminati,
Through Mirabeau, set up the guillotine,
And King Louis' head rolled in sawdust and
A spectator jumped up on the scaffold,
Dipped his fingers in the King's blood and yelled
190 To the crowd, "I baptise you, people, in
The name of liberty and of Jacques de
Molay." Weishaupt's French Revolution aimed
To dethrone the Bourbons and give the French
Throne to the Merovingian Lorraine-
195 Habsburgs, kings of Jerusalem, who were,
After the dethroning, kept out by New
World Order republicanism, which
Targeted the Romanovs and all crowns
That overshadowed the Merovingian
200 Lineage. Illuminati Freemasons
Have still to carry out the Templars' curse
And destroy the Popes' power and end their line.
The Illuminati like the Cathars
Admired the dualistic conflict in
205 St. John's *Gospel*. They greeted each other
By placing their right hand across their eyes,
As if blinded by sunlight, and though they
Took the side of Light and of sun-worship,
They followed Lucifer and his Darkness
210 And were opposed to all religion and
All forms of Freemasonry that grew from
Christianity. They resurfaced in
Eighteen eighty, when Leopold Engel
Reorganised their cell in Dresden as
215 Ordre Rénové des Illuminati
Germaniae (to which Rudolf Steiner
Later belonged) and soon afterwards, when
Engel's centre had moved to Berlin, in

The eighteen eighties Vril Society
220 Or Lodge of Light, linked with Theosophists
And Golden Dawn (founded by Mathers), where
Jacolliot read Swedenborg and Boehme
(A founder of late Rosicrucians) and
St. Martin, the French Illuminist, and
225 Where the faithful bowed down to the sunrise
· In temples that displayed the swastika.
The Illuminati had flowed into
The British Order of the Golden Dawn
Whose Berlin branch started the racist Thule
230 Society, Thule Gesellschaft, formed as
A fragment from the Germanenorden,
The Germanic Order of nineteen twelve,
In the same year by von Sebottendorf
(Who a year before had become leader
235 Of the Order for Bavaria, which
Now displayed the swastika and Wotan)
And a front for: the Illuminatist
Hammer Union, whose leader Fritsch was his
Master, from which came Hans Frank, Governor of
240 Poland; and the *Völkischer Beobachter*,
Bought by Eckart when he received a large
Sum of cash from an unknown source. Good, to
The neo-Gnostic Thule Society,
Was Aryan and evil Semitic,
245 And Eckart its Manichaean high priest.
All Illuminist cults met on neo-
Manichaean ground: Mathers' Hermetic
And magic Order of the Golden Dawn,
Hammer Union of Thor, Wandering
250 Comrades, Seekers of the Grail, which boasted
Rahn, and the Thule, whose guiding principles
Were the same as the NSDAP's
And were shaped by Hitler and Rosenberg.
The main Thule ritual involved a Gold Cup
255 In which a Nordic race drew water from
The Styx, which was used by gods for their oaths.
Hitler's Illuminist, Cathar symbol,
The black swastika, sun-sign, proclaimed he
Was of the Illuminated Ones and
260 Supreme Initiate of Zoroaster
And Mani, Aryan sun-cults, all racist
Anti-Semitic, anti-Christian cults,
And embodied the pagan tradition

Against the Christian one, and once Eckart,
High priest of Mani, Illuminatus,
Devotee of Satan against the Church,
Had opened his initiatory
Centres, Hitler had sought to be possessed
(Believing he could still serve Light and sun)
By Lucifer, Satan, so he in turn
Could possess his people, mesmerise them
With volkish hypnotism and hold sway
Over Europe as the dread Antichrist
Of the *Apocalypse* dear to Cathars.
From the Thule's restatement of the German
Troubadour Wolfram von Eschenbach's Grail
Myth, Hitler took the Germanic legend
Of Charlemagne, and later Frederick
The Second, which was at last applied to
The First Reich of Frederick Barbarossa –
Who was proclaimed Dominus Mundi, or
Master of the World, in Roncaglia fields,
Italy, in eleven fifty-eight –
Of the Emperor asleep in a grotto
In Thuringia (then between the Harz
Mountains and Danube), who will awake to
Proclaim a Thousand Year Reich through Europe
(After the Second Reich of strong Bismarck)
And the supremacy of Germany
Through a Teutonic Messiah's Third Reich,
Awake one day to reign over Europe
As the Antichrist over all peoples.
Possessed with Satan's help by the spirit
Of Frederick Barbarossa, sleep-walking,
Hitler now knew the Emperor would awake.
So like an alder by a dark river
Hitler took root by the flow of Gnosis.

Tell, Muse, how Hitler drew on the Gnosis
That flourished in the Germany he knew
Through secret societies and the arts,
And how he was hailed as the Antichrist
Despite his early feeling for the Church,
Yet how he still lived like an austere monk.
As a boy aged ten at Lambach Abbey
Who led his classmates through the cloister and
Submitted with delight to Offices
In the Abbey, in each corner of which,

Strangely, had been sculpted a swastika,
Hitler received initiation from
310   A newly arrived Cistercian monk, Lanz,
Future founder of the anti-Semite,
Hyperborean periodical
Ostara, who pursued mysterious
Research in the monastery library,
315   Then left, discarded his frock and founded,
In nineteen hundred as von Liebenfels,
A Rosicrucian secret order called
The Order of the New Temple, having
Been initiated as a Templar
320   By a successor of Jacques de Molay.
Lanz stirred the divine in initiates
(Which Lucifer turns into the occult),
And Hitler loved Lambach's quiet arcades,
Its echoing courts and tombs. After his
325   Abbey upbringing Hitler read widely
In Oriental and Tibetan works,
The origin of Christianity,
Anti-Catholic Reformation, Dante,
Goethe and esoteric authors, and,
330   Following Lanz's example, turned to
Rosicrucian anti-Zionist texts,
Heresy and the Cathars, kept in touch
With Lanz, visited his office to buy
Back numbers of his periodical,
335   Became his esoteric pupil and
Found his way to Gnosticism, became
Cathar in his outer life, abstained from
Meat, practised continence like the Pures, swore
An oath of chastity, like Petrarch and
340   Dante had platonic relationships
With Stephani, his niece Geli Raubal,
Who killed herself with a revolver, then
Eva Braun, who in nineteen thirty-five
Tried to shoot herself using a little
345   Revolver she carried in her handbag
(Like Unity Mitford, who shot herself
In the head under his office window).
His disciplined, platonic loves kept his
Channel within pure so he would not lose
350   The supranatural powers that flowed in when
He went into a mediumistic trance
And spoke, or rather let the Antichrist

8

Speak through him. He first glimpsed his destiny
As Antichrist in 1906 when,
355 After Wagner's *Rienzi*, excited,
He climbed out of Linz above fog and saw
The stars and clasped his friend Kubizek's hands,
And spoke about the mandate he would have
To lead the people from servitude to
360 Freedom as a prophet and tribune, and
When Führer held that "it all began there".
He knew of the racist Theosophists'
Gnostic Declaration in nineteen eight,
Which drew on the Sanskrit *Vedas*, not on
365 Hebrew scripture like the Kabbalah. To
The Theosophist Vril Society
Belonged Haushofer, the first Nazi, who
In 1908 in Tibet had met
The Martinist Rosicrucian agent
370 Of the Priory of Sion and the Tsar's
Police, initiator of Stalin,
Gurdjieff, the Russian-Turkish occultist,
Whose Community of Truth Seekers held
There had been one single world religion
375 In ancient times, which fragmented into
Religious beliefs and occult doctrines,
The unfragmented lost experience
Of which they now sought to re-establish –
A groping towards the one religion
380 Of the Light. Haushofer had brought back from
Gurdjieff the notion "Germany Awake"
And passed it to Eckart, from whom Hitler
Would obtain the idea that Germany
Was sleep-walking. An Illuminatist
385 And anti-Semitic Rosicrucian,
Eckart of Vril and Thule and the Nazis
Was a Basilidian Gnostic as
Goethe had been, and as were Rosenberg
And the rest of the Thule Society.
390 To Basilides, chaos was the work
Of the demiurge, a creator who
Imitates God; God animates matter,
Through spirit man can remove himself from
Chaos and possess Light, so Gnosis saves
395 Man, not pistis (faith). Eckart raised spirits:
The Thule Society held séances
Organised by Eckart at which Prince von

9

Thum und Taxis materialised, who had
Been murdered by Communists in nineteen
Nineteen, and had belonged to the Order
Of Bavarian Mystics, which claimed descent
From the Illuminati. Eckart saw
Chaos as Christian debris, escape from
Chaos was through spirit and black magic.
During one of these séances, at which
Gurdjieff was present, Eckart was informed
The German Messiah would soon appear,
A Lord Maitreya, representative
Of the sun-god Lucifer who would reign
For a thousand years and bring in Crowley's
New Age and the millennium. Eckart
Told his fellow adepts in the Thule he
Had received a Satanic announcement
Or Annunciation that he must now
Prepare Hitler as the chosen vessel
Of the Antichrist, the man inspired by
Lucifer to conquer the world and lead
The Aryan race to glory, and set up
A religion of Lucifer that would
Regard Adonai, God of the *Bible*,
As evil, and Lucifer, the black god
Considered evil, as good; Nietzschean
Revaluation of all values that
Replaced the Church's teaching on morals
With prospects that man could become a god
By initiation in Mysteries,
And know good *and* evil, escape Eden
For spiritual advancement to godhood,
Just as fallen Satan transformed himself
Into an angel of Light (deceptive
Idea that lures men into darkness so
The real transforming must be done in Hell).
As Hitler's mentor, Eckart had opened
His seer's initiatory centres
And introduced him to Weishaupt's black art,
Careful to open his occult knowledge
Centre but keep his heart centre closed up.
Hitler took the Thule's "Sieg Heil" greeting and
Its eagle emblem, and made them Nazi;
And later by the "Heil Hitler" greeting
He superimposed his identity
As the Teutonic Messiah on Christ's.

He shaped himself into a god-man who
By Gnosis would lead his people out of
445 Demiurge Jehovah's Christian chaos,
Guided by spirits of dead heroes and
The black art of the Illuminati
And any help Lucifer could give, to
An Aryan Promised Land, as Antichrist.
450 Hitler's neo-pagan philosophy
Turned to black magic, and opposed Steiner's
White magic or anthroposophy. Now
He opened to malefic influences
He could not master, which mastered him, and
455 Creatures – demons, not spirits – fed off his
Creative strength and gave him energy.
In due course his SA broke up Steiner's
Meetings and burned his Goetheaneum
In Dornach and scattered his supporters
460 And caused his broken-hearted early death,
Just as much later his Gestapo smashed
The Steiner movement's offshoot, the White Rose.
The Third Reich was initiated by
Wagner and Nietzsche. Wagner's Lohengrin
465 Sought the Grail at Montsalvat in Heinrich
The Fowler's day. Parsifal found it and
Healed Amfortas the Fisher King's wound with
The Holy Lance, then, crowned King of the Grail,
Held the Emerald Cup on high. Hitler knew
470 Wagner's tunes, which he often whistled, and
The Manichaean Catharism of
The troubadours' Grail. He chose Nuremberg
As the site of Nazi ceremonies
And cathedrals of light because it was
475 The city of the Mastersingers, and
Thought of Wagner as his one precursor.
Nietzsche proclaimed "God is dead", echoing
Wagner's Twilight of the Gods, who had lost
Their divine omnipotence, and offered
480 His man-god substitute, the Superman.
Hitler held that "National Socialism
Is the will to create the Superman"
Through biological selection, and
He himself was the Germanic man-god
485 Which Christianity always condemned,
Knowing Nietzsche's last work *Antichrist* states
There must be excess of evil. Hitler

Consciously became Nietzsche's Antichrist,
From *Beyond Good and Evil* came death camps,
490 Will to power, nihilism and evil
As war freed men from civilisation's
"False thinking" and de-Christianised Europe.

Like a prophet (like blind Tiresias,
Cassandra or possessed Cumae Sibyl)
495 Hitler said of the Antichrist, himself:
"I have seen the man of the future, he
Is cruel." Sitting with his entourage
In the great hall of the Berghof, before
The high fireplace where tree-trunks flamed, during
500 The Christmas Eve before D-Day, Hitler
Spoke of how Christianity destroyed
The ancient priesthood's templed Mysteries,
And, with respect for Christ and for St. John
But hatred for Paul (a "pre-Bolshevik"
505 Who mixed Romans and Jews and created
An evil system, Manichaean view),
Of the antiquity of the Germans,
Who migrated to Greece and fought at Troy,
And how the German tribes had saved Europe
510 By sacking Rome and the Roman Empire:
"German-Nordic struggle against Roman
Universalism then rejected
The notion of a single God ruling
Over the universe – a Jewish lie –
515 In favour of many gods, rejected
The Pope's supremacy over Emperor,
Effeminate love over knights' honour.
Morality has now been stripped away.
Jews, Slavs and gipsies have betrayed Aryan
520 Hyperborean civilisation
And so Germany and Europe should be
Rid of them into camps and further east.
Judeo-Christian thought will soon perish,
National Socialism will soon remove
525 Germany from its enemies' chaos.
We are barbarians because we have
To sack the old world and its rottenness,
The bourgeois decadence of the West and
Its banal talk, so that the new order
530 Can rejuvenate civilisation.
Like the German tribes who sacked the Roman

12

Empire, we shall save civilisation.
I say that the ends justify the means.
Beyond good and evil, there must now be
535 Excesses of evil without remorse."
And now, standing outside on the terrace,
Turning his back on snow-clad Watzmann and
Looking up at his eyrie, eagle's nest,
High above the world on the Kehlstein ridge
540 Like the Cathar Montségur, Hitler felt
Completely at ease with the logic that,
Through Christian upbringing and Gnostic thought,
Challenged human values with the new way
And sacked a thousand cities to renew,
545 And massacred with a warlord's shrug, and
Butchered millions, all necessary deaths.
This gentle man on the Berghof terrace,
Who cried when his canary died, loved dogs,
And abstained from meat and all women's flesh,
550 Lived like a Pure, because of how he saw
The Germans' and Gnostics' tussles with Rome –
Because of how he understood history –
And because Light had not opened his heart
Centre, which Eckart had left closed (raising
555 His Kundalini serpent energy
Imperfectly so it turned venomous
And pitilessly terrified), and he
Was crippled in his spirit and feelings,
Like a choirboy picking the heads off flowers
560 Sent millions to their deaths without a thought.

Satan diverts all seekers from their goal
As a jailer foils escapes to freedom.
Especially he watches Gnostic groups
And tries to entrap the unwary there,
565 This one with wrong ideas, that one a girl
Who will tempt him away from purity,
And during meditation fills all minds
With darkness to divert them from their path.
So when a group such as the Thule meets and
570 Invokes Mani and the Cathar Parfaits,
Alarmed, Satan influences the mind
Of the group's leader towards black magic
As he did Eckart's, tries to change the group
For the worse, corrupt it so its fine aims
575 Degenerate into a travesty

Of what it set out to do. Thule began
With Hyperborean Light and ended
With millions dying in Europe's death camps.
Satan congratulated himself on
580 What he had done to Thule, whose noble aim
And Gnostic aspirations had become
A force for mass-murder, and Eckart's soul
Firmly consigned to reflection in Hell.

Satan preserves his Empire in Hell by
585 Influencing enough human spirits
With temptations to remain in darkness
As a publican detains merry men
In his tavern with a free round of beer,
And not escape their imprisonment in
590 Bodily matter and glimpse the Light which
Entitles them at death to return to
The Realm of Light, Heaven. So they are drawn
To the Realm of Darkness, Hell, where, sadly
Reflecting on what they missed in their life,
595 They understand how they must improve and
(Despite Satan's attempts to keep them there)
Be sent again to the earth's training-ground
To raise themselves towards the Realm of Light.
Satan is doing well as is seen from
600 The increase in the world's population –
One billion in eighteen hundred, nearly
Six billion by the twentieth century's end,
A constant increase in the souls not fit
To dwell in the pure Realm of Light, who have
605 Had to return to earth, reincarnate
And strive to raise their spirits from impure
Bodies, from Darkness, suggesting a new
Religion of Light is desperately
Needed now. God knows well how slow to be
610 Illumined man is, how impure modern
Souls are beside the medieval ones,
The Pure Cathars who brought the Light into
Spirits imprisoned in impure bodies,
And returned through the Montségur pyres' flames
615 With lit spirits, while the priests who stoked up
The fires later dwelt in their own darkness,
Reflecting in Hell, returning to earth.
God is happy that Hell should remain as
A permanent refugee camp for all

14

Spirits released from earth, who must reflect
And, when understanding dawns, can return
To be illumined and eventually
Dwell in the Realm of Light in Heaven with God.
And nor are the regions in Heaven or Hell
Like concentration camps, but rather as
Marquees souls move between, drawn to each one
With involuntary inclination.
Each spirit can progress from inner Hell
To outer, or outer Heaven to inner
As each opens its petals more to Light.
On earth, in Hell, in Heaven, all is self-help
And the example of the Pures, seen in
An impure world that can ensnare the weak
Till they develop discipline and strength,
Leaving Satan free to de-pure the strong
As a wayward lady waylays good men.

Tell, Muse, how Hitler, after ordering
The "deportation" of Jews from Poland
In July nineteen forty-one, mindful
Of an Allied invasion in France and
Wincing at massive thousand-bomber raids
On Cologne and Hamburg, in November
Nineteen forty-two lost North Africa
And, after Russian tanks shocked him when they
Encircled Stalingrad, went out onto
The stone terrace above the garage block
Of the Berghof at night, and looked out at
The twinkling lights of Salzburg by the slope
Of the mountain and his home town beyond,
And, desperate for a success, turned round
And peered for the eyrie on the Kehlstein,
Manichaean temple like Montségur,
Solar octagon disguised as tea-house,
Above Dietrich Eckart's mountain retreat
Near the road that led from the Vorderbrand,
Above the log-cabin Eckart lent him,
The Kampfhaus just above the Platterhof,
Where he lay low, hid after the failed putsch
And dark riot of nineteen twenty-three,
And sensed Eckart's soul in a woodpecker
That clung, quite still, to the bark of a fir,
And sighed, "I will make a pact with the Lord."
And suddenly, above his garage block,

It seemed that Dietrich Eckart's ghost beckoned.
Startled, he followed to the open door
Of the air-raid bunker, its lights switched on,
And descended steep steps two hundred feet,
And walked to where the passage widened by
The gated cell built for his dog Blondi,
Which had been dug before the groined tunnels.
There Satan waited, a towering black shape.
"The pact," said Satan in a relaxed voice,
Low and reassuring, soothing almost.
Five candles flickered in a fire circle
On the red tiles of the deep passage floor.
Without a word Hitler stepped in and said,
"Lord, I am ready. Deep within the earth,
Down in your underworld, I, who have raised
A wide earth-girdling band of magnetic
Bio-electrical energy, Vril,
From vast rallies, a sea from marching men
Among the four thousand five hundred stones
At Verden, and later at Nuremberg,
Which our adepts have directed at will
By the Devil's Table on Mount Brocken,
The holy mountain of Freyja, where their
Transmitter beams high energy drawn from
The etheric currents, that matches low
Frequency oscillations in the brain
And controls minds, for its energy field
Flows round the round earth at the speed of light
And invades brains with electrically
Charged thoughts, magnificent invention of
German discoverers of gyrating flight –
Flying saucers – and rockets, jet fighter
Planes and guided missiles, which the British
Tried to steal in the Battle of Britain
When covens of their witches raised a cone
Of power over their island to obstruct
The operation of my Vril forces,
Counter-magic ordered by dark Churchill –
I, I say, through such awesome achievements,
Can now make massive blood sacrifices:
The whole Jewish people an offering.
I have started shootings within mass graves,
Thousands lie on corpses and are then shot,
I send them down to you and your Kingdom.
Now I am trying a new form of death:

Gas lorries. And I will build gas chambers
And burn the corpses in a holocaust,
A ritual burning of a whole people,
A sacrifice to you that will bring power."
To which Satan replied: "A pact, Hitler,"
(He would not stoop to use a Christian name)
"Is a magical contract. For a price
The demonic Empire gives a service.
The needy must make a sacrifice, yes,
But the sorcerer must give me his soul,
As Eckart here once gave me his for good.
We have worked well together, to us both
God's Light is loathsome and should be erased.
Your energy will be a higher power,
A Vril of darkness which you will release
By your burnings, and by my strong support,
With Eckart's help, your mentor still at hand.
You must pledge your immortal soul to me
As he did once, and you will be with him."
Tears came to Hitler's eyes at Eckart's name,
Love of his mentor leapt within his heart,
The dark shadow that lurked by the cell gate,
Indistinct, formless, an aura in shape.
"I will give you my soul," he said, "if you
Can turn the Allies back in Africa,
And drive the Russians back from Stalingrad,
Scatter them as a stone scatters sparrows,
And prevent the Allies invading France.
I ask the higher powers for victory."
Hesitant, evasive, duplicitous
Satan replied: "I cannot guarantee
Any event, only that the broad sweep
Of all you do will further the ends of
My Demonic Empire. What seems to you
A reverse – losing Stalingrad – may be
The turning of the tide in your favour,
A Russian over-reaching of their power
Which will withdraw like many ebbing waves.
So is it with the Allies. Trust in me."
So the arch-deceiver, teller of lies,
Allayed Hitler's fears and reassured him.

Like a novice making a profession,
Who prostrates himself before an altar,
As if self-justifying, Hitler spoke:

17

"I grew up with the depth psychology
Of Freud, Adler, Jung and Rank, and their view
Of the unconscious of the will, and how
A therapist can take patients to health.
Jung wrote of the racial unconscious and
The archetypes, I saw each person was
A cell within the body of the Volk,
A living cell. I saw Germany was
Sick with the trauma of the lost Great War,
Confused, unsure of her identity.
I acted as her analyst as she
Projected an archetype on my face
And then, when this "transference" was complete,
And the German masses had trusted me,
As therapist, released her will to power,
Awakened her racial unconscious, which
Was Aryan, and led her into war
To restore her to health. I had once been
An artist. With Rank I saw the artist
As hero, not neurotic. With Jung I
Grasped that my nation's unconscious was part
Of Nature, Vril; not the reason's dustbin.
Adler showed me my nation's will to power.
I had no time for Freud, who reduced man.
I needed to magnify each man's will
And raise the stature of his dreams, and I
Achieved that through the occult, which gave birth
To the perceptions of psychology.
The occult has always known unconscious
Energy and will, just as Crowley did.
I had already found the insights of
Psychology as an initiate
In Eckart's Thule Society meetings.
I became a hypnotist, put myself
In trance and sleep-walked my nation's yearning,
Let the power of magicians' energy
Flow through my veins till I became a mage
Like Gurdjieff, who taught me to awaken
From sleep and feel my way towards waking
Consciousness. Then I mesmerised others
And finally became the figurehead
Of an ancient Mystery cult with its own
Order – the SS – like the Teutonic
Knights or Templars, but unashamedly
Luciferian, performing mass acts

Of ritual magic like a high priest who
Controls minds by whipping them up into
800 A frenzy, and then calming them again.
From an initiate, hypnotist and
Cult-leader I have become an adept,
A practiser of magic on earth's Vril
And therefore on all wills that live in it.
805 I established National Socialism
As the German people's sole religion.
I fed its spiritual hegemony
With volkish Teutonic occultism
And Wagner's Parsifal, freed from madness
810 And shown the way to the Gralsburg. Bayreuth,
The city of Wagner's great Festivals,
Is now a national shrine. I have founded
A new religion for you, Lucifer.
I am your Christ, *Mein Kampf* is your *Bible*,
815 And I have overturned Christian ethics
In the death camps dedicated to you!
I am the Antichrist as Eckart knows.
You have my soul in life, it is but one
Small step to pledge you my immortal soul
820 For all eternity as well as time.
See, I draw blood from my thumb with this knife
And offer you my hand to seal the deal."
He spoke half-aware he had projected
Lucifer as *his* therapist, as if
825 He were passing the German masses' trust
To the rightful recipient of their awe.
With a blustering braggart's bravado
At a time that required solemnity
And anguished thought, Hitler drew his penknife.
830 Blood oozed and trickled down his wrist, Satan
Extended a dark arm and sucked the blood.
"Now you are mine," he said, "all will be yours.
We have our pact, victory is now assured."
So Hitler consented to give his soul
835 To Satan in return for a promise
Of higher power that would seek Satan's end,
Ambiguous boon for a desperate man,
Empty inducement to his damnation.
In awesome tones, and loud incantation
840 That flickered the candles, Satan's dread bond
Was formalised, witnessed by dark Eckart:
A holocaust to release victory's power.

O Goethe, o Marlowe, tremble and weep
For this Faust is the terror of the world,
845   A slave to Death who, sleep-walking, performs
As if under an evil hypnotist
The dark will of the caverned underworld.

At Rastenburg's Wolf's Lair, chosen for its
Nearness to the Teutonic Knights' stronghold
850   And ley-line through Rastenburg's high point and
Church to Karlshof, to Kurhaus well and spa,
To a graveyard, to Tautenburg and to
Schwiddern village, a geomantric grid
Which transmitted Vril like electric power,
855   An energy field flowing round the earth
At speed of light into which brains transmit
And receive thoughts, and may become brainwashed,
To which chapels are built on mountain tops
That copy Elbruz, the world mountain that
860   Is sacred to Ahura Mazda, god
Of light, to control the earth's energy;
Hitler sat like a spider in a web
While Himmler's SS made arrests, took names,
Interrogated round the clock to seize
865   All known conspirators and torture them.
The Prinz Albrechtstrasse cellars were filled
And under Kaltenbrunner's expert eye,
As in the Catholic Inquisition,
Bodies were racked and rent, and shrieked out guilt,
870   And details were sent down wires to Bormann
Who laid them before Hitler's peppered arms
With an ingratiating, wheedling air.
Hitler found evidence that the bankers
Who had financed him to obtain the world
875   War they needed for their world programme had,
Now that he had served their purpose, plotted
From London with traitorous Stauffenberg to
Assassinate him and blame the Army.
Hitler had ordered a V-1 attack
880   On London to discount all compromise.
Now he said: "A higher power protects me.
Providence kept me safe. Now there must be
Blood sacrifice as I thank Providence.
In Warsaw Stroop gave me for my birthday
885   The ghetto, now I want you to give me
All the conspirators on meat-hooks, all.

They must be hanged like cattle. On thin wire."
Bormann spoke: "I will attend to it, I
Will use piano wire, and have them filmed.
890 Führer, a message from Eva. She sends
Her love and has written from the Berghof.
She says she will follow you everywhere,
Even unto death." Hitler nodded once.
Alone, Hitler looked at the photo of
895 His beautiful "mistress" and said aloud,
Consumed with pain in every limb and joint,
Throbbing in his head, ears, arms, hands and legs,
"We will watch them suffer, my dear. There will
Be more blood sacrificed, my Lord, as I
900 Spear my enemies with your Holy Lance
Whose tip will pierce their side as it did Christ's."
And in Rastenburg's windowless bunker
Whose walls now had a four-metre thick shell
Of steel and concrete and whose two bombproof
905 Ceilings were at least seven metres thick,
Satan loomed dark and said, "A higher power
Preserved you as your work is incomplete
Till you've destroyed the entire Jewish race
And our enemy Jehovah has no
910 Worshippers. Know that we have kept our word."

The Germans were replacing tanks round Caen,
Aiming to hold the entire bridgehead, and
Bradley had taken St.-Lô to open
The main road west the Americans would use
915 In the coming break-out to Brittany.
To keep the German tanks focused on Caen,
Where they expected a second landing
In the Pas de Calais to head, Dempsey
Had probed the Odon valley west of Caen,
920 And in Goodwood, after four and a half
Thousand aircraft bombed German positions
East of the Orne, on the southern outskirts
Of Caen, where Tiger tanks were set ablaze,
Flung upside down, British armour went in
925 (Not infantry because the War Office
Had warned Dempsey that casualties could not
Be replaced), and seemed to break through as seven
Hundred and fifty tanks punched a way through
The Orne cornfields east of Caen and captured
930 Bourgébus ridge. Falaise was Dempsey's aim,

And though Montgomery said armoured cars
Would merely spread alarm towards Falaise,
Eisenhower and SHAEF believed Dempsey would
Break through to Falaise and then to Paris
935 And were angry with Montgomery when
Progress was slow across British minefields
And Rommel defended the ridge against
A new landing. German defences were
Over six miles deep. In a huge battle,
940 The biggest of the Normandy campaign,
Tigers and Panthers held off Shermans and
Cromwells, until the Allied troops forced back
The German front from Caen, took villages.
But four hundred Allied tanks were lost, and
945 The Desert Rats and infantry were slow.
Then an afternoon thunderstorm drenched all.
Dempsey, with five thousand casualties for
Just a few yards gained despite three armoured
Divisions and no headway, now withdrew,
950 And Goodwood ended without a breakthrough.
Montgomery cabled Eisenhower that
The day's operations were a success
And then spoke to the press of his "breakthrough".
Learning this, Eisenhower, in Bushey Park,
955 Raged, "The truth is, the German defence is
Tenacious and Monty has failed. It has
Taken seven thousand tons of bombs to gain
Seven miles. The Allies cannot hope to go
Through France using a thousand ton of bombs
960 Per mile." Tedder said, "Monty should be sacked."

Eisenhower's blood pressure was up. He lay
In bed at SHAEF's HQ in Bushey Park
With ringing in his ears, still angry at
The British withdrawal after Goodwood,
965 Furious with Montgomery for being
Cautious. Towards evening Tedder rang and,
Ever disloyal to Montgomery,
Said: "Monty stopped his armour from going
Further. The British air commanders are
970 Disgusted. The British Chiefs of Staff will
Support any recommendations you
Make, that you, for instance, should take over
Field command, Alexander replacing
Monty in charge of Twenty-First. Chief Big

Wind can be made a peer, or be given
The governorship of Malta. I could take
Leigh-Mallory's place and command the air
Forces." Eisenhower made no comment and,
Fuming, lay with the implications of
Replacing Montgomery with himself,
An option he then put to Bedell Smith
As if hoping to be contradicted.

SHAEF was full of rumours about Goodwood.
Hearing them, Brooke visited Churchill, who
Was in bed in the underground war rooms,
Wearing a blue and gold dressing-gown, with
A canary on his head. Churchill said
Furiously: "Goodwood has failed and now Ike
Says that General Montgomery banned all
VIP visits during the battle.
Who is he to dictate to me, stop me?
When I was Minister of Munitions
In the First World War, Haig always allowed
Me to visit." He said he had written
To Eisenhower asking to be shown round
By a Staff Officer, and that he would
Not visit Montgomery's headquarters.
Alarmed, Brooke immediately went to see
His protégé Montgomery in France.

Urged by Brooke, Montgomery invited
To his headquarters at Blay Eisenhower,
Who heard a logical explanation
For Goodwood: Montgomery did not want
To take Caen but to keep pressing on it
To bring the Germans to him so Patton
Could swing round, as the original plan
Required. When Eisenhower returned he seemed
A changed man. He now threw away his blood
Pressure pills and went fishing, piloted
A liaison plane. He said he was "more
Than happy" with the conduct of the war.

Brooke took back a personal invitation
To Churchill, who next day arrived at Blay
In pouring rain near Cerisy forest
In his blue naval coat and blue cap, and
His pocket held an order dismissing

Montgomery. All TAC HQ knew he
Was angry at being kept out of France.
Montgomery, now alerted by Brooke,
1020 Greeted him warmly and showed him his dogs
And canaries. Churchill sat in "A" Mess
Dining-marquee and asked Henderson to
Leave, and as he went to the kitchen tent
(And listened through the tent flap with the chef)
1025 Churchill said, "Monty, SHAEF – Ike, Tedder – want
You dismissed. We've had setbacks." "What setbacks?"
Montgomery asked. "The battle's going
Excellently." Churchill said, "They say we're
Losing the war, and you're panicking. They
1030 Want Alexander to take over. And
I'm Prime and Defence Minister, and I've
A right to be here." Montgomery said,
"It's dangerous, sir." Churchill retorted,
"Let me be the judge of that." "There is no
1035 Panic here," the beret-wearer said. "Come
Into the operations caravan
And I'll show you a map. The Germans are
Doing exactly what we want. I don't
Want to take Caen but to lure the Germans
1040 Forward, so that Patton can swing round." As
He took Churchill into the caravan
He said, "I'm not just fighting the Germans
And Italians, but the Americans
And British as well, the only people
1045 I'm not fighting are the Russians." Churchill
Replied, "Monty, I know the feeling well."
Montgomery promised, "In four to five
Weeks you will have all France in your pocket."
He briefed Churchill in the caravan, and
1050 In due course Brigadier Williams knocked on
The door, Montgomery's Intelligence
Officer, and reported that Ultra
Suggested that there had been "a sort of
Revolution in Berlin". Pointing at
1055 Two red despatch-boxes, Churchill said, "There's
Something about it in here. See what you
Can find." Montgomery and Williams searched
Through the red boxes. Williams said, "These are
Ultra signals. Sir, have you read this?" "No,"
1060 Churchill said. Williams said, "Sir, this could mean
The end of the war." Montgomery said,

"There could be a surrender this morning.
The American Cobra attack may
Not be needed. We've got the Germans on
1065 The run." All smiles, the two leaders emerged
From the caravan, and Montgomery
Said, "When you get angry in the future,
Sir, you're to send me a telegram and
Find out the truth." Churchill promised he would,
1070 And, all smiles, they parted. Henderson thought
That like a prisoner smiling at a stay
Of execution who is still condemned
Montgomery had bought another month.

Eisenhower was rung by Churchill that night,
1075 And immediately asked, "What do your
People now think about the slowness of
The situation over there?" He meant,
'Are you after Monty's scalp, like Tedder?'
He spoke with Churchill for half an hour, then
1080 Observed to Butcher, "He is 'supremely
Happy' with the situation. Monty
Obviously sold Winston a bill of goods."

Hitler sat in his room in Rastenburg.
Dr. Giesing examined his bomb wounds.
1085 Hitler said: "My right ear is bleeding, my
Eyes flick to the right, I keep thinking I
Am falling to my right, but the shock has
Got rid of my nerve complaint, my left leg
Does not tremble now. But my hearing's worse.
1090 Cauterise my ear again. Ignore my
Pain. I stopped feeling pain long ago, pain
Exists to make a man of you." Near him
Stood Sonnleithner, Ribbentrop's liaison
Official. Hitler told him: "I had *both*
1095 Ear-drums perforated, yet I did not
Feel a thing, it happened so quickly. That
Is probably how it is when you shoot
Yourself. Even if you shoot yourself in
The mouth, not the brain, I now know you don't
1100 Feel a thing." Dr. Giesing said, "It is
Amazing you were not more badly hurt."
Hitler said: "Providence protected me.
I am immortal till I've completed
My Providential task." Now he ordered

25

1105 Bormann to exhume Stauffenberg and his
Three colleagues: "I want proof they died, I do
Not trust Fromm or the Army, who may have
Invented the execution to put
Me off their track." Next day, he told Goebbels:
1110 "I am indebted to you for crushing
The Army putsch by the officer corps.
You are now to be Reich commissioner
For total mobilisation of all
Resources for war, with power over all
1115 Civilians and Party authorities."
Goebbels thought the move, though right, was too late.

From the top of Bourgébus ridge and Hill
112 the sun sparkled through mist on
The Channel, under the barrage balloons,
1120 Where ships lay offshore like a school of whales.
A million and a half men had landed
In Normandy, mostly Americans.
Round St.-Lô's high ground, among the hedgerows,
The US Third Army under Patton,
1125 Assistant to Bradley's break-out, and west
"Lightning Joe" Collins (who won his name in
The Pacific, having led the Tropic
Lightnings at Guadalcanal, Solomon
Isles) waited on the road to Perriers to
1130 Attack and begin Cobra, the break-out.
Ahead waited German Army Group B,
Thinned by losses, a hundred thousand men,
Panzers with too few tanks and no Luftwaffe
Flying overhead in support with three-
1135 Quarters of the German armoured corps pinned
South of Caen to block a British attack.
The Allies knew from Ultra intercepts
That the Germans had too few tanks and men
To stop the coming American drive,
1140 But all was eerie quiet as troops, dug in
Within hedgerows or houses, tense, waited
As tanks, jeeps, artillery moved slowly
So as not to raise dust and give away
Their positions. An empty landscape with
1145 Shell-holes and ruined farmhouses waited
In complete silence, with no sound of birds,
While the Americans ended German
Resistance in St.-Lô. Then a storm broke

With driving rain all day, mist and low cloud
1150 Sixteen hundred US bombers raiding
From England could not see their targets and
Flew home. But three hundred high aircraft droned
And dropped their bombs along the front line road
To Perriers, on American and
1155 German positions. Tanks and men waiting
To attack were blown apart in roars of
Smoke with a hundred and fifty US
Casualties. Alerted, the Germans
Bombarded with artillery and killed
1160 Many more. Next day, nearly two thousand
Bombers, flying high, bombed the Panzer Lehr
And dropped napalm and white phosphorus, and
Again bombed their own side, flinging bodies
From the slit trenches where dazed and frightened
1165 Americans quivered with six hundred
Casualties and killing McNair, who
Commanded US Army Ground Forces.

Eisenhower had flown to Normandy to
Witness the start of Cobra. But it poured
1170 With rain for two days, and he returned to
London. Soon he flew back to Normandy
And visited Montgomery at Blay,
And told him thinly, "I did not expect
American planes to bomb US troops
1175 Two days running with over seven hundred
And fifty casualties. The lesson is,
Heavy bombers cannot give tactical
Support." Montgomery said, "We are still
Trying to find out why this happened, Ike."
1180 Eisenhower now asked him for an all-out
Second Army attack to help Cobra.
Irritated, Montgomery declined.
He later expressed his reason to Brooke:
"Ike has the very vaguest conception
1185 Of war. If everyone attacks, no one
Will have the strength to make a decisive
Breakthrough." Eisenhower said: "Monty, you should
Know there's a strong feeling in the US
That American troops are doing more
1190 Than British troops as Americans have
Suffered more casualties and captured more
Prisoners." Bristling, Montgomery rejoined:

"Your bigger casualties – ten thousand to
The British-Canadian six – are due to
1195 American lack of skill in fighting,
For example, bombing their own side." Now,
Eisenhower, aware that Cobra might be
Failing, said: "That's not right. I am under
Pressure from General Marshall. There's feeling
1200 That there will soon be more American
Troops than British, that they are doing more,
And if Cobra fails – and the battle is
Touch and go at present – then shortly there
May be criticism of your command."

1205 Along the front line road outside St.-Lô
Panzer Lehr fought in bomb-craters and wrecks
To the last man, and as Germans mingled
With American units, much killing
Took place with only two miles gained. A push
1210 To their west won half a mile and, through smoke,
The Germans pulled back, and soon VII Corps
Was through the German line, and Patton's old
2nd Armoured "Hell on Wheels" now broke out
And moved south and west down the roads of France
1215 Without opposition. Tanks thrust down roads
With clouds of dust, fighter-bombers above.
After two months' stillness all was movement,
As when ants hatch and an old garden path
Is full of scurryings to left and right,
1220 And after the diversionary Goodwood
Cobra had struck out towards Brittany
As an upreared snake strikes at a mongoose
As Patton's US Third Army broke out.

Eisenhower lunched with Churchill and expressed
1225 Dissatisfaction with Montgomery.
Churchill had him to dinner the next night
In his underground HQ, to repeat
His words in the presence of Brooke, British
Chief of Staff, who said: "These criticisms
1230 Are defeatist and do not accord with
The picture I have received from General
Montgomery today. He is fighting
Hard on the eastern flank now to assist
The Americans on the western side.
1235 I am quite certain that his strategy

28

Is about to pay off, and anyone
Who doubts that" – he looked at Eisenhower – "knows
Nothing of strategy. If the Supreme
Commander has some criticisms of
1240 The way his Land Forces Commander-in-
Chief is directing the battle, he should
Return to Normandy and put them to
His face, rather than complain to others
Behind his back." Eisenhower, narrowing
1245 His eyes, said: "I am shy of doing that
In such a sensitive matter. I want
To maintain the best relations between
The British and Americans and win
The war." Churchill then ruled: "We cannot make
1250 A public statement on our strategy
In making the German leaders believe
That the British are trying to break out
When they are not, as this would be read by
The enemy. Silence is best." Smarting,
1255 Eisenhower came away feeling that he
Had got nowhere in tackling the problem
Of a too slow British commander in
Charge of huge numbers of American
Troops, and half-resolved to take the command
1260 From out of British hands, and to himself.

Eisenhower flew to Normandy in his
B-25, and, driven by Kay, went
To Bradley's French HQ. Montgomery
Was there, and now Cobra was succeeding
1265 And he recognised victory was in sight,
In good heart, he said to Montgomery:
"It is excellent news that Brad's armoured
Divisions have caused the German front to
Disintegrate." Montgomery described
1270 Dempsey's next attack from Caumont, and said
Von Kluge would be out of position
As he expected a thrust for Paris,
And, "We all agree, the plan is working
Well." Eisenhower, ever diplomatic,
1275 Asked, "Did you get my signal, that I am
Delighted your basic plan has begun
To unfold brilliantly with Brad's success?"
Montgomery nodded, and, elated,

Eisenhower said: "I have told General Surles,
1280 The American censor, that I am
Responsible for strategy and all
Major activity in Normandy,
And that any criticism of you
Is criticism of me." As Eisenhower
1285 Turned to talk to Bradley, Montgomery
Said to Henderson, "O-o-oh, did you hear that?
He smells triumph, he's taking the credit."

Meanwhile at night, at 3.30 a.m.,
Like a wild cat prowling for pastured prey
1290 Crerar's Canadian swift First Army
Attacked Panzers south of Caen to suggest
Breakout was to the east, not to the west
(Spring), but was stopped with heavy casualties.
The German defences held and Tilly
1295 La Campagne had not been taken. Quickly
Montgomery moved British armour next
To the Americans, and soon attacked
From Caumont heights, through hedgerows towards Vire,
But British troops were now weary, punchdrunk
1300 And lacked enthusiasm, and despite
Heavy bombers and artillery, their
Infantry only covered five miles of
The way towards Mont Pinçon's steep craggy
Slopes, thickets and rocky earth. The Germans
1305 Were dug in beyond minefields. The British
Assault opened at midday, the air thick
With dust and smell of dead cattle. Tanks crossed
A bridge to La Varinière, from where
Six tanks crawled up a narrow track and reached
1310 The summit. Exhausted men climbed all night
And, picks in hands, fell headlong into half-
Dug trenches and slept till the sun woke them
To parched throats and empty bellies in graves,
Proud to have weakened the German Army's
1315 Panzer defence of Caen. Now the British
Ground slowly forwards while the US dashed.

The Russian Rokossovsky had advanced
Four hundred miles in six weeks and was ten
Miles from Warsaw. At the direction of
1320 The Polish Government-in-Exile in

London, the Polish Home Army rose up,
The Warsaw Uprising of the Free Poles
Against the Germans. Koniev had taken
Lvov and Russians were in North Poland and
1325 Lithuania, but Rokossovsky told
Stalin in his Kremlin office he had
Lost a hundred and twenty-three thousand
Men on his way to Warsaw, that his troops
Were exhausted, that he feared a German
1330 Attack from the south. Stalin said: "Stay put.
Do not move on Warsaw. The Uprising
Is led by a General Bór, real name
Komorowski, who wants a pro-British
Democratic Poland. He is against
1335 The Red Army and will fight you if you
Go in. Sit tight, let him fight the Germans.
When they are both worn out, and street-fighting
Is no longer a danger, then go in."

Bradley had put VIII Corps under Patton.
1340 Armour speared their thrust, engineers cleared mines
From German minefields where the infantry
Fought. The armour reached Coutances and VIII Corps
Captured seven thousand prisoners. With hands
On heads they marched out of the war. Slowed down
1345 By prisoners, the Americans attacked
Avranches and crossed the River See near where
Mont-St.-Michel's monastery towered in quiet,
And, urged on by Patton, advanced ten miles
A day throughout Brittany, ballooning
1350 Outwards south to the Loire, east to Le Mans
Where they could pincer up towards the held
Canadians south of Caen. Overlord
Now had a new momentum. The Germans,
However, kept control of the main ports.
1355 Bradley's HQ now became 12th Army
Group, equal with Montgomery under
Eisenhower, though Montgomery remained
In charge. With his approval Bradley told
Patton to send the Third Army towards
1360 The River Seine. The German front had cracked
From Cherbourg to Caen, before the US
First Army and British Second Army,
And Kluge, knowing the Germans had lost

The Battle of Normandy, described his

1365   Position to Command as "a madhouse".

Montgomery studied maps at Dempsey's
HQ and saw a possibility
He had hoped would present itself. He said
To Dempsey: "Now the plan is working and
1370   The Allies have Rennes, and while you, Crerar
And Bradley tie Kluge down between Caen
And Mortain and swing his right flank towards
Paris, outflanking the Germans, forcing
Some back to the Seine; it is possible
1375   You and Hodges can outflank the Germans
To the north in this Falaise gap. And if
Crerar strikes south towards Falaise we can
Surround the enemy in a pocket.
This is the consequence of sticking to
1380   The plan for two long months. The struggle for
Normandy has been the longest ever
Battle in the West, surpassing the twelve-
Day battle of El Alamein." A few
Days later Montgomery, in his new
1385   TAC HQ at Forêt de Cerisy,
Put this idea to Bradley, saying, "I
Want a full encirclement of the Seine."
Bradley modified the idea: "Sir, time
Is critical, that would take too long. I
1390   Advise a short encirclement all round
Falaise. I can't believe that Hitler has
Sent four Panzer divisions right into
Our trap. We should spring it as soon as we
Can. Kluge does not seem to know what we're
1395   About. It will be a present to Ike,
Who's setting up SHAEF HQ near Tournières –
In an apple orchard outside – today."

In Rastenburg, poring over his maps
In his fortified bunker at Wolf's Lair,
1400   Moving pins as if his divisions were
At full strength, with fuel and ammunition,
Ignoring Allied air strength and tank power
And how Allied artillery shot up
The tattered morale of his troops, Hitler
1405   Ordered a counter-attack near Mortain.

"Here," he declared, "our forces will break through
To the sea at Avranches, cutting Patton
Off from the Allied armies. Our armoured
Drive will be like those on the Eastern front
1410 And recapture the lost Cotentin lands,
Sever the Americans from their supplies
And restore their beachhead in Normandy."
His Generals looked at each other, but since
Stauffenberg's plot and the SS arrests
1415 The Army was under suspicion, and
They said nothing, knowing the Panzers would
Be in hedgerows and short of fuel, without
Much air cover. Even if they captured
Troops and tanks, the suicidal attack
1420 Would weaken the front. Von Kluge agreed,
Shocked and resigned to a massive defeat.

After midnight, through dark misty hedgerows,
Crept a hundred and forty Panzer tanks
Like frogs migrating from a foggy pond.
1425 Forewarned by Ultra, under Michael's gaze,
The Allies lay in wait like alert snakes.
Mortain was defended, but fell before
An SS Panzer attack. A dawn fog
Hung over rocky hill three-seventeen,
1430 Which was held by infantry. Allied planes
Swooped and bombed the German armour and fired
Rockets, and no Luftwaffe appeared, and though
Three hundred men were lost, the Allies had
Remained on the hill, taken three hundred
1435 And fifty prisoners, and destroyed all
But thirty tanks. The highway littered with
Wrecked German vehicles and blackened corpses,
Fields strewn with dead swollen farm animals,
Amid burning fires Patton exulted
1440 To Codman beside him with glee unknown
To Marlborough, Wellington, Napoleon:
"Just look at that, could anything be more
Magnificent?" Now the German troops in
Normandy could not withdraw, and no tanks
1445 Could rescue them. Next day Patton's tanks pushed
South and east to Le Mans. The German Seventh
Army was all but surrounded. Trapped by
Hitler's orders, von Kluge sent the 9th
Panzers to Mortain to try to break through.

1450   Hausser, commander of the German troops,
Said: "This will deal a death blow to Seventh
Army and the entire western Wehrmacht."
Von Kluge, having to show loyalty
As the SS probed for conspirators,
1455   Frightened but having to accept the plan,
Said tiredly, "It is the Führer's order."

The terror Hitler promised had begun.
Hundreds of Army officers had been
Arrested. Guderian, appointed
1460   Chief of General Staff, pledged the Army would
Now give the Nazi raised arm salute in
Loyalty to Hitler. In Prinz Albrecht-
Strasse, the Gestapo cellars were crammed
With new prisoners who were tortured: their legs
1465   And fingers were encased in metal tubes
Lined with spikes which were screwed to their flesh, and
Their heads were put in helmets and blankets
To muffle their screams. Kaltenbrunner was
In charge, under Himmler, and Bormann took
1470   The lists of names to Hitler, wheedling in
Some he would bring down, making sure he spoke
Of von Kluge and Rommel. Soon seven
Thousand had been arrested, along with
Their families as the Nazis applied
1475   The Teutonic "Sippenhaft" (detention
Of kith and kin) to outlaw all bad blood.
The first group of conspirators was tried
In early August.
                In the People's Court
1480   In Berlin Field Marshal von Witzleben,
Generals Hoepner (Fromm's friend), Stieff, von Hase,
Lieutenant-Colonel Bernardis, Captain
Klausing and Lieutenants von Hagen and
Von Wartenburg stood before judge Freisler,
1485   Who wore a blood-red robe. Swastika flags
Festooned the first-floor hall and hid cameras
Which Freisler started and stopped by signals,
Screaming and shouting abuse for the spool.
The eight were unshaven and dressed in clothes
1490   Worn by concentration camp victims to
Make them look like criminals. Witzleben's
Trousers were too large; he had to clutch them.
"Why are you fiddling with your trousers," screamed

Freisler, "you dirty old man." His false teeth
1495   Had also been removed. Wartenburg spoke:
"I have nothing but contempt for National
Socialism. Man has a moral and
Religious duty to oppose regimes
That lack respect for the sacredness of
1500   Human life." Freisler shouted "Enough" and
Stopped the film cameras. On the second day
Of the trial, all eight were sentenced to hang,
Were denied "the honour" of beheading.

At Plötzensee prison that afternoon
1505   The eight were led to the execution
Building, a large high room with two windows
Under a beam with eight hanging meat-hooks
Concealed behind a black curtain. One by
One, the half-naked men were led before
1510   The Public Prosecutor, Hanssen, who
Read sentence: "Accused, the People's Court has
Sentenced you to death by hanging. Hangman
Do your duty." Two hangmen, one grinning,
Led Witzleben to the first meat-hook, placed
1515   A figure of 8 noose of piano wire
(Dreamt up by Bormann when Hitler, to spread
Terror, said "They must be hanged like cattle")
Round the victim's neck as he scathingly
Said, "Piano wire, for a human being?"
1520   And, lifting him, looped the top of the 8
Over the meat-hook, then let him fall, and,
While he strangled slowly, the wire biting
Into his neck in a collar of blood,
They drew a short black curtain under which
1525   Could be seen feet twitching and jerking in
Death-agony, and returned through the large
Black curtain to Hanssen, to whom the next
Was brought. So during the coming months five
Thousand plotters would die at Plötzensee.

1530   In a night attack American troops
Cleared the ruins of Vire of all Germans,
And the Canadian First Army pushed
South towards Falaise to sew the German
Seventh and Fifth Panzer Armies like rats
1535   In a bulging pocket closed on three sides:

The west and south by US First and Third
Armies, the north by the British Second
Army. Crerar now launched Totalize down
The road to Falaise, with Polish units,
1540 Kangaroos (turretless Sherman tanks) and
Unfrocked Priests (gun platforms) which carried troops
In armour. A thousand bombers attacked
By artificial moonlight (searchlight beams
Reflecting from clouds). They advanced five miles,
1545 Some toppling into bomb-craters, all in
The dark running into tail lights ahead,
But the Germans reinforced their Panzers,
And US planes bombed their own side again,
Causing three hundred Canadian and
1550 Polish casualties. The Germans fought hard,
Knowing retreat would doom Army Group B.
Wittmann, the victor of Villers-Bocage,
Led his Tiger against five Shermans and
Was smashed at close range. Smoke billowed round him,
1555 He died, his mangled, charred body slumped by
The notches he had carved for each tank kill,
And floated like a puff from a tank gun
To a twilit place where he would reflect
That the aim of living is love, not hate.
1560 After one skirmish, German tanks withdrew
And the commander of the 12th SS
Panzers Kurt Meyer stood in their path and
Shouted, "Must I face the enemy alone?"
And the Panzers turned round and fought again.
1565 As in Goodwood, the Allies were delayed
And the Canadian tanks fought all night
For a hill between Cintheaux and Falaise
And some lost their way and were attacked by
Tigers at dawn: forty-seven were knocked out
1570 With two hundred and forty men. In woods
Thirty-five German tanks held the Laison
Against seven hundred Canadian tanks.
Half way to Falaise, the advance ended
When "overcautious" Montgomery failed
1575 To send reinforcements to add more weight.

Having sent orders from his Tournières tent
Eisenhower walked through the apple orchard,
Past a gold-brown cornfield splashed with poppies

Scarlet as soldiers' blood. A harvest mouse
Swung on an ear of wheat. Elders, hawthorns
And holly had berries that had turned red.
He noticed the drupes of a guelder rose,
Passed a wayfaring tree and then dogwood.
Birches and limes were turning yellow, and
Hedgerow brambles were tinted purple-red.
Two caterpillars crawled like a·convoy,
Swifts swooped and soared like German fighter-planes.
He spotted a charm of goldfinches on
Ripe thistle heads; one flitted with tinkling
Cries. A wood-pigeon cooed, corn bunting sang
From a telegraph-wire. And as twilight
Crept down the sky, above dancing gnats, bats
Darted and swerved like Allied air cover,
And a crane-fly descended slowly like
A helicopter. By the damp roadside
Fleabane grew near young wasps, and in a stream
Beyond, minnows darted. Round its reed bed
Gathered swallows as if in conference.
Eisenhower stood and watched in long silence,
Breathless, with awed thoughts of holy peacetime.

From Le Mans, Patton wheeled to Argentan,
Northwards, to trap the German Seventh Army
In place of the Canadians – Bradley's
Plan, which Eisenhower welcomed; a left hook
That would open the way to the German
Border and a swift advance. French armour
Blocked roads and the Germans reinforced their
Position north of the town, and Bradley
Refused Patton permission to drive on.
Canadians and Americans were near
Each other, and Eisenhower was afraid
They might fight as they closed the Falaise gap.
Von Kluge saw the danger to his troops
And asked Hitler for permission to send
A Panzer group from Mortain to counter
The Canadians. Hitler refused, still
Set to hurl the Allies into the sea,
Urging an even stronger armoured force.
Almost enveloped, Kluge told Hitler
Loyal Hausser and Eberbach agreed
That no attack from Mortain could take place

And that the Seventh Army should withdraw.
Hitler, ignoring the German Army's
Weariness and lack of equipment, how
1625   SS commanders terrorised Generals,
And the Allied bombing, agreed but said
The Seventh Army should then resume its drive
Westwards towards the sea, and no one dared
Tell Hitler his troops were ragged, morale
1630   Low; not even Sepp Dietrich, who, approached
By officers to tell Hitler the truth,
Said, "That is the way for me to get shot."

Bradley flew to Montgomery's HQ
In the Forêt de Cerisy, where bold
1635   Montgomery said: "Patton's raced away
And will reach Paris and the Seine. Do you
Still favour the short encirclement at
Falaise?" Bradley said: "Yes, sir. Once Patton
Starts racing, he can find he's going in
1640   The wrong direction as at Palermo.
We have Germans in a trap, it's wiser
To spring it now, rather than let them get
Out." Montgomery said: "In that case, no
Germans must cross the Seine without being
1645   Mauled. The plan is: the Canadians will
Attack, supported by heavy bombers;
Dempsey will seize Falaise and thus allow
The Canadians to push towards Trun and
Argentan, where Collins will arrive from
1650   The southern flank; and Patton will act as
Long stop east of L'Aigle." Bradley nodded.

At noon Crerar's Canadians attacked
Through smokescreens, heading for the red sun which
Showed blood-red through smoke, as if through burning
1655   Farm stubble, while a thousand RAF
Bombers struck their German flanks, some again
Hitting their own side. They broke through and pushed
Seven miles in two days through dust and smoke
Towards Falaise, their aim to pass east and
1660   Close the pocket towards Argentan and
The US Third Army. Kluge, driving
To see his troops in the Falaise pocket,
Was caught in a traffic jam of tanks, trucks

And carts and strafed by Allied aircraft like
1665 Rommel. His car and radio truck hit,
He hid in a roadside ditch for twelve hours
Like a rabbit frightened by a huge plough.

In the Wolf's Lair at Rastenburg, Hitler,
Bent over maps, cotton wool in his ears,
1670 Saw the German Army was in a trap
And raged to Bormann at Kluge's lack of
Contact: "Patton is now rampaging through
Brittany, all day the Americans
Have attacked us near Falaise, and still no
1675 Sign of Field Marshal von Kluge. We learn
His radio truck has been silent all
Day, and he's mentioned in an enemy
Radio signal. Either he is dead, or
He is surrendering to the British,
1680 Joining forces with Russia, an absurd
Notion. SS General Hausser will now
Take over the command of Army Group
B and stop the enemy." Later, with
Kluge missing, his Army trapped, Hitler
1685 Received a second blow which made that day
"The worst day of my life". Shocked, Hitler learned
That near Toulon thirty thousand Allied
Troops landed in operation Anvil
(Renamed Dragoon by a disapproving
1690 Churchill, who wished to target Italy)
To invade Southern France. They took Marseilles
And moved up the Rhône valley to link up
With Allied troops from Normandy, and would
Become Sixth Army Group under Devers.
1695 Taken aback, depressed, that night Hitler
Did not sleep. His sedatives did not work.
Eberbach's headquarters reported that
Kluge had just arrived in the middle
Of the trap with no explanation for
1700 Where he was the previous day, and again
Demanded to retreat. Suffering from
A thumping headache, Hitler resisted
Until next afternoon, when he gave in.

Falaise fell when Hitler at last agreed
1705 To withdraw Seventh Army across the Orne
At von Kluge's requests. The Polish troops

Crossed the Dives at Jort but were held by
Panzers a mile north of Falaise. Troops from
Canada entered the ruined town of
1710 Falaise, home of William the Conqueror.
The Hitler Jugend would not surrender,
And sixty Germans fought to the death from
The local high school buildings. Allied bombs
Had obliterated streets with rubble
1715 And Canadian bulldozers clearing routes
For traffic after the battle had great
Difficulty identifying streets.
The gap in the pocket was now between
Falaise and Argentan, and in the fog
1720 Of war – the Canadians and Poles slow,
The Americans rushing northwards from
Argentan, others heading for the Seine –
The closing would be east between Trun and
Chambois. The Canadians and Poles crossed
1725 The Dives, and now a hundred thousand
German troops were bombed and shelled in a ten
By twenty mile pocket with a narrow
Six mile gap near Chambois, and sought escape.

Now at Bradley's headquarters at Fougères
1730 Montgomery told Bradley: "We must keep
A grip on the battle, not be carried
Away. Patton has charged towards Paris
Like a bull – Palermo again – and now
The Poles are trying to close the jaws of
1735 Our trap without Patton. We have taken
A hundred and fifty thousand prisoners
In Normandy, and another hundred
Thousand Germans are in the Falaise bag.
Meanwhile Leclerc has raced to beat Patton
1740 To Paris; another hole. Gerow has
Pulled him back. We now need to think ahead
Beyond the Seine, which we'll reach tomorrow.
As I see it, both Twelve and Twenty-one
Army Groups should keep together as one
1745 Solid moving mass that need fear nothing.
The British and Canadians should hug
The coast and go for Antwerp and capture
The rocket sites that threaten England. You
Should form a right flank, press towards Aachen,
1750 Cologne and then the Ruhr. Together we

40

Will form a single, narrow thrust." Bradley
Said, "I agree entirely." The beret-
Wearer then said: "I have not yet discussed
The plan with Ike. I want to put to him
1755   That the US Seventh Army, driving up
From the south of France, should target the Saar.
Ike is not likely to have any great
Objections, and he will undoubtedly
Accept what we say." Bradley thought he was
1760   Deluding himself with wishful thinking
In believing Eisenhower would agree.

Now Falaise had fallen Kluge received
His last order from Hitler, to go home:
"There are reports that he has contacted
1765   The British. Signal that he is to leave
The area at once. I can no longer
Trust him. Contact Field Marshal Model and
Appoint him as von Kluge's successor."
Model was now Supreme Commander West.
1770   Awaiting arrest for conspiracy,
Kluge wrote to Model of the hopeless
Task, then to Hitler urging surrender:
"You have fought an honourable and great fight.
The German people have borne so much it's
1775   Time to put an end to this frightfulness.
Show yourself great enough to put an end
To a hopeless struggle." It was the act
Of a man who had already chosen
To die, a lone, brave, posthumous gesture.

1780   As waves sparkle in summer sunshine and
Dazzle with leaping light, so crowded two
Billion spirits, excited at their Christ's
Return to report back to them on his
Mission to the earth to save troubled man
1785   From Satan's Antichrist. From a distance
They resembled a sea, but closer up
Their angelic Light bodies rippled and
Shimmered, each like a gorgeous swallowtail,
Aura of breathtaking beauty, content
1790   As Red Admirals settled on buddleia,
Basking in summer sunshine, fumed with scent,
Drowsily happy, at peace, pleased to be
At one with their own kind. Mellifluous

41

Humming of approval greeted Christ as,
1795 In his giant Light body he stood on
A rock and spoke words heard and understood
At once by all spirits, whatever their
Last life's language, to a concerned Heaven
That was still a concert of harmony,
1800 Aware of Christ's efforts from Heaven's news,
Now confirmed by direct democracy:
"Angels, I have come back to give you my
Progress report from the earth, and to ask
You to approve the next step. As you know,
1805 The earth is a training-ground to bring man
To the Light, and Satan's activities
Are beyond our control: the Light cannot
Act negatively and, though by its law
Of constant harmony evil-doers
1810 Destroy themselves eventually, we have
Taken the view that we must endeavour
To hurry the process up in Hitler's
Case, the brutal Antichrist. Our greatest
Fear is that Hitler, Antichrist, will soon
1815 Possess an atomic bomb. I have been
Successful in heading this off so far.
I can report that newly beloved
Heisenberg, who has the know-how to work
His calculations to a formula
1820 That can give Hitler the bomb that he seeks,
Has agreed to undermine his efforts
And those of his colleagues. We can all rest
Easier for that." A humming of assent
Wafted from the rippling rose of Heaven
1825 (Rose-garden of roses that seemed one rose).
"As to the attempt on Hitler's foul life
By our beloved Stauffenberg, who stands
Among you, he did his best but Hitler
Is protected by Satan's dark powers, and
1830 His efforts were not successful. You will
Know that the battle of Normandy is
Going the Allies' way. I hope Generals
Close to Hitler will take his impending
Defeat as cause to overthrow him, and
1835 Stop the slaughter of millions more pure souls
Who will increase our refugee problem
Here just as the influx of impure souls
Is already expanding another

42

Place. But I have to say, under Satan's
Guidance, Hitler's reign of terror is now
Very effective, as some here will bear
Out, victims of corrupt Freisler's 'justice';
And his Generals are under pressure to
Stay silent. Hitler is on the verge of
Sending his latest reprisal weapon,
The V-2, against London. He can be
Expected to retaliate for all
Reverses in Normandy. I will now
Approach level-headed Eisenhower, who
Is running the war for the Allies, but
Under orders from Satan's agents round
Roosevelt's White House. He is now debating
Whether to take over field command from
Montgomery, and he, I know, will do
All he can to destroy the V-2 sites.
I will try to detach Eisenhower from
His bosses, who are under Satan's dark
Influence." An approving humming came
From the animate sea of Light. "I know
That Satan has approached Stalin, who is
In league with Satan's internationalists,
And Satan is hurrying up Stalin's
Offensive just as the clique round Roosevelt
Want. Now I will share my dilemma with
You, openly and frankly as always.
So far, our strategy and policy
Has been to end the war as quickly as
We can, to speed the Allies to Berlin
Before Hitler obtains an atomic
Bomb, to hurry up the Allied victory
Which Roosevelt's clique want to protract for their
Own purposes, which are also Satan's.
But our strategy is also to seek
To confine Satan in one place before
Binding him, and until he is bound our
Millennium cannot begin. Satan
Already has Bolshevik Russia, which
Has three million troops on the move. And now,
Outnumbered and exhausted as they are
From the fighting, the Allies cannot match
That force. We can make our priority
The immediate end of Communism
(Doctrine of Weishaupt's Illuminati

43

Under a new name), which means we must speed
1885   Eisenhower towards Berlin and then push
The Allies towards the Urals, so that
Eastern Europe is Allied; in which case,
Satan, who is stronger, will rampage back
Through Eastern Europe as Stalin's goal is
1890   Poland, and will be tempted to go on
To the Atlantic, and there will be more
Conflict, between two of the Allies and
Russia, which at present the US and
Britain, exhausted from years of fighting
1895   And outnumbered by the Red Army, just
Cannot win, and the whole of Europe will
Fall to Stalin, who will occupy all
The liberated lands including France
And Normandy, and there will be endless
1900   Warfare after Hitler has fallen, and
No stability there. Or, we can make
Our priority the end of Nazism,
And allow Stalin, who's still an ally,
A treacherous one but still an ally,
1905   And stronger on the ground than Britain and
America, to take Eastern Europe,
For which he craves, give him Berlin and stop
Him there and Satan's influence with him,
And confine Satan in a ring behind
1910   A wall he will want to build himself to
Safeguard his gain. Behind that wall he will
Remain, while we free the rest of the world
From his tyranny, and we can begin
To bind him later when Communism
1915   Ends, as it will, for the laws of history
Show that a unified conglomerate
Is but a stage in the long decline of
A civilisation; and Satan, bound
Without a big power-base, will present no
1920   Problem. In fact, Satan will then have done
Us a favour by moulding the Soviet
Union's regions into one bloc, which we
Can inherit as a large ready-made
Province in our Order that will assist
1925   Our world government and millennium.
So, do we continue the policy
Of hurrying up both Eisenhower and
Montgomery to end the war and reach

Berlin? In which case we should now support
Montgomery as field commander. Or,
Do we slow down the Allies – go along
With Roosevelt's clique's orders to Eisenhower
To impede their progress, to allow (just
As they wish) Stalin to take Berlin – and
Thus have a strategy for bringing in
The millennium? In which case we should
Support Eisenhower as field commander.
Montgomery has served us well, but he
Now wants to end the war quickly and we
Must put our strategy before all else.
And you must not forget, as I have said
Before, that the laws of history require
Our millennial world rule to grow out of
The present expanding, world-wide stage of
The American civilisation,
The youngest extant civilisation
Which is only a quarter through (whereas
Europe's is two-thirds done and in decline,
Though it will rally into a province,
A United States in our New Order),
The sole one with a global stage ahead,
The same stage the Roman Empire was in,
And world rule in this stage always reflects
The orthodox religion, in this case
Protestantism – not the occult, so
Satan's effort with Hitler or Stalin
Is doomed in terms of the laws of history,
As is his effort with Freemasonry;
So is any Pope's talk of a Catholic
World rule: the Vatican can only be
A part of my universalist Light
Millennium, which will include all known
Religions that point to the Light, and will
Shine round America's Protestant Light.
It may be wise to support Eisenhower
As he is a Protestant in the young
American civilisation which
Hosts our millennium's seeds and first growth.
Eisenhower can bring in what is to be,
Can help us bring in our New World Order,
Whereas Montgomery is at the end
Of a declining Empire, and as part
Of declining Europe cannot help us.

Do we want a short-term solution but
1975 A long-term problem that endangers peace
And which cannot be solved without a war,
Or do we want a long-term solution
With a short-term problem that can be solved
Without a war, by an internal change
1980 (The end of Communism in due course)?
A problem we can see the end of, and
For two generations throw the free world's
Energy into confining Soviet
Communism and destroying Satan's
1985 Power-base in tyranny? We will now vote.
Hum if you favour the Allies taking
Berlin under Montgomery's command
And, given the current state of their armies,
Eventually yielding all Europe to
1990 Stalin." There was an uncertain noise that
Could not be called a hum. "Hum now if you
Favour the Allies letting Stalin take
Berlin under Eisenhower's field command
And stopping Stalin in Eastern Europe
1995 And confining both him and Satan there."
A loud humming was heard and the Light flashed
Out from the sea of beings around Christ.
It was a clear decision in favour
Of confining Satan in Russia. "You
2000 Know the outcome," Christ said, when he could make
Himself heard. "That is what I shall now do.
I shall visit Eisenhower and urge him
To take field command from Montgomery
And restrain him, and make sure he seeks out
2005 The V-2 sites. I shall restrain him with
A heavy heart, for the foul Antichrist
Hitler is increasing the pace of his
Genocide of the Jews, as many of
You know from direct experience. We
2010 Have tried to stop this, but Himmler's SS
Is in league with Satan's forces, and we
Cannot make much headway in the death camps
However, our beloved Dorebus
Is making an attempt to put an end
2015 To the genocide, and we shall give him
All our support. To be completely clear,
Our policy is to stop the war, stop
Hitler possessing an atomic bomb,

Stop genocide and bind the Antichrist,
All as quickly as possible. But we
Must also stop the war on the best terms
For the Allies, and it would be the worst
Outcome if, after their sacrifices,
They ended as they were before D-Day,
Completely out of Europe and back in
The British Isles. We must also confine
Satan's activities on earth behind
A Communist wall, and bearing in mind
How tired the Allies have become, we must
Settle for what is possible: Western
Europe free, and Eastern Europe given
Up to the Antichrist in the short term,
A hard decision which makes me sad, but
One that is for the best. The same thinking,
Which you have just now so wisely agreed,
Applies to the Pacific war. There our
Priority must now be to defeat
The Japanese who have occupied parts
Of the British Empire and behaved with
Contemptible barbarity, as some
Of you know all too well. The Japanese
Will be a difficult enemy for
The Americans to vanquish as they
Will fight for their "god-man" Emperor to
The last man in Japan. But when they are
Conquered, Satan will be confined within
The USSR. Angels, although we
All want this World War to stop as soon as
Possible, we must have a plan for peace
At the end of it, while we create our
Millennium; otherwise Satan will
Break out everywhere and destroy our chance
To bring in our New World Order. Angels,
Coalition of souls, you have come through
Many traditions, religions and sects,
And you know they were all routes to the Light,
You know all nations are present within
The folds of our great Rose of Light, just as
You know that I am with you all, Christians,
Moslems, Hindus, Buddhists, Taoists, any
Faith the founders of religions here have
Found for you like pioneer pathfinders
In a jungle. You know all routes lead here,

Eventually, for all beings, spirits
2065 Of our brothers and sisters, even those
Who will not be ready to join us for
Whole ages yet. Keep to your spirits' fore
This vision of Heavenly peace which we
Want to bring down and place upon the earth."
2070 A loud humming of appreciation
Greeted his words, a humming full of love.

At Marshall's suggestion, and to appease
The British Montgomery, Eisenhower
Flew to London for a press conference and
2075 Lifted censorship on Patton's command
Of Third Army, which meant there were now two
American Armies in France and that
Bradley would soon become Montgomery's
"Co-equal" – which Butcher leaked to AP's
2080 Gallagher. Now the BBC broadcast
News that Eisenhower had taken over
Personal command in France, with the two
Army Groups under him. The impression
Was Montgomery had been demoted.
2085 Directed by Eisenhower, Smith denied
That Bradley had become co-equal with
Montgomery. Next day the BBC
Retracted the story. With the *Mirror*
Demanding a public apology,
2090 Brooke spoke to Churchill in his underground
HQ: "It is clear to me Eisenhower
Wants to be Field Commander of Allied
Army Groups in France once he has set up
Battlefield headquarters. He is now in
2095 Normandy, but Monty is treating him
Like a VIP, he's forbidden him
To attend meetings with Bradley, Patton,
Dempsey and Crerar – inviting trouble.
His latest letter is quite disturbing:
2100 'Ike is apt to get very excited
And talk wildly at the top of his voice.
He is now here, which is a very great
Pity. His ignorance as to how to
Run a war is absolute and complete;
2105 He has all the popular cries, nothing
Else. He is such a decent chap that it
Is difficult to be angry with him

For long. One thing I am firm about; he
Is never allowed to attend meetings
2110 Between me and my Army Commanders
And Bradley.'" Churchill shook his head and sighed:
"He is digging his own grave." Still smarting
From being kept from France, he was appalled
That Montgomery should be rash enough
2115 To exclude his Supreme Commander from
Meetings with four Allied fighting army
Commanders. But neither he nor Brooke could
Tell him so as the Anvil landings near
Marseilles the previous day had an impact
2120 On Italy, and they had to visit
The Italian front, and the Pacific
Also required their attention. And so
Montgomery had to fend for himself.

Eisenhower had reported to General
2125 Marshall, his boss, on his dire dinner with
Churchill and Brooke and their rejection of
His criticisms of Montgomery.
That year there would be a Presidential
Election, and the President's campaign
2130 Was under way, and Secretary of War,
Stimson, and his Chief of Staff, Marshall, were
Concerned that Roosevelt should receive credit
For the victory in Normandy now that
American troops outnumbered British
2135 By two to one, and, alarmed at reports
That following Falaise the Germans might
Collapse as in nineteen eighteen and that
The war in Normandy might be over
In September, before the election,
2140 And bent on boosting Stalin's post-war role,
And convinced that the British were fatigued
And defeatist, haunted by the shadows
Of Passchendaele and scuttling from Dunkirk,
Mad at the nationalistic British press,
2145 Decided the time had come to remove
The supreme command from Montgomery
And emphasise that the Americans
Were running the war. At Bradley's HQ
Eisenhower read a communication
2150 From General Marshall: "The Secretary"
(The brash, bellicose Stimson) "and I and

Apparently all Americans are
Strongly of the opinion that the time
Has now come for you to assume direct
2155   Command of the American Contingent.
The astounding success of the campaign
Has evoked emphatic expression of
Confidence in you and Bradley." Taken
Aback, Eisenhower showed Bradley. Shrewdly
2160   Knowing Allied unity would be strained,
He sent Butcher – his role as confidant
To Eisenhower now untenable – to
Replace the sick Davis as Head of SHAEF
Press Relations in London, exiling
2165   Him to a post that would soon be crucial.

Knowing the Germans were now encircled
Model ordered a German withdrawal
Through the gap, across the Dives. Panzers
Tried to keep the gap open around Trun
2170   But Canadian tanks fought their way to
St. Lambert-sur-Dives, in the centre
Of the German Seventh Army's retreat,
And the Fifth Panzer Army's, and held it
(Having in the square silenced a Panther
2175   Which had knocked out fourteen Canadian tanks)
Under the brave leadership of Major
Currie (who was later made a VC),
By shelling the village and the Germans
Approaching from the Dives with horse-drawn
2180   Wagons and guns, so horses stampeded
To the river which was filled with floating
Corpses and wheels, and stopped the retreat till
They were reached four days later, and were found
Amid hundreds of dead Germans, burned-out
2185   Tanks and vehicles, dying transport horses.

Like a small boy sucking a peppermint,
On his way home, near Metz, Kluge swallowed
A poisoned capsule of potassium
Cyanide and, like a diver, plunged from
2190   The top board of a bleak, distasteful earth
Into the wide invisible sea of
The next world. In Rastenburg, Bormann told
Hitler: "My Führer, Kluge's dead. Army
Doctors say that he had a cerebral

2195 Haemorrhage. He was shocked by the failure
Of his counter-attack on Avranches, and
Then Falaise." Hitler listened in silence
And then remarked: "It is scandalous that
The Canadians have taken Falaise.
2200 That was largely Kluge's fault for he was
Defeatist and pessimistic. But could
He not have committed suicide? He
Was linked to the putsch, along with Speidel.
I want a second army autopsy.
2205 Model is to be congratulated
On saving German forces from total
Encirclement. *He* is one who does not
Know the meaning of abject surrender."

Seeing Eisenhower in the throes of his
2210 Decision, and seeing its importance
To mankind, Christ knew he could not postpone
Appearing before him any longer.
He discussed with Michael as to how he
Should approach Eisenhower, seeing that he
2215 Was known for his bluff commonsense approach.
"He has minor vices," Christ observed, "he
Smokes, plays cards, reads Western novels, drinks and
Has a mistress of sorts, to relax and
Counter his blood pressure. Spiritually
2220 He is an average, sensual man, or as
The French say 'Homme moyen sensuel', and
Such men have a rational explanation
For everything, impose their sceptical
Views on all aspects of experience.
2225 If I approach him as I appeared to
Heisenberg, he will not recognise me,
Not wandering in that apple orchard,
It is not in his closed soul to do so."
Michael said: "You must go in a form he
2230 Will recognise, and appear in a place
Which defies rational explanation, where
Your appearance will seem miraculous.
He is visiting troops, then looking at
Granville as a site for his next Shellburst
2235 HQ. It looks out on Mont-St.-Michel.
I will draw him to my Holy Island
Where Satan's forces cannot penetrate,
Which is impregnable, protected. I

Will lure him there, out of uniform, and
2240   Arrange for him not to be recognised.
Once he is there I will isolate him
And then you can appear to him in an
Inaccessible place, just as you did
To the fishermen on St. Michael's Mount.
2245   The place must be precipitous, and you
Must materialise out of air, so he
Knows he is with the supranatural."
And so as Kay drove him back from Granville,
Eisenhower was suddenly overwhelmed
2250   By an urge to go to Mont-St.-Michel.
The granite Abbey with a grandiose spire,
The monastery clustered above the town,
Mysterious, the sea all round, drew him,
Called for the elevation of his soul,
2255   Called him to rise like a pilgrim and climb
To the topmost turret of Paradise.
"Kay," he said, speaking formally, as his
Aide sat by him, "I would like to visit
The monastery on that rock. The tide's out,
2260   I think we can go over now. Could you
Detour and drop me off so I can climb
And sit in silence up there? I want to
Be alone and think." Kay said, "You will be
Recognised in your uniform, General.
2265   You will be mobbed, you won't be much alone."
Gault, who had replaced Butcher as his live-
In aide said, "I've got some casual clothes in
The back you can borrow as a disguise.
On security grounds I must keep you
2270   In sight, but I can give you space." And so
Half an hour later Eisenhower, wearing
A sweater, fawn trousers and a knitted
Climber's hat, pursued at a distance by
His aide and driven by a compulsion he
2275   Did not understand, walked up the Grande Rue,
A narrow, steep lane past medieval
Houses, and climbed the ninety stone steps of
The stairway called Grand Degré and wandered
To the West platform where, suspended like
2280   An angel in the sky, he looked across
Wet sands and salty pools, part land, part sea
To where the Couesnon meandered and
Where sea-gulls wheeled, and high above his head,

A hundred and fifty metres above
2285 Sea level, Saint Michael fought the dragon,
A distant statue on top of the spire.
He entered the dark Abbey, his aide not
Far behind him, and found a quiet corner
And sat and wrestled with his decision
2290 Until he felt compelled to climb some stairs
In a spiral staircase in a buttress.
He came out on an outside platform where
The view was breathtaking: across the stone
Lacework Staircase, flying-buttress footbridge,
2295 Was the sweep of the bay from Granville to
Cancale. His soul, opened by the beauty
Of the stones, opened to beauty, he now
Returned back down to the chancel. His aide
Had gone. He wandered down the Grand Degré
2300 To the terraced Abbey Gardens and went
Through the gate on his left, his soul raised by
Aesthetic feeling, open and intense,
And, leaving the ramparts and North Tower
Behind him, walked down a path through woods to
2305 A rock that hung above the Fountain of
St. Aubert. He was quite alone, and there,
Envying monastic serenity,
He found a crag high up, and as he sat
In anguish at his decision and looked
2310 Down at the sea sparkling in the sunset,
A shape appeared on the ledge before him
And said, "Dwight." Startled, Eisenhower said, "How
Did you get here?" Christ said, "I knew you would
Discount an apparition in a place
2315 Which has a rational explanation for
You are a rational, sceptical man. I
Have chosen to convince you here, where no
Rational explanation is possible,
Just as I appeared on St. Michael's Mount
2320 To a fisherman fifteen centuries back.
I've come in a form you will recognise."
And the shape gathered to a body which
Showed the wounds on his bloodied hands and feet
And the gaping hole in his side. "It's you,"
2325 Eisenhower said, stunned. "You believed in me
Once," Christ said half-reproachfully, "when you
Were a River Brethren Mennonite and

53

Then when you were a Jehovah's Witness.
You've not had much time for the world beyond
2330 Of late. I do not blame you for that. But
I want you to know, we in Heaven support
You, and back your judgement. Montgomery,
Maddening though he must have been for you,
Has been a good friend of ours, and always
2335 Prays each night. Even so, we support
You in the choice you are making because
You can help bring in the new Order we
In Heaven are working towards. You are
Loyal to General Marshall, I know, and
2340 He is loyal to Stimson and Roosevelt,
Who want to carve up the post-war world with
Stalin, Lucifer's agent of influence,
To further their Illuminatist goals.
I realise I have just shocked you, shaken
2345 The way you see things, but don't get me wrong,
We in Heaven do not mind that. We are
Happy for you to proceed as Marshall
Wishes, and after the end of the war
When there is a United Nations and
2350 Soviet hegemony of Satan, our
Adversary, you can be President
And can cajole the world towards our post-
Soviet New World Order, which cannot come
To pass unless Eastern Europe succumbs
2355 To Russian rule. I can tell you, there are
Men close to Roosevelt who are working for
Satan, just as do men close to Stalin,
And Satan already wants the post-war
World to be an American-Russian
2360 Alliance disguised as hostility.
Dwight, know that though you may have doubts about
Bringing such an alliance in, it is
A necessary half-way stage towards
The Order Heaven wants, which will emerge
2365 From it. Satan does not realise what our
End is, he does not grasp that he is our
Instrument. So we can let him do what
He thinks advances his dubious ends.
Choose to be Land Commander, and through your
2370 Victory in this battle of France become
President and work, by establishing

Its opposite, towards the new Order
Heaven desires. The choice is yours, I point
Towards a potentiality or
2375 Tendency. Nothing is fated, human
Freewill is absolute. This time I have
Just made contact. Next time I appear, I
Will show you the true situation round
Roosevelt, your destiny and a vision
2380 Of the dream Heaven has for the rich earth,
And the alternative one Hell has, as
Possibilities, which freewill can make
A reality." With that he faded
In the evening air, and Eisenhower was
2385 Left looking at the sparkling waves alone,
Wondering if he had hallucinated.
His aide approached and said, "I was alarmed,
I have been looking for you everywhere.
You vanished, sir." Eisenhower asked Gault, "Did
2390 You see someone leave here just now?" Gault said,
"No sir, just you sitting on this high rock."
Eisenhower was disturbed by what he'd heard.
That night he lay awake and, abstracted,
Went over each word in his waking soul.
2395 He was still the bluff, genial extrovert
Who, though alert in scanning and planning,
Switched off in his spare time with distractions,
But now there was new awareness within.

At Tournières, the Falaise trap still not closed,
2400 Eisenhower, still blaming Montgomery
For being slow and letting Model's troops
Escape, finally made up his mind to
Implement the urgings of Stimson and
Marshall. He convened a meeting "to draw
2405 Up plans for future conduct of the war".
Strangely Montgomery did not attend
But sent his smooth Chief of Staff, de Guingand.
Eisenhower said: "I have here a letter
From Montgomery to Brooke, which arrived
2410 After Brooke left for Italy, saying
The two Army Groups should keep together.
However, Brad favours an eastward drive
To Germany, not north via the Lowlands,
Monty's preference, and yesterday the Red

Army launched its Romanian offensive.
The balance of Allied troops has changed. On
D-Day America had fewer troops
Than Britain. Now America has twice
As many – three-quarters of all forces.
2420 Now it is impossible not to change
The command structure. I have decided
To change the system of command on first
September. I will take command of both
The two Army Groups, and Bradley's Twelve Group
2425 Will drive across the Seine for Metz and Saar.
The British under Montgomery can
Go north to destroy V-bomb rocket sites,
While the Americans proceed into
Germany. The two Army Groups will now
2430 Separate. Cable the Combined Chiefs of
Staff and send a directive to Monty."

De Guingand brought news of Eisenhower's shock
Decision to Montgomery's new TAC
Headquarters at Condé. Devastated,
2435 Hurt, wanting to curl up like a hedgehog
But extending prickliness to its full,
Montgomery said: "Tomorrow – tonight –
The battle of Normandy will be won.
I do not agree with the decisions
2440 Reached. I'm sending you back to Eisenhower
With *Notes on Future Operations*. You
Are to tell General Eisenhower that these
Notes express my views and that Bradley has
Expressed his agreement with them. Then ask
2445 The Supreme Commander to lunch with me
The day after tomorrow. He should come
And see me." The *Notes* showed Montgomery's
Desire that Eisenhower should abdicate
Command over both of the Army Groups.
2450 After de Guingand left, Henderson said
Gently, "I said you had bought a month." Still
Devastated, Montgomery said: "But
When I've just won. Eisenhower wants to scoop
The reward. I thought he was too decent
2455 To do this. I was wrong. This, in the hour
Of my greatest triumph. It is dangerous
To swap horses in mid-stream. And just when

The Germans are on the run, and the war
So nearly won. If only Brooke were at
2460   The War Office, not with Alexander."

Montgomery battled to remain Field
Commander. De Guingand returned and said,
"I spent two hours with him in an apple
Orchard. I said commanding the Allied
2465   Force was a 'whole-time job' for one man, and
That to change the system of command now,
After having won a great victory, would
Be to prolong the war. He would not budge.
The Allied Force must split, the British to
2470   The north, the Americans perhaps to
The east. He says the British cannot count
On any Americans in the north."
Montgomery sighed, "Procrastination,
'Perhaps'. I disagree with any plan
2475   Which splits the Allied Force." In Brooke's absence,
His deputy Nye said, "I beg you not
To split the Allied command while Churchill
And Brooke are out of England. The Alliance
Must come first."
2480   Montgomery flew early
Next morning to Laval, Bradley's latest
HQ, and said: "On August the seventeenth
You agreed with me that both Armies should
Go north." Bradley, for the first time dropping
2485   The 'sir' to which the Land Commander was
Entitled, said, "No, I did not. I see
That the British should go north because of
The V-1 sites, but I've always wanted
To go east to Germany." The beret-
2490   Wearer said: "You were got at yesterday,
When you went to visit Ike." Bradley said
Defiantly, "No, the American
Army has now put behind it the poor
Performance at Kasserine Pass, Anzio
2495   And Salerno, and has new confidence.
We're pouring fifty divisions into
Europe while fighting in the Pacific,
We've come of age. We have double the troops,
We want to go east to Germany. We
2500   Can do it on our own." Montgomery
Said sadly: "I trained you, and now you want

To race off like Patton. It's a mistake
To split the Armies. It will not shorten
The war but prolong it." To which Bradley
2505   Retorted, not equal to equal but
Superior to inferior, "We don't
See it that way. And as regards training,
I'm 'the military Lincoln' in the press
Back home. Good day." An hour after they had
2510   Both left Patton jauntily arrived and
Asked General Allen, 12th Army Group's Chief
Of Staff, where everyone was, and said: "I
Have just thought up the best strategical
Idea I've ever had. Write it down now.
2515   Third Army will cross the Seine at Melun,
And the Yonne at Sens, swivel north across
The Marne and the Oise and cut off German
Troops fleeing from Dempsey and Hodges at
Beauvais. In other words Third Army now
2520   Abandons Saar and takes part in Monty's
Northern thrust." Support for Montgomery
That arrived just an hour too late for him.

As Montgomery returned at noon to
His Condé HQ, Eisenhower arrived
2525   For lunch as Montgomery requested,
Along with Bedell Smith and General Gale.
Bristling at his "misused" authority,
At once Montgomery said abruptly:
"I must see you alone and obtain your
2530   Decision on some points of principle.
The staff should not be present." To humour
Montgomery, Eisenhower meekly told
Smith to stay outside while he went into
The map caravan with Montgomery,
2535   Who stood before a large map, feet apart
Hands behind his back, eyes darting, and said:
"You know I want a northward thrust of both
Armies, who would be so strong they need fear
Nothing. The immediate need is for
2540   A firm plan. I think it was a mistake
To split the Armies, and for you to take
Field command. The Supreme Commander should
Be on high, on a perch with a detached
View of land, sea, air, civil control and
2545   Political problems, should not descend

58

Into the intricacies of the land
Battle, someone else should do that. And it
Is a whole-time job for one man. Today
The Falaise trap is closed, and we are now
2550 Bombing the Germans caught inside. We've won
A great victory because of land control,
Not in spite of it. If American
Public opinion is the problem, let
Bradley control the battle, and put me
2555 Under Bradley." Eisenhower looked at him
With dislike, but said patiently: "No, that's
Not my intention. I do not favour
A single thrust to the Ruhr. The Germans
Are in confusion, I want two thrusts with
2560 The flexibility to reinforce
Either, depending on which of the two
Is succeeding the most." Montgomery
Interrupted: "I do not think either
Will be strong enough, alone. The British,
2565 Alone, need additional forces for
The northern thrust to the V-1 sites." To
Humour, diplomatic Eisenhower said,
"They can have American assistance,
But it should be kept to a minimum."
2570 Montgomery then asked, "Who should command
The northern thrust?" Eisenhower said, "There must
Be one commander. You." Montgomery
Said: "Twenty-first Army Group only has
Fourteen divisions." Eisenhower asked, "How
2575 Many American divisions would
You need for your thrust north?" Montgomery
Said, "An American Army of at
Least twelve divisions on our right flank." Now
Eisenhower was speechless. After a pause
2580 He collected his thoughts and said, "If that
Happened the Americans would only
Have one Army, and public opinion
Would object." Montgomery asked, "Why should
Public opinion make you want to take
2585 Military decisions which are unsound?"
Eisenhower, keeping calm, said patiently,
"You must understand, it's election year
In the States. I can take no action which
May sway public opinion against our

2590 President, and lose him the election.
And so we must now separate the two
Army Groups, and I must take command of
The ground forces and send the two Army
Groups in different directions so there is
2595 No question of Americans being
Under the operational control
Of a British General." Montgomery
Contradicted: "Military logic does
Not base itself on public opinion."
2600 Eisenhower stared at him, put out at his
Narrow military view and lack of
Diplomatic sense, which did not grasp that
He had to do what Marshall and Roosevelt
Wanted, that how they both perceived public
2605 Opinion was a pressure on him. He
Could only agree to a single thrust
In the north if there was separation
Between Americans and British as
His masters wanted. Now he felt his blood
2610 Pressure rising, and wanted to leave. As
Patiently as he could he said calmly:
"The American Army Group will now
Become two Armies, so we have three in
All: an Army Group of the North, Centre
2615 And South. I will be Generalissimo
In the field." Montgomery looked at him,
Eyes darting, convinced that SHAEF were behind
This mess, and Bedell Smith, sure that talk of
The American election was just
2620 An excuse, that deep in his heart of hearts
Eisenhower knew he was wrong. He said: "So
The British are on their own in the north,
But are not strong enough to thrust without
American help, which must be under
2625 The command of an American." He
Shook his head. "We've split the Allied effort
On the day it triumphed, that it achieved
Its greatest victory in World War Two, at
Its highest point, just when it could shorten
2630 The war. This is a mistake and it will
Lengthen the war." Bristling, Eisenhower said:
"Bedell Smith and I will go off and draft
A directive I will show you before

It goes out." And Eisenhower turned and left
The map caravan. He sensed Christ at his
Elbow, grateful that he had stood so firm.

The Polish tanks fought up a ridge above
Chambois, and then blocked the exit road, while
In Warsaw the Germans were putting down
The July uprising, arresting Poles.
From the wooded high ground, they saw below
A vast and level plain of armies, where
Thousands of armoured cars, tanks, half-tracks, cars,
Horse-drawn wagons, gun-carriages and carts
Queued bumper to bumper in every road
With ten thousands of mud-covered soldiers,
All stuck in a massive traffic jam as
All pressed on the narrow, blocked bottleneck
Whose roads were still held open by Panzers
For the tiny columns of crawling things.
Above, the Allied fighter-bombers flew
At will, bombing, strafing and battering.
Among the explosions and burning carts,
Piercing screams and yells, whinnying horses
With legs blown off, still harnessed to their shafts,
Tired men cowered under cover, pleading,
Crying for help, crouching next to the dead,
Whose faces were still screwed in pain. Some pushed
Them off wagons and flopped down in their place,
Sheltering, huddling under smoke that rose
From burning vehicles and hung like a pall
Over the columns of this carnage, and
Gave some air cover as the Thunderbolts
And Typhoons fired rockets and bullets, swept
Over the burning plain time after time.
As misty rain sweeps over meadows from
A grey-white cloudy sky, and green hills and
Woods hang in mist, so the bombs and scorch-fires
Left a veil of smoke on the rolling field.
That night Americans and Poles entered
Chambois, but next day SS Panzer tanks
Under Hausser sought to open a route
And added to the flaming wreckage and
Men fleeing eastwards. In the end they cut
The Polish armour holding the ridge from
The Canadians, who broke back next day
And found, among burned vehicles and strewn dead,

The Poles still holding what was called "the Mace"
From the shape of the contours on the map,
2680 Crying with joy, hugging the relief force.
The Falaise pocket was now closed, and though
A few men and vehicles slipped through Allied
Lines at night, including Hausser, whose jaw
Was shot away, in a tank, and "Panzer"
2685 Meyer, head bound with bandages, nothing
Could save the German troops in Normandy.

The pocket sealed, Allied troops now moved in
And found a dreadful sight. In that foul Hell,
Ten thousand lay dead among nine thousand
2690 Burned-out tanks, guns, vehicles, trucks, cars, while, dazed,
Fifty thousand soldiers sat, some wounded.
Thirty thousand had escaped to the Seine
With just a hundred and twenty tanks. But,
From Trun to St.-Lambert and Chambois smelt
2695 Of death, a stench of dead troops and horses,
Cattle and burnt vehicles. The heat shimmered,
Flesh soon decayed, flies swarmed on swollen limbs,
Maggots crawled, flesh hung in the hedgerows with
Bits of uniform. Corpses stared, legless
2700 Trunks propped, blown-up horses lay in heaps, blood
In dry pools. The Germans had suffered a
Worse defeat than at Stalingrad, and now
US Third Army was across the Seine
The Allies could drive towards Germany.

2705 Hitler woke up shouting, yelling for help
In his dim-lit bunker room. He sat on
The edge of his bed, as though paralysed,
Like a child just woken from a nightmare,
Terrified of a shadow on a wall;
2710 Panic-stricken, he trembled so much that
The bed shook. A guard rushed in but just heard
Confused, unintelligible words as
Hitler gasped for breath, then stood, stumbling and
Looking about him, muttering, "It's him,
2715 It's him, he's here!" His lips were blue, sweat dripped.
Then he uttered some numbers without sense,
And strung terms together in a strange way.
The guard, frightened, backed to the door. Hitler
Stood silent, his lips moving. Then he screamed,
2720 "There, over there in the corner." He howled.

The guard rushed to the corner of his room
And said, "There's no one here." Not listening,
Hitler said, "More, asking for more." Slowly
He calmed down, reassured that the presence
2725   Had gone, but realising he was now in
The power of a force he could not control,
That he had gone too far in the occult,
From Basilides and the Cathar Pures
He had dabbled and explored a dark way
2730   To Eckart's black magic that had destroyed
Steiner, and that he was now entrammelled,
A victim of demoniac possession.
As soon as the guard left he was aware
Of a black presence in the dark corner
2735   And shuddered, was filled with dread and panic.
He did not gabble numbers to appease
It. He spoke, "I know you're there." Satan said,
"You know why. I'm your Providence, you have
Achieved nothing without me, you sleep-walk
2740   While my voice through your lips conquers the world.
You want me to speak through you as Pythian
Priestesses wanted me to speak through them
At the Delphic Oracle." Divided,
Hitler muttered, "I did not want this, you
2745   Lurking in dark corners, on the edge of
My consciousness. I always knew that I
Must be pure in body, soul and spirit
To communicate with other-worldly
Entities, but though I wanted to be
2750   Possessed by a strong will to power, I sought
To bring in the era of the Cathar
Paraclete, Holy Spirit, deliverance
From the chaos of evil enemies.
I wanted beauty and found ugliness.
2755   You promised you would bring me victories,
But what about Falaise? And now the Seine?"
To which Satan said, in scathing contempt,
"Call yourself the god-man, a Superman?
Without me you are a whining, snivelling,
2760   Whimpering child. Did I not save you from
Stauffenberg's bomb? We at least keep our word.
Falaise was my trap, I lured them across
The Seine. You can burn Paris and attack
Their flanks. The pact, Hitler, our agreement.

63

2765 I want the Jews, if you can't deliver,
I will not go on supplying. There are
Others with larger empires than yours who
Can, and who do not talk of ugliness.
Deliver me the entire Jewish race
2770 And I will take care of blind Jehovah."
Reluctant Hitler knew he must comply,
And offer more to the unsatisfied
New possessor of his tranquillity
While outwardly still living like a Pure.
2775 The black presence now went, but left Hitler
Divided, and with tension in his jaw.

After the carnage, Eisenhower, driven
By Kay, visited the battlefield at
Falaise where the Allies killed ten thousand
2780 Germans and took fifty thousand prisoners,
Wandering like a tourist from his car.
What he saw appalled him: the great field was
Covered with tanks, guns, vehicles, horses and
Thousands of dead German soldiers still in
2785 Uniform, overhung like a morning
Mist with the foul stench of death that entered
His throat and sickened him. It was a field
Of decaying flesh. He could walk hundreds
Of yards stepping on dead flesh. It was as
2790 If the top had been skimmed from a burial-
Ground, exposing the rotting corpses of
The hidden dead. The men who'd got out were
Stragglers without vehicles or equipment.
He stood in an inferno confronted
2795 With the reality to which his plans
Had led, loathing war as his pacifist
Parents had done, despising the victory
He had won over these now dead humans,
Disgusted at being involved in and
2800 Primarily responsible for this
Slaughter, this massacre. It was as if
He had to clear out a cesspit, and had
To wade in muck and inhale sickening
Stench in order to finish the job, but
2805 While he did it he hated what he was
Doing. Back at the car he said to Kay:
"The odour of war nauseates me, Kay,

64

And I feel ashamed to have ordered that
These young men should be bombed and strafed into
2810 Lifeless carcasses. Civilisation
Is not pretty when it resorts to war
And deeds of unfeeling barbarism."

German Army Group B was now wiped out,
With three of thirty-eight divisions left.
2815 As Germans raced for the Seine, the Allies
Were too cautious, lost time disentangling
US, British and Canadian troops
And halted every evening to regroup
Like boys in a cross-country race gasping
2820 For breath, bent double, waiting for their friends,
Though Patton's Third Army drove east and crossed
The Seine at Mantes-Gassicourt at night, though
More reached Melun, and Hodges crossed northwards.
Through delays the Germans built a pontoon
2825 Bridge and, floating it at night, ferried tanks
And vehicles across the Seine. Their defeat
In Normandy eroded the German
Occupation of France. The Allies chose
To bypass Paris, feeding which would take
2830 Food from SHAEF forces bound for Germany,
But wanting to avoid street-fighting and
Destruction as at Caen and with de Gaulle
With the Americans and French troops in
SHAEF, Eisenhower was in a quandary. Then
2835 Thirty-five Frenchmen were executed
For defying the occupation, and,
Contrary to de Gaulle's orders the Free
French rose, three thousand men tore cobblestones
And seized weapons from the Germans and, while
2840 One third were killed and still more wounded, waged
A guerilla war against the Germans
Whose military commandant, von Choltitz,
Using a Swedish go-between, arranged
A truce, with joint German-Free French patrols
2845 To curtail the sporadic fighting. He
Told Kluge the truce would keep the bridges
Open and strengthen Paris's defence.
Brooding on Warsaw, where resistance would
Be punished by demolition, Hitler
2850 Ordered: "Anti-German actions must be

65

Suppressed with utmost force. The Seine bridges
Will be prepared for demolition, for
Paris must not fall into the hands of
The enemy save as a field of rubble."

2855 The Elysée Palace and forty-five
Bridges were wired with charges that would cause
A fire-storm and burn the city down, but,
Not wanting to go down in history as
The barbaric destroyer of Paris,

2860 Choltitz phoned Speidel and, talking in code,
Denied he had resources to blow up
Seventy Paris bridges, said he had
Placed explosives in Notre Dame and the Arc
De Triomphe, and would topple the Eiffel

2865 Tower into the Seine to block it, that his
Troops would have no food in two days, and that
The Free French held the key buildings. Meanwhile
Leclerc sent a hundred and fifty tanks
Towards Paris, and Bradley heard the truce

2870 Would end bloodily next day but Choltitz
Would withdraw before Allied troops. De Gaulle
Appealed to Eisenhower, who decided
Leclerc should take Paris under SHAEF, and
Be reinforced on military grounds.

2875 He sent Gerow with US infantry.
Leclerc's tanks were fêted in a great march
Of liberation, which Germans opposed.
As Gerow prepared to go in with tanks
A small patrol reached the Hotel de Ville.

2880 Nearby von Choltitz rang Spiedel, so he
Could hear the cheering, and then surrendered.
When told that Allied troops were in Paris
Hitler asked, "Is Paris burning?" When told
"No", and that all its cultural treasures

2885 Were still intact, he raged, "I do not trust
The officer corps. They withdraw. I want
More Party men who will observe all my
Orders to the letter." Flushed with anger,
He ordered bombing, V-1s and shelling,

2890 None of which happened. And de Gaulle's parade
Took place to nearby sniping, the streets lined
With Leclerc's troops under Gerow's command.
Later Americans from Omaha
On their way to battle, marched down the Champs

Elysées past de Gaulle, Leclerc, Gerow
And Bradley. No British troops attended.

Like a disputatious neighbour who knocks
Down a garden wall and then shouts insults
And rude words across it, insisting it
2900 Was cracked before, or cuts down a yew hedge
Because a surveyor has miscopied
A figure on his plan, or declares he
Will be driving across newly bought land
Because he wrongly thinks he has a right
2905 Of way, or, just moving to an eighteenth
Century port near an old china-clay shoot
For loading boats, complains about the dust
To Environmental Health, saying it
Is a health hazard and should be ended,
2910 Whose distant figure is enough to make
The poor owner shake with put-upon rage,
Montgomery's presence irritated
Eisenhower, who was glad Montgomery
Refused his invitation to attend
2915 The liberation ceremony in
Paris (which was "in the American
Zone" and thus no concern of his) and laughed:
"It's just as well, the less I see of him
The better it is for my blood pressure."

2920 At Eisenhower's advance headquarters, which
Were codenamed Shellburst, Kay lived in a tent
Pitched in a meadow near Eisenhower's big
Wooden-floored office tent that stood under
Trees. Kay breakfasted with Eisenhower each
2925 Day, glowing in the warmth of his presence
As from a log fire. The weather was fine.
Kay drove him to the front to visit all
The commanders and talk with the men. He
Was always accompanied by an aide.
2930 Next day they flew to Portsmouth and she drove
Him, and his aide, to London to confer
With Churchill or SHAEF at Bushey Park, and
They would sometimes visit the Cottage for
An hour or two and return with armfuls
2935 Of marrows or beans from his vegetable
Garden there. When they were alone he would
Put an arm round her shoulder and draw her

To him, but usually there were fleeting
Caresses and quickly squeezed hands under
2940 The breakfast table, and exchanged glances
In the rear view mirror of the car. Each
Day he scribbled a message on a scrap
Of paper and tucked it into her hand,
But though they were always together from
2945 Breakfast to bedtime, she now almost felt
Lonely, and she could not write messages
Back in case Mickey found them when looking
After his wardrobe. "You don't have to write
To me," Eisenhower told her, "every time
2950 You look at me, I see a love letter
In your eyes." Huge events were happening
Round them, but their lives were almost routine
Now that the extraordinary appeared
Commonplace. The day after Paris was
2955 Liberated Kay drove him for five hours
Past mounds of abandoned German vehicles
To Chartres, where Bradley had moved his HQ
To a barnyard almost in the shadow
Of the great Cathedral. They were mobbed by
2960 Jeeploads of jubilant correspondents.
They had dinner with Bradley (rations and
A bottle of wine) and the next day they
Drove in to Paris and, through cheering crowds
Lining the Champs Elysées, to the Arc
2965 De Triomphe, where Eisenhower and Bradley
Paid their respects to the unknown soldier
And were mobbed by excited French people.
On the way back to Chartres, Eisenhower talked
About the year he spent in Paris when
2970 John was small, how they lived near the river
And how he had often walked with John to
The Arc de Triomphe. He was now wistful,
Thinking of Mamie among falling leaves.

Devastated, Montgomery had sunk
2975 Into deep depression, staring as if
Looking for faces in a leaping fire,
Pondering their meaning. At the end of
August Brooke visited him at his new
TAC HQ at Avernes, and said: "It is
2980 A pity this all happened while I was
Away. It will add three to six months to

68

The war. But you can look back with pride on
A staggering victory, perhaps the most
Outstanding military victory in
2985   The whole of human history, and all through
Your plan. Our political chief, Grigg, thinks
The same." Montgomery tiredly rejoined:
"Overlord has reached a successful end,
But what now? I go north with six or eight
2990   American divisions now under
Hodges, in all less than half what I have
Had. Patton now says it's a mistake for
Hodges to turn north, that he could now end
The war in a few days by driving hard
2995   Eastwards. I am now out of telephone
Communication with Bradley, and know
The Germans are not finished by any
Means." In despair he said wearily: "I
Have isolated myself to perfect
3000   The art of field command from the front, with
TAC HQ separate from Main, and I
See with my military eyes, not through
Political or national antennae."
Brooke said quietly: "We are seeing the rise
3005   As a great power of the United States,
To whom events now pass. I fear we shall
See the decline of the British Empire.
If so, it will be dated to our loss
Of land command, the first of September
3010   Nineteen forty-four."

                    The next day Brooke went
To the underground HQ, where Churchill
Lay in his blue and yellow dressing-gown
And announced he had a temperature of
3015   A hundred and three and pneumonia.
He asked, "Did you see Monty?" and, hearing
That he was "bearing up", though still distressed,
Said: "I want to make him a Field Marshal
On September the first, so as to mark
3020   The approval of the British people
For his leadership." Next day the King came
To his sick-room and signed the submission,
Using Churchill's pillow as a table.
Churchill said: "It is the highest rank in
3025   The British Army. It now puts him on
A par with Wellington, Haig, Kitchener –

And Brooke, and higher than any four-star
American General like Eisenhower."
He added sadly, "He is now paying
3030 The penalty for being unable to
Communicate with his superiors."

On the evening of September the first
Montgomery sat on a canvas chair
In a field at his new headquarters at
3035 Dangu, being painted by James Gunn. He
Looked like a medieval English king
Surveying lands won at Agincourt or
Crécy. He went to his caravan and
Sat alone. He had been elevated
3040 To Field Marshal, but demoted from field
Commander to Twenty-First Army Group,
And by a man who had not seen a shot
Fired in his life before Overlord and
Who did not understand strategy, who
3045 Had failed to impose a clear strategic
Plan on the battlefield, squandering all
The Allies' gains and who was useless as
A field commander. He'd been demoted
After the greatest invasion ever
3050 And a three-month battle resulted in
Victory, when he was across the Seine and
Heading for Brussels. It defied sense. It
Was unjust and would prolong the war. He
Did not understand and prayed to the Light
3055 To enlighten him, and nearby felt Christ's
Compassionate strength, but was still baffled.

Two million Allied men had landed in
Normandy, most were American, and,
With the creation of 12th Army Group,
3060 Bradley was almost free from the command
Of Montgomery and his Overlord.
For the Americans, the Caen stalemate
And caution at the Falaise pocket made
Montgomery suspect, and Eisenhower
3065 Was glad he was to take command of all
SHAEF land forces and that Montgomery
Would now command 21st Army Group.
It is a law of the universe that
Overweening egos must be humbled

3070 As they obstruct the Light's entry into
The soul. The humbling of Montgomery
Was necessary for his spiritual
Good, and now that his egotistical
Pride had led to an inevitable
3075 And necessary fall, Christ stood near him,
Like a father giving encouragement
And strength to a son whose self-esteem has
Received a blow as a result of his
Own unwise actions. So far-sighted Christ,
3080 A pragmatist seeking to bring in his
New World Order that, unlike Satan's, would
Rule mankind well, supported Eisenhower,
Who did not pray, against Montgomery,
Who did, whose desolation he Lightened.

3085 Heaven and Hell have different politics
And different policies towards mankind.
The policy of Heaven offers the Light
To all disillusioned by Darkness who
Repent of evil and prefer the good;
3090 Hell's policy offers false promises
To self-deceivers who believe untruth.
One forgives, the other flatters with lies.
Hitler sat in despair in his bunker,
His forces routed, and felt betrayed by
3095 Satan, for Paris had not burnt. He had
Made a pact, sold his soul for victories
And world dominion, which had not happened.
He felt deceived, cheated. He hoped Paris
Was a trap, like Falaise, to embolden
3100 His enemies and lure them forward so
He could deliver a crushing defeat
And stop the Allies with a mortal blow.
Evil deceives by flaunting promises
A man longs to embrace, lures his yearning
3105 To believe in what is meretricious
Till he consummates consuming desire
And trusts promising possibilities.

~ BOOK 4 ~

THE ALLIES ARE REPULSED

O   John, evangelist of love's vision,
The son of Zebedee and Salome,
Sister of St. Joseph, you who with James
Became a fisherman and by the trees
5   Of Lake Tiberias and in Jordan's
Desert, had visions, the disciple of
John the Baptist until you spent a day
With Jesus, who called you to be the first
Fisher of men at Gennesaret, you
10   Who with James he nicknamed "sons of thunder"
("Boanerges") for your great passion, and
Who with James and Peter were closest to
Jesus, witnessed the Transfiguration,
His raising of Jairus's daughter,
15   Agony in Gethsemane's Garden,
The Last Supper you and Peter prepared
When you reclined "on Jesus' breast" and asked
Who would betray him; you who followed him
Into the High Priest's hall and heard his trial
20   And went to Golgotha and at the cross
Took charge of his mother ("woman, behold
Thy son") and took the body down and bore
It to Joseph's tomb, who first saw linen
Cloths, the empty shroud, and ran and told them
25   In the upper room, where the doors were closed,
And saw Christ enter, Thomas touch his wounds,
And saw the Ascension and Pentecost,
Your baptism in the Holy Spirit,
Then preached the Gospel with Peter and James
30   In Samaria while Aramathaea
Took Mary to Glastonbury, and when St.
Paul the Turk was martyred, you who went to
Ephesus, some say with Mary, the new
Artemis (whose devotees had booed Paul
35   In the theatre and imprisoned him in
The tower on the hill above Celsus's
Library) – although some say after her
Dormition; who preached twenty-seven years
Till during Domitian's persecution

When he built a Temple to himself in
Ephesus, you were summoned to Rome and
Immersed in a pot of boiling oil and
Banished, you who were exiled to Patmos
For eighteen months: a convict island with
No water and few trees to build a house,
Ruled by the high Temple of Artemis.
There, your chains off, you preached the one true God
Who unlike Artemis cannot be seen,
Who is spirit and love, and defeated
Cynops, the magician of Darkness, and
Prayed in this Cave where now I queue in heat,
Wearing a towel tucked in my waist to hide
The knees below my shorts. Here where I edge
Down steps between white walls and tiny domes,
In the Cave of the Apocalypse you
Heard a great voice like a trumpet, which cracked
The cave wall into three parts, rent the rock
With three fissures, say "I am Alpha and
Omega, the first and the last: and, what
Thou seest write in a book" and you turned,
Saw the Son of Man and fell at his feet
And saw, your head in this railed-off corner,
Your domed eyes shut above your tangled beard,
The supernatural events of Heaven
Unfold, and dictated your vision to
Your follower Prochorus, who stood here,
And made a book-rest on this sloping wall
Near where you scratched this sign of the true cross,
And took dictation as your lips gave words
To the substance of your visions, compiled
The last book of the *New Testament*, your
Revelation of Satan's fate, triumph
Of Light over darkness, your glimpses of
The Light of the World – of your *Gospel* and
Three *Epistles* – now shown in this fifth book;
Here you reconciled Christianity
And Gnosticism in your Light Gospel
(As I now reconcile conflicting Lights
Of Christian and Gnostic sects in the One),
A site now guarded by your Monastery
High on the hill above, your Gnostic Light
That later appealed to Pope and Cathar;
When Domitian was murdered and Nerva
Became Emperor and permitted all

85　To spread Christianity, you returned
　　To Ephesus, leaving this Cave to be
　　A Christian church, dedicated to you,
　　And, alone of the Twelve, were not martyred
　　But led forward Paul's Church of Ephesus.
90　You became so old and frail that you could
　　No longer walk but had to be carried
　　To services and meetings, could only
　　Say repeatedly, "My little children,
　　Love one another," your final pared down
95　Simple message of love in peace and war.
　　You lived to be a hundred and four. Then,
　　With a premonition of your own death,
　　You left Ephesus at dawn with seven
　　Disciples, prayed at Selcuk, then asked them
100　To dig your grave in the shape of a cross
　　And laid your cloak in it, and then lay down,
　　Requested them to cover you with soil
　　Up to your knees, and then to shroud your chest
　　And cover it with soil. As the sun rose
105　You died, and now you rest in a marble
　　Tomb with four columns, and five steps lead down
　　To your crypt. Justinian built this Church
　　Of St. John in the sixth century, you lie
　　Between the Seljuqs' castle and their mosque,
110　The infidels who fought the Crusaders.
　　As storks wheel overhead in the blue sky
　　I sit in shade under a fig-tree and
　　Think of your testimony and how you
　　Took over from St. Paul and handed on,
115　And added your visions, demanding to
　　Be more believed than the carpet-sellers
　　Who tout for custom around Ephesus
　　And say, "Hello, how are you, I honest,
　　Believe what I tell you and buy my wares."
120　O John, visionary who knew the Light
　　And knew history is a tussle between
　　The Light and the Beast's Darkness, and valued
　　Visionary images, help me as
　　I tell of the plan to sprint tanks and troops
125　Through Nazi-occupied Holland, and cross
　　The Rhine and thrust deep into Germany,
　　A lightning stroke to topple the Third Reich,
　　Arrest the Antichrist, put him in chains
　　And end the war in nineteen forty-four;

130　And describe Eisenhower's revelations,
　　How Christ poured visions of the future in
　　To his domed head, so he knew that the war
　　Could not be ended at Arnhem, but must
　　Bring in a new European order,
135　A prelude to your New Jerusalem
　　Which, nineteen hundred years after your glimpse
　　In 94 AD, can come to pass
　　At the start of a new millennium
　　In a world government, triumph of Light.

140　Tell, Muse, how in the transcendent Fire which
　　Reconciles apparently conflicting
　　Forces of Darkness and immanent Light,
　　There is just one revelation of Light,
　　Many glimpses of one reality,
145　And tell how St. John unites opposites.
　　Throughout recorded history there have been
　　Two conflicting traditions of Light thought,
　　The Gnostic one from Egypt to the Thule
　　And the Christian one which made war on it.
150　Both share the Light and look back to St. John,
　　Both Catholics and Cathars who fought for it.
　　Initiates such as Zoroaster,
　　Pythagoras, Christ, St. John, Mani, de
　　Molay, Cagliostro, Weishaupt, Crowley,
155　All sought the pure Light, some with perfect aims,
　　And some with impure ends; some filled with love,
　　Some to manipulate; some in God's Will,
　　Some with a god-man's rage and murderous hate.
　　The true experience of the Light invades
160　And conquers self-will with its loving Will.
　　Just as a forked pollarded willow puts
　　Out shoots which grow thin branches in a year
　　Which wave their leaves in wind, and when it is
　　Cut back again, puts out more though the trunk
165　Is rotten and leaning, till a tree shaped
　　Like a flame flickers in the evening sky,
　　So from one fire-like trunk and two massive
　　Branches have grown many thin sects or groups,
　　All of which, though different, make up the flame-
170　Like shape of the whole tree, and pruning makes
　　No difference to the leaping round its stems.
　　There is one Light, which if received with due

Emptiness of soul and passiveness, grows,
As does the sun the seed, but if received
175 With the will of national aggrandisement
Intent on destroying human beings,
Turns against that will and destroys it as
Does its outer symbol, the Emerald Cup
In wrong hands. There is one power of God, Fire,
180 Which seems two in conflict of opposites –
Gnostic and Christian clash of Lucifer,
Alternative god of Gnostics, and Christ –
Or many as Fire differentiates
Into the multiplicity of time,
185 But track each life-form back and there is One.
Division and difference are illusions.
Just as God, Fire, contains Darkness and Light,
Apparently conflicting opposites,
So the One Light contains all local sects'
190 Lights, and St. John's bright Light and Hitler's pale
Glow are the same Light seen through differing
Souls – one transparent, one cloudy as smoked
Glass; one submissive, one arrogant; one
Love, one hate – in polished or distorting,
195 Opaque mirrors, each glimpse a different mix
Of conflicting shades of both dark and light.
St. John's love was less dark than Hitler's hate.
As the Lights of Ephesus and Berghof
Show pure Christian and impure Gnostic souls,
200 So those of Montségur and Templar stakes
Show impure Christian and pure Gnostic souls.
To see the Truth and know good from evil,
Satan's darkness and grime must be dispelled,
Light must shine, opaque mirror must be clean.

205 Tell, Muse, how Light that draws to Heaven relates
To Christian or Luciferian doctrines.
All who actually see the Light, whether
Christian or Gnostic, transmute their souls to
Less dense, more subtle, airy Light substance
210 (The gold of the philosopher's stone) that
Is drawn to one of the regions of Heaven
As up one of the bands of a rainbow.
As when the sun shines through rain, a rainbow
Forms that spans the curved sky in red, orange,
215 Yellow, green and blue bands, a perfect arch

That, when you try to drive through it, travels
With you, both of whose arcs rise to apex,
Its coloured opposites reconciled in
Symmetrical beauty that at first seems
220 So tangible a sign of God's pleasure,
But which will fade, so all souls from seven
Religions turn into coloured air and
Travel up one curved band, which attracts souls
From sects within a religion, to Heaven.
225 It is not the tradition we are in
That draws to Heaven or Hell, but the degree
Or intensity of Light. The doctrines
In religions or Gnostic sects about
Christ or Lucifer are only ladders
230 To take us to the Light, and they can be
Discarded once the Light is seen. The Light
Is from God and divine; Satan, ever
Claiming what is God's (just as a leader
Of an Opposition political
235 Party steals the Government's policies
To be elected), deceptively claims
It is his form Lucifer's and places
Obstacles in the way of the Light, to
Stop seekers seeing it, and offers them
240 Ladders which are faulty. As with the Lance,
He who sees the Light in unready soul,
Before it is properly awakened
And purged from sensual attachments, detached
From desire and worldly ambition, and
245 Does not use it for good, will find it can
Destroy him, as it did Eckart, Heydrich
And Hitler, who were deceived by Satan
And more concerned with Antichrist doctrines
Than to experience the Light itself.
250 As in an examination system
Attainment of grades leads to the college
Of our first choice, but falling below them
Can lead to a different college, so, too,
The level of Light we achieve draws us
255 Automatically to a region
In Heaven or Hell. The lower the level,
The more removed from Light is the region.
Eisenhower's soul was being purified
In the privations of Normandy, whose
260 Wartime austerity and suffering

Acted like the Scetis desert, and was
Being transmuted, and nearly ready.

Tell, Muse, how the disaster of Arnhem
Came out of Eisenhower's injury and
265   Montgomery's requests to race towards
Berlin. Now field commander, Eisenhower
Flew to Versailles to see Bradley, Hodges
And Patton, an American meeting,
On September the second. Patton said
270   He had patrols on the Moselle and in
Metz (an exaggeration), and asked to
Push on to the German frontier and
Rupture the West Wall. Eisenhower granted
Him additional gasoline and gave
275   Him permission to head towards Mannheim
And Frankfurt, agreeing that Bradley should
Stay on Patton's left, south of the Ardennes.
Hodges should leave Montgomery's right flank.
On his way home to Granville, Eisenhower's
280   B-25 broke a muffler, and he
Changed to a small L-5 one-passenger
Liaison plane. A storm broke, the pilot
Became lost and, running out of fuel, not
Seeing the airstrip, landed on a beach
285   Near foaming waves. Eisenhower jumped out and
Helped the pilot push the L-5 above
The tide line and slipped in the wet sand and
Badly twisted his knee. The pilot helped
Him limp across salt marshes to the road,
290   And Eisenhower returned in a GI's
Jeep to Granville. Two GIs carried him,
Wet and exhausted, up to his bedroom,
Where Mickey stripped him to his pants, washed him
And put him to bed with a hot-water
295   Bottle. He ate his supper from a tray
While Kay and Shellburst staff sat round his bed.
His knee swelled, a doctor flew from London
And ordered him to stay in bed a week.
And until the swelling went down and his
300   Knee could be put in plaster, Eisenhower
Lay in bed in pain and looked out at Mont
St. Michel, irritated at having
To hobble round his bedroom on crutches,
A ringing in his ears, which he would not

305   Let the doctor examine lest he was
       Sent home, peeved he was out of action on
       His second day as SHAEF's field commander.

       When Montgomery learned that Patton was
       Receiving more fuel and that he would be
310   Losing Hodges, he grasped that there were not
       Enough supplies for two offensives, and
       He was enraged and, while British tanks took
       Brussels, he flew to Dempsey's HQ at
       Lailly, near Amiens, and met Bradley,
315   Who in the presence of Hodges, said: "At
       Yesterday's meeting of American
       Commanders with General Eisenhower just
       Before his unfortunate injury,
       It was agreed the main American
320   Effort will be to Frankfurt, through Metz and
       Nancy. Monty, we strongly felt Hodges'
       5 US Corps should be switched from you to
       Cover Patton's left flank as he thrusts to
       Saar south of the Ardennes. We felt you don't
325   Need help with your effort north of the Ruhr
       As you won't find much opposition there,
       And that First US Army on your flank
       Should be depleted. The Americans
       Don't need British help with an airborne drop
330   Near Liège." Montgomery replied, "We are
       Getting away from the original
       Plan of one thrust of forty divisions
       Who need fear nothing. I've not seen General
       Eisenhower for nearly two weeks, and have
335   Had no orders from him, so I'm drawing
       Up plans to advance to the Ruhr, and I
       Need your help, Brad. Brussels is falling, but
       The Canadians are stuck on the Seine and
       The Somme, and now Dempsey has to approach
340   Antwerp and attack the whole of the Ruhr
       Without significant American
       Help. And Hodges is going east. It is
       Not going to work." Bradley frowned, ill at
       Ease before his superior of three
345   Days ago and now equal, wishing that
       Eisenhower were present. "I'll tell you what,"
       He said, "I will make two simultaneous
       Thrusts towards the Rhine, one south, one north of

80

The Ardennes. That will help you, Monty, in
350 Place of Hodges. There can be a pincer
Attack on the Ruhr." Then Montgomery,
Thinking aloud, replied: "The British must
Still cross the Meuse and the Rhine. We will need
An airborne drop to secure the bridges
355 Ahead of my thrust. Given the withdrawal
Of American support, and that I
Have no orders from the field commander,
An airborne drop seems very essential
In the region of Arnhem." And so, in
360 The anarchic atmosphere of fighting
Without a land commander, was conceived
The Comet Plan that became the airborne
Assault on Arnhem. A chain of events
Was set in motion with Montgomery's
365 Order to de Guingand to bring Browning,
Corps Commander of First Allied Airborne
Army, to see him the very next day.

Ignoring the doctor's order that he
Should stay in bed a week to rest his knee,
370 Eisenhower hopped on crutches to a room
Where he could meet with Bedell Smith, Morgan,
Gale, Strong and Whiteley of SHAEF's HQ. Smith
Said: "The German Army is retreating
Along the coast. Antwerp has fallen, but
375 Not the approaches to Antwerp harbour
From the North Sea. Should you give the order
For these to be taken?" A telegram
Arrived from Montgomery, which Smith read
And passed round. He said, "It says one thrust to
380 Berlin can now end the war, and it should
Go through the Ruhr rather than the Saar as
The American plan states. He wants to
Meet you, sir. He wants your decision by
Tomorrow." Grimacing, Eisenhower said,
385 Exasperated, "He has not spoken
To me for nearly three weeks, and now he
Wants a decision by yesterday. No.
No, I can't meet him, I've got too much on:
My broadcast to the peoples of North West
390 Europe; linking the Italian campaign
With Overlord; a conference with General
Devers on our control of the Franco-

American forces; and there is Greece.
He's four hundred miles away, and my knee
395 Will make travelling awkward. What should we do?"
Strong, SHAEF's British Intelligence expert,
Said, "I vote for one strong thrust through Belgium
To the Rhine." Eisenhower looked at him and
Said, "Can we go outside?" He hobbled to
400 The door and showed Strong a telegram from
Stimson, urging him to take full command
Of all Americans. "What can I do,"
Eisenhower asked, "in the face of this? I
Have to take account of political
405 Ramifications. If I put Monty
In charge of British and Americans,
Stimson will be angry, not to mention
Brad and Patton. There must be two thrusts for
Political if not military
410 Reasons." Back in the meeting, Eisenhower
Ordered Smith to draft a written reply
To Montgomery: "Say that I like his
Idea of a full-bloodied thrust towards
Berlin, but that I do not agree that
415 It should be initiated at this
Time to the exclusion of all other
Manoeuvres. There can be no question of
A thrust to Berlin until both Le Havre
And Antwerp harbours are operating.
420 The Allies will advance to both the Ruhr
And the Saar. I believe Montgomery's
Thrust to the Ruhr will be via Aachen, and
This can be tied to Patton's thrust via Metz."
Strong asked, "Sir, shouldn't you meet him?" To which
425 Eisenhower replied, "And be insulted
By the new Field Marshal? No thank you. No,
The telegram will carry my message."

In Rastenburg Hitler lay in bed in
His bunker room with jaundice, a result
430 Of Stauffenberg and living below ground,
The Supreme Commander of the German
Armed Forces and Commander-in-Chief of
The Army laid low like Eisenhower, Heaven's
And Hell's leaders mirror-images. He
435 Complained, "Why have my Generals withdrawn from
France, defying my orders to fight on?"

Goebbels, his visitor and the new Reich
Commissioner, sitting by his bed, said,
"My Führer, you are a thousand miles from
440   The action, and cannot appreciate
That the German force is short of fuel and
Ammunition. Under Montgomery
The British and Canadians have covered
Two hundred miles in four days, and are in
445   Belgium, have taken Brussels and Antwerp.
Hodges has moved as far and is in South-
East Belgium, and has Liège. Patton has reached
The Moselle and has linked with the Franco-
American Army from the south coast.
450   We need to prepare the defence of our
Fatherland. The Siegfried Line is largely
Unmanned, the West Wall, and many guns have
Been stripped. The British and Americans
Are only four hundred miles from Berlin.
455   The Russians a mere three hundred. In three
Months since D-Day we have lost a million
And a quarter men, dead, wounded, missing –
Fifty divisions in the east, twenty-
Eight in the west. We have no guns, tanks or
460   Lorries, our allies have deserted us.
Germany stands alone. The Allies have
Two million men in Europe, the Soviets
Five hundred and fifty-five divisions.
We need a defensive plan. I will raise
465   A new army of a million men, and
All our industry will produce the arms
And equipment we need to repulse our
Enemies." Hitler muttered from his bed,
Sallow, "No withdrawal. We must keep on
470   Fighting until, as Frederick the Great said,
One of our enemies tires and gives up."
Goebbels, sitting by the sick-bed, wondered
At how uninformed, uncertain Hitler
Seemed, that the man who was the terror of
475   The world, whom thousands of helmets, planes, tanks
And ships obeyed, should look so vulnerable,
And he felt protective and knew he would
Follow him to the end of life itself.

Now that Eisenhower was supposed to be
480   Housebound, Kay breakfasted with him, then went

To the office for the morning, and she
Returned to the house to have lunch with him
And go over anything that might have
Come up. After lunch they sat and talked and
485   Sometimes held hands or kissed, hastily in
Case the door opened and someone came in.
Often he was alone with time to think.
Eisenhower lay in bed and pondered how
Stalin could have Generals Zhukov, Koniev
490   And Rokossovsky competing, whereas
Montgomery, Patton and Bradley all
Demanded priority over each
Other. Holding Montgomery's message,
He pondered his insubordinate, brash
495   Egotism and self-esteem, his vain
Arrogance. Montgomery had written:
"One really powerful and full-blooded thrust
Towards Berlin is likely to get there
And thus end the German war." He required
500   All the fuel and transport, and took the view
That Bradley would have to do the best he
Could with what was left. He weighed the Ruhr and
Saar, wrote: "If we attempt a compromise
Solution and now split our maintenance
505   Resources so that neither thrust is full-
Blooded, we will prolong the war." While he
Bristled, Eisenhower thought of Stimson, and
Knew there would have to be a compromise:
A broad front with resources split between
510   Montgomery and Bradley. There could be
No thrust to Berlin before the ports of
Antwerp and Le Havre were taken, could there?
And the Americans must be kept quite
Separate from the British, mustn't they?
515   Lying alone, Eisenhower questioned his
Policy and past firmness became doubt.

The Eisenhowers, then spelt Eisenhauers,
Had come from Bavaria – the name meant
"Iron striker" or "armoured Knight" – where they
520   Had been pacifist Brethren in Christ
(Who were Mennonites, Anabaptists led
By Menno Simons who drew on Zwingli's
Swiss Bretheren, *Bible* disciples in
Brotherhood and love who saw Jesus Christ,

Not Caesar, as Lord, followed right reason
And the Enlightenment and spread throughout
Holland, Switzerland and South Germany,
From whose mass split the enclosed Amish Church)
And, persecuted in the Thirty Years
War, migrated in the eighteenth century
And settled in Pennsylvania by
The Susquehanna river, where they were
Known as River Brethren. Eisenhower's
Grandfather was Minister in the church
Of the River Brethren and farmed midweek.
The River Brethren moved west to Kansas
After the Civil War, and soon prospered.
Eisenhower's father and mother were both
Brethren in Christ, and were bankrupted when
A partner absconded with cash, and then
A lawyer overcharged. They went out to
Texas, but returned to Abilene to
Work in the River Brethren's creamery.
At each meal Eisenhower's father led his
Family in prayer and explained Scriptures
To the children in the evenings. Later
Eisenhower's parents became interested
In the Jehovah's Witnesses. Meetings
Were held in Eisenhower's home, after which
He prepared the noon meal. He loved cooking.
Eisenhower, then, was of Bavarian stock,
And came from Hitler's Palatinate. His
Father spoke German with his grandfather,
And he had as German a temperament
As Austrian Hitler. And, having been
A Protestant Jehovah's Witness, he
Instinctively respected Jehovah,
And from the Brethren absorbed brotherhood
And what it meant to mount a Great Crusade,
And knew about divine revelations.

Often an accident or injury
Is Providence's way of slowing down
An active man, giving him time he would
Not otherwise have in which to reflect,
Ponder on destiny. So it was with
Eisenhower. After Falaise, seeing that
Montgomery was pressing for a fast
Drive to Berlin, Michael deftly arranged

For Eisenhower's plane to lose its way and
570 Come down on a beach, and for his knee to
Be wrenched so he could be confined to bed
And ponder the future direction of
The Allied advance. Now, lying in bed
One morning after Kay had left for work,
575 Looking out on Mont-St.-Michel, he had
Fallen into a reverie, and saw
Icky, his first son who died aged three of
Scarlet fever caught from a young maid who
Was recovering from it; the greatest
580 Disappointment – disaster – of his life,
The one thing he had never forgotten
Though he was now almost fifty-four. As
If yesterday, he was buying the toy
Wagon for his last Christmas, waving to
585 Him through the quarantine window. Knowing
This, Christ appeared as a shape and said, "Dwight,
I can show you Icky in gratitude
Because you did what I asked and became
Land Commander and Overlord." At once
590 Eisenhower was transported to a field
Of Light, and saw, in transparent, undense
Spirit body, the ageless face and form
Of Icky on a knoll, smiling, waving
Happily. Wet-eyed, Eisenhower breathed, "I'm
595 Sorry, Icky, I blame myself, we should
Not have hired that maid," and Icky smiled, and
Gently Christ drew away the sobbing man
And soothed him into tranquillity. "At
Least I know he's happy," Eisenhower sniffed,
600 Completely accepting Christ's presence as
If he had been visited by a friend.
"You know, every January the second,
The day he died, I send Mamie flowers." Christ
Said, "I know. He's in my care now, and is
605 Doing well. I will look after him. But
I want to show you Roosevelt. Your parents
Were pacifist Jehovah's Witnesses
So you are familiar with the battle
To unseat Satan, Armageddon, and
610 The establishment of the Kingdom, which
Russell wrongly put at nineteen fourteen,
Counting 2520 years from the date,
607 BC, the Israelites

Were conquered by Nebuchadnezzar, which
615 You never believed in, as you told Kay
When you walked in Gethsemane last year."
Eisenhower said, "You know a lot about
Me." Christ said, "We have been watching you and
Protecting you. But the point is, you know
620 About Satan. So, Roosevelt." Eisenhower
Found himself watching a meeting outside
Roosevelt's room. He could see the head of his
Crippled President through glass, and he saw
Baruch, Stimson and Marshall, Alger Hiss
625 And others with John D. Rockefeller
And Lord Rothschild poring over the new
Design for the one-dollar bill, which had
A pyramid and eye at the capstone.
He saw Vice-President, Henry Wallace,
630 An occultist, approach the President,
Who ordered that the Great Pyramid and
All-seeing Eye should be put on the bill.
On the floor was a pentagram, round which
Were candles. Into the room came Stalin.
635 Eisenhower frowned. "What does this mean?" he asked.
"That is Bernie Baruch, a friend of mine,
Whom I wrote to, as did Winston Churchill."
"Your rapid promotion followed during
The next three years, as did Churchill's," said Christ,
640 "And it is to your credit you are not
A Luciferian Mason like him,
A fact that's not escaped Heaven's attention.
But you see he worships at the eye of
Satan, which you see being put on your
645 Currency: the Illuminati eye.
The USSR's in effect governed
Not by the high Central Committee of
The Communist Party of the Soviet
Union but the Council of Elders, which
650 Is a secret body from a secret
Masonic society (Grand-Orient's
Supreme Council in our France) and behind
The Universal Brotherhood, a world
Council of just nine wise men. You should know
655 That Stalin's five-year plans have been funded
By the House of Warburg (the rich pawns of
The Gentile Templars in their battle with
The Priory of Sion, in whose dark hands

The Rothschilds are rich pawns), that the Elders
660   Of English Freemasonry who include
Baruch, a thirty-third degree Templar
Scottish Rite Freemason, seek to expel
The French Grand Orient lodges from Paris
To Moscow, far from London, and so are
665   Stalin's allies; they are behind your boss
And close to Roosevelt now. Ever since your
Jefferson brought back knowledge from Weishaupt
Of the Illuminati, there has been
A strong Masonic-Illuminati
670   Influence in the new American
Civilisation. French Illuminists
Sent your statue of sun-spoked Liberty,
Goddess of Illuminati Reason.
You should now know that orders you have been
675   Given, for example, to take command
From Montgomery, which as you know I
Approve, were to advance not your country
But the internationalist dreams of
A hidden hand, shadow world government.
680   Much of the responsibility for
This war lies with the internationalists
Who financed Hitler's rearmament and
Encouraged his designs. Know that English
Freemasonry funded him to destroy
685   The French Freemasonry. Know the anti-
Semitic Priory of Sion which
Created English Freemasonry through
Weishaupt and the Rosicrucians and ran
Rasputin, had links with and shaped Hitler
690   Through rosy cross and Grail and through Gurdjieff,
Who talked all night with him, probed and condoned
The Final Solution. American
Non-interventionism had to be
Turned into interventionism, and
695   The American people had to want
War. The planned attack by the Japanese
On Pearl Harbour, which was known to those men
You have just seen, your boss General Marshall
Included, was kept from the commanders
700   In Hawaii. The Committee of Three
Hundred ordered Roosevelt to engineer
(Using the Institute for Pacific
Relations) the Japanese attack on

Pearl Harbour to draw the US into
705 The Second World War. Once America
Was in a war 'to save democracy',
It was kept going rather than finished
Quickly. After Italy surrendered
In September nineteen forty-three, you
710 Could have attacked Germany through the 'soft
Underbelly' of Europe, Churchill was
Right, but at Marshall's request you withdrew
Heavy equipment from the war front and
Turned Britain into an armed fortress and
715 For nine months bombed German industry and
Reduced German cities to rubble. Thus,
Little action took place on the ground, and
Allied commanders urged political
Leaders to attack the Reich from the south
720 And west. But this would have resulted in
A sweeping victory, and the Allies would
Have occupied all Germany and East
Europe, whereas the scenario required
Bolshevism – dark Illuminism –
725 To seize East Europe. So Marshall, under
Orders, slowed things down. You were asked to stop
Allied forces crossing the Po Valley,
And open up another front in France,
Which would give Stalin more time to go west.
730 He will order a halt at the German
Frontiers, and you will be instructed to
Refuse all German pleas to surrender.
Internationalists meanwhile built up
The Communist forces by sending them
735 American supplies, matériel.
They delayed the Normandy invasion
Until the Russians were on their way west."
Eisenhower, frowning, interjected, "We
Needed a second front, we did not want
740 Another Dunkirk." "Dwight," Christ said, "you know
You could have invaded in the Pas de
Calais, where Hitler expected you. You
Know it was not in the interests of speed
That you invaded where you did, look at
745 Caen." Eisenhower, still frowning, said, "But we
Got off the beaches, and we might not have
Done so in the Pas de Calais." Christ said:
"You defend Marshall, all right. We in Heaven

Are not now concerned with what might have been,
750 We work with what is, and although we were
Distressed by the delays, we now welcome
An opportunity with Russia we
Did not have before. But you must grasp that
The internationalists' aim is not to
755 Make Eastern Europe American; it's
To create a new order for Satan,
From which expanded Communism in
Eastern Europe can confront the Allies.
With this purpose they weaken Germany,
760 Bomb its cities, put Russians on its soil,
So bankers can lend billions to rebuild.
Reconstruction, that is the air raids' end:
So buildings can be blitzed and bankers can
Make more billions out of their rebuilding.
765 The bankers have invested hugely in
The Bolshevik Revolution and have
Used Stalin's dictatorship as their 'foil'
In their plan to conquer the world by their
Hidden hand. Their shadow world government
770 Now has power over Roosevelt and Stalin,
Who are both Masons, like Churchill – Roosevelt
A thirty-second degree Mason, and,
As such, bound to maintain the Masonic
'Religion' in the purity of its
775 Luciferian doctrine. (The thirty-
Third degree Masons learn the 'secret', or
Rather, deceptively revealed lie, that
Lucifer is the Great Architect and
Secret god of the universe, and that
780 The Light is from him, not God-Fire.) Among
Those men you saw Alger Hiss. You will one
Day know he is the link between Roosevelt
And Stalin, and can found a United
Nations. I say 'can', not 'will', for future
785 Events are not predetermined, ordained
And inevitable, and now exist
Only as conflicting tendencies or
Potentialities, which I see. I
Have no power to arrange which tendency
790 Finally becomes an event and thus
Happens, though I can lobby and persuade
And influence an event's arrival,
As I do now, with those who have freewill

And freely choose. Now it is time for you
795　To see the two potentialities
Of future world Orders. The success of
One of these you will influence by your
Decisions. They fork out in opposite
Directions from a common origin,
800　Like two branches from a tree-trunk, and first
You must see the trunk, which has not happened
Yet and which is itself a tendency.
Dwight, look within now." Eisenhower gazed at
A potentiality in his mind.
805　As if a cosmonaut in outer space
Looking down at the earth from great distance,
He saw twin giants America and
Russia straddle the globe, bristling with arms,
Like mirror images, from Atlantic
810　And Baltic to the Pacific's two sides
(Russia covering half of Germany).
He saw himself in Washington's White House,
An older man with less hair – Christ murmured,
"We support you as Land Commander as
815　America now has a global role
And is more important than Britain now."
The British Empire fractured to pieces.
He saw the USSR crack into
Fragmented states, and then a gathering
820　Of the continents' peoples into new
Regional blocs: a North American
Bloc, with Mexico; a United States
Of Europe from Ireland to Turkey; then
A Pacific bloc round Japan and with
825　Australia; blocs for Africa; South
America; India, Pakistan and
South-East Asia; Arab states and Israel;
Russia's states; and China – ten blocs in all.
And then he saw ten leaders talking through
830　Ten film screens on their walls, talking live via
Satellites whirling round the earth, carried
By rockets like V-2s, pictures of which
Intelligence had sent. "That is what both
World Orders have in common," Christ said, "that
835　Is the tree-trunk from which both Orders branch,
Provided Satan does not win victory
Through the Antichrist, Hitler, his ally,
Now, in which case there is a different trunk.

But now I will show you the two branches,
840   Two scenarios, starting with Satan's."

Eisenhower saw a war in the Balkans –
Moslems fighting Christians and Orthodox –
After a failed peace, a rearming truce,
Blaze into a huge conflagration with
845   A task force of Arab Moslems fighting
Task forces from Europe and Russia, all
Fighting on different sides in confusion.
He saw an annual meeting hosted in
Great secrecy by the House of Orange
850   (Whose Protestant Prince William the First had
Led the Dutch revolt against Habsburg Spain),
One hundred internationalists talking,
He saw from a great distance three hundred
Who called themselves "Olympians" after
855   The Greek gods who lived on Mount Olympus:
A few monarchs, billionaires and leaders
Of industry and communications,
Internationalists who ran the world
As a Secret Brotherhood, for themselves,
860   And nine veiled men behind them, the real power,
Under an East India Company coat
Of arms (two lions rampant with flags each
Side of a crossed shield and armour helmet),
And they greeted a Tyrant, bowing down,
865   A handsome, youthful man dressed as Satan.
He saw across the globe all churches, mosques
And temples burnt down and replaced by one
Religion of Lucifer or Satan.
A Pope was dethroned and then replaced by
870   Satan's Pope, who had a bent cross, and men
Who wore a skull and bones and bowed down to
A huge eye carved in a stone pyramid.
He saw a corner building in New York,
The Council on Foreign Relations, where
875   United Nations representatives
Met to control rising population.
He saw wars, famines, diseases killing
Millions, who died at the Tyrant's command,
All the non-productive Africans and
880   Asians mainly, carried away by plagues
(From fifty strains of germs that were man-made
In labs and deliberately released),

Starvation and conquests in regional
Wars. He saw the ten bloc leaders talking
As on a newsreel film to each other
And co-ordinate the killing and then
The United Nations sanctioning it,
Appearing to keep peace but planning war,
Deceptive genocide while appealing
For massacres out of control to stop,
Under the guidance of the Council on
Foreign Relations. Now he saw public
Executions in many cities, he
Saw shootings against sandbags in London's
Trafalgar Square. He saw a great machine
In Brussels labelled 666, in which
Were details of every world citizen.
And, implanted under each person's skin,
On the back of one hand it seemed, there was
A metal chip that was read by a beam
At certain entry points – each held-out hand
Labelled with a number, identified.
He saw everywhere, men like zombies, slaves
Who shuffled in gangs to labour with stones,
Their minds controlled by some ray that, broadcast,
Matched their brain rhythms, which they all obeyed
For the time of their work – a world of slaves.
He saw cameras on motorways that ringed
Cities like moats, patrolled by tanks that put
Down local revolts against the Tyrant
And kept the world government intact, while
The tyrannical leader, the World-Lord,
Czar of the New World Order, autocrat,
Strutted like Nero or Caligula
And with cruel orders exterminated
Millions in each regional bloc, and burned
Their bodies in crematoria whose
Chimneys towered in each hospital, then took
Part in a Black Mass at a pyramid,
Worshipped the eye of Satan-Lucifer.
He saw colonialists loot the diamonds
Of Africa, resources of Russia.
He saw oil revenues given to men
In a Masonic ceremony, dressed
In Freemasonry's highest degree, who
Piled up riches in one earth currency
And ran the World-Lord as their puppet, who

All came from secret societies. He
Saw the cross burned, all images of Christ
930 Toppled and burned, and the Tower of Babel
Rebuilt with upside down stars – pentagrams –
All round it, and a Nazi-style field with
Millions of troops hailing the World-Lord as
Their dictator. Eisenhower said aloud,
935 "It's neo-Nazism, Hitlerism
In a new form. Everything we have fought
Against in Normandy and Europe is
In their new Order." And then he saw barbed-
Wire enclosures, prison camps, and barbarous
940 Mass executions, shootings and hangings,
As hundreds of thousands of prisoners were
Herded on to waste ground and shot, and their
Bodies flung on trucks and driven away
Through seas of rotting flesh, and Eisenhower
945 Cried out involuntarily, "It's Hell,
The Tyrant has made a Hell on earth." Christ
Said, "That is what Satan's world-rule will be,
And population reduction will lead
To that potentiality, peaceful
950 Living will be a cruel deception as
Knowledge and intellect are deceived by
Ravenous, raw power. The New Age of
'Religionless' worship you saw will be
A New Age of worshipping Satan, led
955 By a so-called Council of Wise Elders,
Nine men and their leader, the World Lord, and
A global committee of thirty-three
Thirty-third degree masons, rulers, and
A circle of three hundred (modelled on
960 The British East India Company,
The richest trading company ever,
Which built an empire with East Indiamen,
Vied with the Dutch East India Company,
Both of which were controlled by a Council
965 Of three hundred shareholders with twenty-
Four directors working through committees)
Known as the Committee of Three Hundred,
And billionaires. And below them in this
Pyramid shape a thousand points of light,
970 The top thousand of the Brotherhood from
All regions of the world, who believe that
The Light is not a force for good, given

94

From God, Fire, through me, Christ, but for evil,
From Lucifer. Like the legendary gods
975   Of Olympus, this secret elite – heirs
Of the Illuminati (Moriah
Conquering Wind), Cults of Dionysos
And Isis, Cathars and Bogomils – call
Themselves Olympians, and, with Lucifer
980   Their god, have set themselves above God and,
The Western world's hidden Establishment,
Pursue the policies of Malthus (who
Was a professor at the British East
India Company's college), cull useless
985   Eaters to keep world population down
Through global wars. It will be a nightmare,
The worst regime ever to have held power,
Beside which Hitler's Nazi terror is
A Paradise. Darkness will hide the face
990   Of the earth. The Beast will rule, and those who
Do not bow down, they were the ones you saw
Being executed." Eisenhower felt
Sick at this future ahead of his choice.

"But that is only one tendency or
995   Potentiality," Christ said. "Here is
The other one, what Heaven would like to see.
It starts from the same place as Satan's but
This tendency is different." Eisenhower
Now saw a sunlit globe as the war in
1000   The Balkans was ended by peaceful talks,
He saw the House of Orange meeting in
Secret, and three hundred self-replacing
Leaders, monarchs and billionaires react
With consternation as a handsome man,
1005   One of the ten regional bloc leaders,
Walked among them, Light shining from his soul,
A young man with Christ's aura, as if the Light
Of the World had made a Second Coming.
Everywhere throughout the globe tyrannies
1010   Collapsed before the Light and changed into
Democracies. Churches, mosques and temples
Shook as if in an earthquake, their doctrines
Cracked and now they were Light-centres, throughout
The world was one religion of Light. Men
1015   With serenity in their faces walked
In crowds in all the capital cities,

And worked before screens in sunlit places,
And, opposites of slaves, could come and go
Just as they pleased, and all were creative;
1020 Tranquil men with half-closed eyes lived at peace
In each bloc, and though religion flourished
In each region, whether Christian, Moslem,
Hindu or Taoist it existed
To contribute to the One Light. The Pope's
1025 Church was within, not above, this global
Movement of the Light of the Cosmic Christ.
Eisenhower watched Light spread across the globe:
A world ecumenism of One Light.
There was no population control, but
1030 There was enough food for all to eat through
Control of world resources, there were no
Famines, wars or epidemics and all
Human beings pursued their livelihoods
And spiritual advancement with guidance.
1035 Universal love and self-sacrifice
Had replaced reason and the will to power.
A universal gentleness prevailed,
The poor were cared for by caring rulers,
The leaders were chosen for their progress
1040 In spiritual enlightenment. He saw
The House of Habsburg restored in Europe
And the earth shone in peace and happiness.
Christ said: "You see Universalism
At work, true Illumination – not false
1045 Illuminatist magic of Satan
But universal mysticism as
Spirits grow in the Light and develop
Enough to go straight to the Realm of Light
Without having to unlearn false Darkness.
1050 This is the universal government
Of the Lighted Ones. Just as the rational
Satanic Enlightenment of history
Was a darkness of soul, which has had to
Be replaced by true Enlightenment, by
1055 The Lighted Ones' Illumination, so
Satan's rational Illuminati taught
A Luciferian darkness of soul
Which true Illumination must replace,
The mystic vision of the Lighted Ones."
1060 "It's a prelude to Heaven," Eisenhower

Said in awe. "It's returned Paradise to
The earth: no war, starvation or disease."
"Yes," Christ said, "it is Heaven on earth, the dream
Heaven has for the earth: global unity
1065   Through the Light." Eisenhower said, "What must I
Do to become a Lighted One like them?"
Christ said quietly, "Be patient Dwight, when you
Are ready the Light will flow into you.
But you must be pure and open within
1070   And wait for it, want it to enter you.
But, and I want you to understand this
Most of all, Heaven's dream for earth can only
Come into being after the binding
Together into blocs of the next stage,
1075   After the growth of conglomerates through
New technology and political
Arrangements. To oppose Satan's new world
Order with our New World Order, we need
Stalin to rule a huge empire. Satan
1080   Thinks he has cleverly recruited cruel
Stalin for his purposes, but we need
To confine Satan in one place before
We bind him for a thousand years. We need
Satan to deliver a united
1085   Bloc from East Europe to the Pacific,
And so it is important you allow
Stalin to be the first into Berlin,
Even though your instincts are to arrange
For Americans to enter Hitler's
1090   Capital, the Antichrist's, you must stand
Back and allow Stalin's Russians to take
Berlin, so he fulfils his destiny
And contributes a unified empire
To our coming New World Order. Therefore
1095   There cannot be a quick end to the war,
Much as we in Heaven would all like it;
Stalin's Red Army offensive is not
Yet ready. But Montgomery dreams of
Ending the war in three weeks' time and will
1100   Approach you. Go along with what he seeks
In Holland, for a new and dangerous
Weapon is being prepared by Hitler
Which Montgomery should seek and destroy,
And he will need to do what he'll propose

On those grounds. If he succeeds, you will have
A useful bridgehead. If he fails, he will
Have demonstrated to all that Berlin
Cannot be taken in a hurry, and,
Well-intentioned though he is, we in Heaven
Who have mankind's greater and more long-term
Good in our care will be pleased. He has set
Himself up and faces more humbling till
His haughtiness is atoned for." And like
An intelligence officer briefing
An agent he recently recruited,
Christ, having given him his mission, now
Ended the meeting unobserved: "That is
Enough for now. Your leg is beginning
To hurt again, I have made sure you have
Not been aware of your knee while you saw
These visions and had this revelation.
I must go now, but I will come again.
Always remember, Heaven supports you, and
Expects you to follow your boss General
Marshall, even though inwardly you know
His course may not sometimes he wholly right."
Suddenly Christ faded, and Eisenhower
Sat up to reach for him, then lay back on
The pillows on his bed and, stunned, looked out
Across the water to Mont-St.-Michel.

From Everberg Montgomery had soon
Protested that he was not receiving
Priority in supplies. The second
Part of Eisenhower's directive reached him
Two days before the first. He demanded
Eisenhower should visit him, ignoring
The pain he felt, the baking and rubbing
Of his knee, and then signalled: "Providing
We can have the ports of Dieppe, Boulogne,
Dunkirk and Calais, and in addition
Three thousand tons per day through Le Havre we
Can advance to Berlin." Now he ordered
Dawnay, "Tell Eisenhower that I must see
Him in Brussels tomorrow, please, after
My 9 a.m. conference with Dempsey." That
Afternoon he received a cable from
The War Office: two V-2 rockets had

Landed in England, would he please rope off
The area they were fired from in Holland.

1150   Montgomery had refused Eisenhower's
Suggestion he should go to Granville, and
So on the afternoon of September
The tenth, with great difficulty, his knee
In plaster, Eisenhower painfully climbed
1155   Aboard his B-25 and flew to
Brussels. Because of his knee he remained
In the cabin on the airfield, where both
Montgomery and Tedder joined him. At
His meeting with Dempsey Montgomery
1160   Had decided to involve the whole of
First Allied Airborne Army, three Allied
Parachute divisions, in the Arnhem
Drop in the hope that Eisenhower would give
Priority of supplies to the Ruhr
1165   Offensive. Montgomery said, "I want
Everyone to leave the cabin, and that
Includes Tedder." Eisenhower gestured and
All left. Tedder remained in the plane but
Out of earshot. Sitting down and waving
1170   Two pieces of paper, Montgomery
Said: "Ike, I have your directive here. It
Arrived in two parts, the second part first,
The first part two days later, so I did
Not get the drift till yesterday. How can
1175   We run a war if we cannot make clear
Where we are going? I had no orders
From you for a fortnight. There has been no
Communication apart from unclear
Telegrams written four hundred miles from
1180   The front line. There's no plan, we in the field
Don't know what we're doing, we're making it
Up as we go along. It seems Patton,
Not you, is running the war, and getting
The supplies. The double thrust will end in
1185   Certain failure. You've dispersed the Allied
War effort, there's no field command or grip."
Montgomery had got increasingly
Worked up. Eisenhower sat in silence as
Montgomery's fury vented itself,
1190   And when he paused for breath, he leaned forward

And put his hand on Montgomery's knee
And said, "Steady, Monty. You can't talk to
Me like that. I'm your boss." Stopped short, sheepish,
Montgomery mumbled, "I'm sorry, Ike."
1195   Then, in a different tone, he said: "A new
German weapon hit London yesterday,
The V-2 rocket, which is silent and
Arrives without warning. It is based in
Holland. The British Government wants me
1200   To find and destroy the V-2 sites near
Rotterdam and Utrecht, and that means I
Need to get to Arnhem. To do that I
Must have priority of all supplies
Over Patton and command in the north
1205   Over American supplies and troops.
It's no good trying to sustain two thrusts.
We must put everything into one thrust
And give it priority. Other thrusts
Can do their best with what is left over.
1210   I think you're wrong, but I'm not insisting
On an immediate thrust to Berlin now.
Arnhem is the gateway to the Ruhr as
Well as to the V-2s, and after that
Berlin. But I need fuel and tanks. Give me
1215   These now and I can get there." Eisenhower
Immediately recognised the V-2
As the new weapon Christ had mentioned, and
Arnhem as Montgomery's approach on
Holland. He had his reply ready. He
1220   Was adamant there must me a wide front
Until they were across the Rhine. There could
Then be a single thrust. But the V-2s
And the British Government's request had
To be responded to. He said: "Monty,
1225   You must understand there are certain things
That I cannot change. The Allied Armies
Must be kept separate; you cannot command
American troops in the north; your Ruhr
Thrust cannot have priority over
1230   Patton's Saar thrust as regards supplies. I
Am now running the war, and that's my view.
As I said in my signal, we cannot
Start a single thrust to Berlin now, with
An army that is still drawing the bulk

1235 Of its supplies over beaches. I know
You think it can be done if you're given
The supplies, but you can't have everything
And Patton nothing. Public opinion
Back home would not accept that. But we can
1240 Look at your bold plan for a new bridgehead
Over the Rhine at Arnhem now, which I
Wholeheartedly support. If you achieve
That, you can cut off the Ruhr and advance
Into northern Germany. There can now
1245 Be a combined Anglo-American
Airborne drop." And as they talked, agreeing
To codename the drop Market Garden, and
Cross the Rhine with the Airborne Army and
British Second Army, massive Allied
1250 Airdrop, Montgomery realised he would
Not have priority of supplies for
The Ruhr thrust over the Saar offensive.
He thought contemptuously that Eisenhower
Was no commander, he did not know what
1255 He should do, he had no experience
Or philosophy of battle, he was
Just a genial fellow who went round and
Talked to everyone and was popular
And then worked out a compromise that pleased
1260 Everyone. He had no plan but found out
What his subordinates thought, collected
Their ideas and reconciled them, liaised
Through conferences, and did not give orders.

At Granville, Eisenhower sat with Bedell
1265 Smith, who said: "There are now three armies, and
The Germans, fighting on three fronts, are far
From beaten. The way to the Saar is blocked
By good divisions. I can see a drop
To seize Walcheren would control the approach
1270 To Antwerp the Navy want, and help to
Open the port. Montgomery's Arnhem
Thrust would secure a Rhine bridgehead and be
Most useful to our present cause." Then he
Received a signal from Montgomery.
1275 Smith said: "He's postponed the Allied airborne
Drop across the Rhine for twelve days, because
He lacks supplies." Eisenhower buried his

Head in his hands, and said, "Do I accept
It? Or do I keep the drop?" Smith rejoined,
1280   "The drop will be useful." Eisenhower thought.
He wanted a bridgehead across the Rhine,
He wanted to use the Airborne Army.
But there were disadvantages. Moving
North rather than east from the Belgian-Dutch
1285   Border would make a gap between Second
Army and Hodges' left, filling which would
Give a broader, more stretched front. Twenty-first
Army Group would be taken away from
The Ruhr. Taking Antwerp would be delayed,
1290   Along with the Scheldt estuary which would
Open the port. He wanted to silence
Montgomery with a "most useful" plan.
But was it a foolish and risky scheme,
A strategic blunder? He said, "Go and
1295   See Monty, and give him all he needs. In
View of the German opposition, we
Will stop the thrust to Saar, we will now give
Priority to the Ruhr and the Arnhem
Drop: Operation Market Garden on
1300   The seventeenth."
                      Montgomery was soon
Explaining to Brooke that his telegram
Had produced "electric results": "Ike has
Given way and he sent Bedell to see
1305   Me today. The Saar thrust is to be stopped."
He would have the transport of three US
Divisions, would co-operate with First
US Army and deal with Hodges and
Felt he had "gained a great victory": "We shall
1310   Now win the war reasonably quickly."
In fact, Bradley flew to Montgomery,
Complained the new plan would halt his supplies
And refused to let him deal with Hodges,
While Eisenhower permitted Patton to
1315   Attack towards Saar: "There's no reason why
He should not keep acting offensively."
And the new plan meant the war would now be
Won more slowly, and with more loss of life.
Eisenhower followed up his half-changed plan
1320   With a signal to duped Montgomery:
"Berlin is the main prize, in defense of

102

Which the enemy is now likely to
Concentrate the bulk of his forces. There
Is no doubt whatsoever in my mind
1325 That we should concentrate our energies
On a rapid thrust to Berlin. But this
Should not be concentrated but be spread
Across the whole front, with combined US-
British forces." Broad front and not one thrust.

1330 At von Rundstedt's headquarters, his Chief of
Staff, General Blumentritt, asked him: "Why have
The Allies not gone for Berlin? There were
No German forces behind the Rhine in
Late August, the whole front was wide open.
1335 Berlin was the Allies' target, the strength
Of Germany is in the north, Berlin
And Prague were there for the taking. Why did
The Allies not take them?" Von Rundstedt shrugged.
On the radio came Goebbels' voice: "Germans,
1340 You know my total mobilisation
Is to find a million men for our war
Effort. I warn you what to expect if
We lose this war. Roosevelt and Churchill in
Quebec have discussed the US Treasury's
1345 Plan which Secretary Morgenthau has drawn
Up. Germany will be dismembered, our
Heavy industry destroyed, much of our
Territory will be transferred to Poland,
The Soviet Union, Denmark, France. Germans,
1350 We will be a pastoral economy,
Existing at subsistence level through
This plan. You must strengthen your will, work with
The Führer and repulse the enemy
Before these things happen." Von Rundstedt winced.

1355 The sun shone on the Lower Rhine, which brimmed
Brown between green banks on the bend from where
German officers lolled at tables in
A round room with windows by each of which
Stood a naked lady sculptured in stone
1360 By a Dutch sculptor, and, at Sunday lunch,
Gazed down towards Arnhem and the steel bridge
Whose grey arcs glinted as if washed in gold.
And further out, in leafy Oosterbeek,

The sun gilded Model's headquarters in
1365 The baroque Hartenstein Hotel, where all
Awaited an amphibious landing
On the Dutch coast and a thrust to Wesel
To cross the Rhine. The nightly bombing raids
Of Lancasters and Mosquitoes had been
1370 Somewhat heavier than usual; at midnight
Four airfields in northern Holland were hit,
Grounding German jet fighters, and at eight
Flying Fortresses bombed anti-aircraft
Positions and more airfields, and at twelve
1375 Another raid bombed barracks. Otherwise
All was normal on this late summer day.
Suddenly the clear sky was filled with specks
As a sky train droned high above, dropping
First Allied Airborne Army, comprising
1380 Three airborne divisions, the British First
And US Eighty-second and Hundred
And First (the Polish First Independent
Parachutes would follow), to seize bridges.
Twenty thousand combat troops floated down
1385 In a corridor from Eindhoven to
Veghel, Grave, Nijmegen and now Arnhem.
Following pathfinders, the glider tugs
And Dakota carriers droned forwards,
Two columns ninety-four miles long, three wide,
1390 While from twelve Stirlings British pathfinders
Drifted down west of Arnhem near Wolfheze
Like popular fluff in a September breeze,
Major-General Urquhart's bold daylight raid,
Even as Americans landed north
1395 Of Eindhoven and near Grave bridge, while more
Landed on anti-aircraft batteries
At Groesbeek Heights. Then followed the gliders,
Skidding on grass west of Arnhem, and as
The last British parachutists landed,
1400 Fearful to be behind enemy lines,
And Lieutenant-Colonel Frost, commander
Of the 2nd Parachute Battalion,
Six foot, with a languid, slow-motion air
And worry lines on his thoughtful forehead,
1405 Moustached, rounded up his troops by blowing
A call on a copper fox-hunting horn,
Model fled from the Hartenstein Hotel

Like a fox hearing the baying of hounds,
Took Army Group B HQ to Terborg
1410 Thirty miles east, aware that British troops
Under Horrocks had bombarded Germans
And broken through from Joe's Bridge and had pushed
Along the tree-lined road through flat country
Towards Eindhoven, and beyond to where
1415 Paratroops had taken bridges, and that
The air armada of Market Garden,
Assembled for a swift end to the war,
Would drive towards the V-2 rocket sites,
The Zuider Zee, and then surround the Ruhr,
1420 Unless stopped by a massive blocking force
In the largest airborne battle ever.

At Rastenburg, hearing the unwelcome news,
Hitler was stunned by the airborne assault,
And promised planes and men to Model, who
1425 Had obtained plans for Market Garden from
A crashed glider. He sent troops to block it
Round Eindhoven, to retake the Groesbeek
Heights, and drive from Arnhem to Nijmegen.

In Oosterbeek the British paratroops
1430 Moved towards Arnhem by three routes, and soon
Met sniper fire and mortars. Urquhart's jeep
Was hit. Urquhart, modest in a beret
And moustache, had lost radio contact with
Gough and Frost, and with Krafft blocking the way
1435 To the Arnhem bridge and high ground, he spent
The night with Lathbury's troops while at Wolfheze
Crossroads, Lathbury's men shot at and killed
Generalmajor Kussin, the commandant,
Who fell out of his car door on his back
1440 And lay, mouth open, showing his eagle.
The Germans charged to defend the bridges.
As Frost's men approached, the railway bridge blew
Up in a spurt of orange flame and plume
Of thick black smoke, and the pontoon bridge was
1445 Dismantled. Thirty vehicles headed for
The Arnhem bridge en route for Nijmegen,
And Frost drove unopposed to the buildings
Whose roofs reached the height of the concrete ramps
And the pillbox at the bridge's north end.

The advance guard waited below the huge
Supports and arched girders that towered above,
And as Germans opened fire from side streets
On Mackay's sappers on the eastern side,
They all ran into a school, seeing that
Whoever held the buildings held the bridge.
When Frost arrived, he ordered the lead men
To take the bridge and commandant's HQ,
But as the men moved, the northern pillbox
Fired on them, as did an armoured car on
The south end. Mackay's men moved through attics,
Vlasto's through cellars, and then flame-throwers
Attacked the pillbox. Ammunition flared,
An explosion lit up the sky, German
Soldiers staggered out. The bridge's northern
End was Frost's, but fires and explosions made
It impossible to take the south end,
And now SS Panzers rolled in defence.
Not knowing of the Heveadrop ferry,
Frost had now lost his chance to cross the Rhine.
Gough arrived and asked where Urquhart was. Frost
Did not know. Gough ordered his tired men in
To a building close to the bridge and climbed
To the roof and watched Frost's men try to seize
The bridge's southern end. An explosion,
And the whole end of the bridge seemed on fire.
Through smoke he saw the pillbox was destroyed.
Frost returned to the building, from which he
Could see the ramp and the whole bridge. He had
Stopped the vehicles heading for Nijmegen
From crossing the river. Bittrich sealed off
The south end of the bridge for the Germans
With armoured cars, and Frost, lacking the troops
To hold the entire bridge, stayed put that night
Beside the fires and debris. Before dawn
More paratroops reached him. Six hundred men
With four anti-tank guns and mortars now
Held the north end, and radio links were made
With British Airborne Headquarters again.
German snipers climbed into the steeple
Of the church of St. Eusebius and
Surveyed the eighteen houses and foxholes
Frost's men had dug in their perimeter,
And watched as twice during the night they rushed

Across the bridge, to be repulsed with fire
1495   That hit Grayburn, who led them, in his face.

Montgomery, furious that Eisenhower
Had not backed the northern thrust, but was now
Pursuing both the Ruhr and the Saar thrusts,
Had sent a signal offering to call
1500   Off the Ruhr thrust, but it was sent too late:
The two columns of aircraft stretching at
Least ninety-four miles long had already
Crossed the Channel. The Ruhr, not the bridges,
Was the true objective of the battle.
1505   His aims were that Horrocks' 30 Corps should
Cross the Lower Rhine at Oosterbeek to
Reinforce Urquhart's bridgehead as if it
Were threatening to seize Arnhem, and meanwhile
O'Connor's VIII Corps would turn eastwards and
1510   Drive towards the Ruhr, while the Germans dealt
With Urquhart; it was a variation
Of the D-Day plan in which the pressure
On Caen was to allow Americans
To break out and swing round. Arnhem was Caen,
1515   And the real drive was to the Ruhr. Although
The planning had gone wrong Montgomery,
Who had proposed this untypically
Risky operation because he had
Despaired of Eisenhower's strategy and
1520   To show the US he was not cautious,
Stuck to his feint, his hopes on O'Connor.

Satan, sensing danger, sent bad weather.
Thick fog that morning grounded all aircraft
In England, France and Belgium, and Holland.
1525   It lifted as the Luftwaffe attacked
From Joe's Bridge up to Arnhem, enjoying
For the first time since D-Day complete air
Supremacy. Emboldened, the Germans
Attacked the Allies at Renkum all day.
1530   Cleminson reached the Hartenstein Hotel
And parachutists entered the cellars
Singly, but found the place deserted and
Signs of a hasty exit by Model.
Then he and Urquhart marched towards Arnhem
1535   To relieve the bridge, but on the bend where

The lower and main roads join just west of
St. Elizabeth's Hospital Germans
Fired on them with guns and tanks, which clattered
With extra armour. Cleminson's men reached
1540   The Rhine Pavilion, riverside building,
Where the Germans hit several paratroops.
Shot at from both front and rear, the British
Scattered to buildings by the Rhine or woods
Or streets of identical brick houses.
1545   Cleminson fell back up the hill towards
The Hospital, and General Urquhart and
Brigadier Lathbury and his hardened men
Occupied a high three-storey house on
The main road. German tanks approached and some
1550   Mortars were fired, and there was now shooting
From houses at the rear. Lathbury's men fired
Back. Now Urquhart was pinned in his house and
As a German tank trundled down the street,
Its commander casually standing
1555   In the open hatch as if certain that
The British were no threat to him, Major
Waddy leaned out of next door's top window
And dropped explosive into the turret.
The tank was blown to pieces. Soon two more
1560   Tanks were destroyed in similar manner.

Urquhart, anxious to return to HQ
To control the battle, wished to break out.
Amid the din of battle he now held
A conference, during which a British
1565   Bren-carrier clattered through the German fire,
Crammed full with supplies and ammunition
For Frost, and stopped outside. Lieutenant Heaps
Ran in, and, having found him by chance, told
Urquhart that Frost was under great attack,
1570   That he himself was reported missing
Or captured. Urquhart ordered help for Frost,
"Who must hold out till Horrocks' tanks arrive",
And when Heaps had left through enemy fire,
Front walls of buildings crumpling under shells
1575   Round piles of dead, the commanders agreed
To break out from the rear of the large house.
And so Waddy left to reconnoitre
At the back. As Urquhart watched, a mortar
Exploded as he crossed a small lawn and

He fell, killed by the blast, his skin unmarked
And joined the crowds of jostling spirits who
Milled in bewilderment near the gates to
The next world like crowds of Christmas shoppers.
He was later buried in the garden.
1585 We reap what we sow, and just as he had
Blown a tank commander out of this life
So he too was blown to eternity,
To reflect in twilit darkness on how
The Light requires men to show charity.
1590 At the front destroyed tanks stood in rubble.
As paratroops laid a heavy smoke-screen
Urquhart and Lathbury dashed out at the back
With a group of men, all in studded boots,
And climbed a fence – Lathbury's sten went off –
1595 And crossed a garden, climbed a high brick wall,
Ran through an arch into a cobbled street
With intersections on the left, down which
German machine-guns were firing. As they
Sprinted past one, Lathbury was hit and fell.
1600 Urquhart and two men lifted him inside
A terrace house, where a Dutch couple watched
As they found he was bleeding from his back,
Paralysed where a bullet snicked his spine.
On the floor Lathbury said: "You must leave me.
1605 It's no use staying. You will be cut off."
With Cleminson and Taylor, Urquhart saw
A German soldier at the window and
Fired point blank. Glass shattered, the German dropped,
His face a hideous morass of blood.
1610 The Dutch couple said they would move Lathbury
To the Hospital when they could. Having
Hidden him in a cellar under stairs,
Urquhart and the two men left the back door
And crossed several tiny fenced gardens, turned
1615 Right and then left, and entered the kitchen
Of 14 Zwarteweg, where a surprised
Dutchman, Derksen, pointed to stairs. Germans
Approached. The three men ran upstairs and found
A window, whence they saw grey-uniformed
1620 Wehrmacht so close they could hear them talking.
They heard the creak of caterpillar treads
And a self-propelled gun halted below.
An attic lay above, with a trapdoor
In the ceiling and pull-down steps, a shelf

1625 Shaped by the roof's slope and the room's ceiling,
To which they climbed, pulled up the steps, and sat,
Holding their pistols and now primed grenades,
Waiting for Germans to burst up the stairs,
Hoping the Dutch would not betray them, and
1630 Settled back. Urquhart said, "We could lob these
On the gun and make a dash for it," but
The other two said, "We'd be killed or caught,"
And, "It's better to wait for an attack
To catch up with us." And so they stayed there
1635 Without food or water, having to soil
The family's home as the Germans had
By now turned off the water at the mains
To preserve supplies during the battle.
Having sheltered the British, Derksen now
1640 Evacuated his family to
A neighbouring house, leaving the three alone,
The General trapped in an attic behind
The German lines, unable to command.

Hicks took command, and by the Arnhem bridge
1645 Frost beat off German infantry attacks
Against the houses his men occupied.
Artillery and armour were brought up.
Now twenty-two German reconnaissance
Vehicles and half-tracks charged across the bridge,
1650 Truck-loads of infantry ramming their way,
Returning from Nijmegen, and were met
By concentrated British fire, by mines
And anti-tank guns, and set on fire by
Flame-throwers. Panzer grenadiers were burned,
1655 Staggered like human torches and, screaming,
Plunged a hundred feet to the Rhine below
Amid the smell of burning rubber and
Thick smoke and debris that now blocked the road.
Frost's men went onto the ramp and brought in
1660 The wounded from among the dead, and lay
Them in the dark cellar of a house, where
They glowed with splinters of phosphorus shells
That lodged like candles in their burned bodies.
The Germans crept up and threw hand-grenades
1665 Into the houses, and fought hand to hand,
And Mackay's men routed them with bayonets
And grenades. Mackay was hit by shrapnel
In his legs, but was still in place. Frost was

110

Running out of food and ammunition
1670 And Hicks' relief was checked by the Germans
Just short of the bridge, and replacement tanks
And guns were arriving from Germany.

Radio signals did not reach Browning as,
With Americans, he probed Nijmegen
1675 Bridge, expecting a German attack from
Groesbeek Heights, and waited for the Welsh Guards
To build a Bailey bridge near Son and keep
Momentum going north of Eindhoven.
At midday a second airlift took off
1680 From England with gliders and tugs, but in
The bad weather many gliders were lost.
Most landed reinforcements and supplies,
Some on Groesbeek Heights, some on west Arnhem
Where German anti-aircraft guns set fire
1685 To the heath below the paratroops, and
Hackett's men dropped on, and routed, Germans.
Hackett went to the Hartenstein Hotel,
Now 1st British Airborne's HQ, where Hicks,
The oldest brigadier in the Army,
1690 Obeying Browning and supporting Frost,
Cancelled his plan to take high ground and called
On him to send his troops towards Arnhem.
Heated words were exchanged between these men.
There was delay. There was delay at Son,
1695 And Model's counter-attack was ready.

That night the fog returned, to lift at dawn
And as the British attacked east along
The Lower Rhine they were caught in crossfire
From anti-aircraft guns on the south bank
1700 And Germans to the north, and were routed
Like fallen leaves blown by a river gust.
No breakthrough to the bridge could happen there.
To the north British paratroops drove back
The Germans till Urquhart, woken by shouts
1705 And the self-propelled gun's rattling tracks
And wheeze as it moved off and Derksen's cry,
"British troops down the road," left his attic,
Ran down the street and greeted South Staffords
And reached his Hartenstein HQ by jeep.
1710 There he reorganised his division.
Hackett attacked north-east and Urquhart warned

111

The Poles not to land on the pre-planned zones,
Which were now held by Germans. Barlow left
To command the street battle in Arnhem.
1715 He was never seen again. Supplies were
Low, the troops were exhausted, casualties
Were high, more German artillery and
Armour arrived. There was news of Horrocks,
Who had now built the Bailey bridge at Son
1720 And, though unwell, reached Grave and with Gavin
Planned an assault-boat crossing of the Waal.
In Arnhem, Hackett withdrew under fire
And the Polish gliders landed without
Having received Urquhart's warning, and all
1725 But a handful of men were now wiped out.

Eisenhower, on his way from Granville's port
To Shellburst's new location at Versailles,
Stopped the car and, his knee uncomfortable,
Stood near a market garden where rows of
1730 Ripe cabbages waited the harvest. In
A recently ploughed field a magpie was
Eating grubs. In the lane juicy blackberries
Invited. He saw elderberries and
Sloes, the wild damsons of the blackthorn, and
1735 Chicory and ragwort. By his damp feet
Conkers peeped from spiky cases like mines.
Ivy was in white flower. He wandered off,
Observed by Kay his driver, and by Gault.
Everywhere there was seed and fruit; insects
1740 Had laid eggs on leaves, drowsy wasps crawled on
Windfalls from a pear-tree, wood-ants scurried
Round a pine like half-tracks. Spiders had hung
Webs on which trembled careless flies, and hung
In mid-air till the cool evening brought them
1745 To earth again. Swallows and martins sat
On wires, and he heard a willow-warbler
And a chiff-chaff. A robin hopped among
Fallen leaves and faded flowers. On a pond
By the road water-boatmen flicked their legs,
1750 And a hive stood in a garden. Had there
Been a massacre of drones? Cow-parsley
Bobbed in the breeze, and near the road he saw
Wild pansies, scarlet pimpernel, speedwell,
Toadflax and camomile. He stared at dock
1755 Leaves and wondered that Nature should provide

Natural remedies. All was bountiful.
Even bee-stings had therapeutic gifts.
In God's great plan for man Nature burgeoned,
All was ripe and top-heavy with autumn,
1760   Full of profusion and harvest and good.
Amazed at plentiful variety,
Eisenhower, full of reverence, loved life.

Round Arnhem bridge a German air raid struck
Like a thunderstorm hailing lightning bolts.
1765   All day Frost had repelled attacks, and then
The Germans tried to burn his men out with
Phosphorus shells from a long-barrelled gun.
Hundred-pound shells smashed into Frost's HQ,
Forcing all into the cellar. But then
1770   British mortars hit and killed the gun's crew.
From burning houses and smoking rubble
Frost's men cheered and hooted as the Germans
Towed the gun away. The wounded mounted,
And still there were no signs of any force
1775   Approaching to relieve them as they yearned.

At midnight Frost left his HQ and walked
(A ghostly figure in an eerie mist)
Round the perimeter, checking his men.
In the school under the ramp Mackay had
1780   Crammed his troops in two rooms. The Germans fired
Machine-guns and mortars. As bullets whizzed
Through windows splinters flew from floorboards. As
Men ducked, flame-throwers set fire to the house
To their north, sparks fell on their roof, which blazed.
1785   Men fought flames with school fire extinguishers,
Dodging the snipers, and put out the fire.
The stone floors were covered with glass, plaster,
Splinters and blood. Then a terrific flash
And thunderous roar knocked all over: one end
1790   Of the school and its roof was blown away
By an anti-tank Panzerfaust. Many
Lay dead in the shattered ruin. Firing
Stopped. Germans stood around outside, thinking
That all inside were killed. Mackay's men threw
1795   Grenades, fired brens and stens, and killed fifty
Germans, who lay, grey shapes on the dark grass.
They then collected their wounded. One man
With fifteen bullets in his chest now died.

Shrapnel had pinned Mackay's foot to his boot,
1800 Which he laced tight to keep the swelling down.

After counting all survivors, Frost had
Two hundred and fifty unwounded men
In ten shelled houses, but they still drove back
The Germans, guarding the wounded, saving
1805 Food, water and ammunition. Harmel
Ordered a truce and sent a prisoner,
Halliwell, a sapper of Mackay's, with
A message to Frost: "Surrender or die."
Frost replied contemptuously, "Tell them
1810 To go to Hell," not seeing Satan stand
Nearby. Now a ferocious bombardment
With tank and artillery shells took each
House down floor by floor till it was heaped bricks.
Buildings collapsed before the tank barrage,
1815 Roofs fell in, top storeys crumbled in dust
Round British who scuttled like cockroaches,
The wounded screaming in the deafening din.
Tanks rammed ruins and levelled them, while shells
Roared in every ten seconds, one thunderous
1820 Pounding, and in this charnel-house, the stench
And din of battle everywhere, Tiger
Tanks firing high explosive shells at them,
A lone voice – Sims' – cried out, "Hold on, hold on,
It can't last much longer," as each shell burst
1825 On men who lay in rubble and falling
Debris, buried like moles. And still Frost's men
Clung on to their positions by the bridge
As floors were dismantled with each salvo.
Outside in bowler hat, with umbrella,
1830 Tatham-Warter led a bayonet charge.
Father Egan was hit by shrapnel and
Fell two flights of stairs, found his clothes on fire,
One leg broken, his back full of splinters.
The German tanks came back, and, looking out,
1835 Frost saw the city seemed to be burning,
The two church spires on fire, and he could hear
The crackle of burning wood and crash as
Each building fell as if in a nightmare.
With courage as awesome as Mackay's, he
1840 Preserved a defiant and unbowed will.
Meanwhile afar the Luftwaffe had bombed
Eindhoven, separating Ridgway, who

Pressed on north, from Brereton, who returned
To Son and then to a SHAEF conference.

1845 A foggy, wet dawn at Oosterbeek, where
Urquhart's division crouched in a pocket
Between the Lower Rhine and railway line,
Germans on three sides, pressing from woods and
Houses in dark unco-ordinated
1850 Attacks which were repulsed, and then snipers.
In the pocket's centre, the Hartenstein,
Urquhart radioed new supply drop zones
And called in a Polish landing at Driel.
Model evacuated all civilians
1855 From Oosterbeek's and Arnhem's battle zones.

Under siege in wrecked and raftered rubble
At Arnhem bridge the gallant Frost had just
One day's water left, and the Germans were
Bombarding the buildings his troops still held
1860 And using flame-throwers in the rubble.
The houses were now wrecks, yet, ringed by flames,
Welded together by their great ordeal,
Small groups of men fought on from the cover
Of smoking rubble, one will to resist
1865 Among their dead or dying friends, bloodstained
Bandages round their heads. Around noon Frost
Met Major Crawley to start a patrol,
And a tremendous explosion lifted
Him off his feet and threw him face downwards.
1870 A mortar bomb had landed between them.
Frost lay groaning, shrapnel in left ankle
And right shin. Crawley hit in both legs and
Right arm, made no sound. Frost's batman, Wicks, helped
To drag the two till stretcher-bearers came
1875 And took them to the cellar of wounded.
Frost looked dejected as if at last he
Had given in. He slept in the darkness
And woke to shell-shocked gibbering and noise,
For the Germans were still pounding above,
1880 And heat from raging fires and pain of legs.
He sent for Gough and told him, "You'll have to
Take over, but bring crucial decisions
To me." Two hundred wounded were roasting,
Coughing from smoke; the building was burning.
1885 Frost ordered Gough to arrange a truce so

The Germans could collect the wounded, but:
"Get fighting soldiers to other buildings,
And carry on till our tanks come." Brave hope.
Now four Tiger tanks crashed across the bridge
1890 From the north, blocking it. There were jackboots
On the stairs, a German officer stood
In the door. A paratroop raised his sten
But was disarmed. An order and German
Soldiers carried the wounded upstairs as
1895 A flaming timber crashed in the cellar.
Frost lay on the embankment by the bridge,
Lit by flames. With a roar the building fell
Into fiery rubble. Germans handed
Round brandy, chocolate and cigarettes
1900 And knelt and congratulated them on
Their gallantry and skill. And the battle
Started again. Gough told his troops, "Disperse
Till morning." As they moved into the dark
He radioed: "This is the First Para
1905 Brigade. We cannot hold out much longer.
Our position is now desperate. Please
Hurry, please hurry." The only answer
Was the roar of shells from a fiery dark.

As a Tiger tank fired shells at the school,
1910 Which was in flames, Mackay and thirteen men
Brought their wounded up from the cellar to
The garden to break out. A mortar attack
Began. Yelling "Surrender" to Simpson,
Mackay led five men through ruined houses
1915 To the next street and faced two tanks and more
Than fifty German soldiers, whom they shot
In a three-second burst of fire. They reached
A house. He told his men to disperse and
Hide. Mackay crouched into the garden and
1920 Crawled under a rose bush and tried to sleep.
He heard German voices and played dead. Then
He felt a bayonet thrust through his buttocks
And hit his pelvis. There was no pain till
The bayonet was withdrawn. He jumped up and
1925 Waved his gun at a ring of Germans but
Had no bullets, was disarmed, searched and marched
To a building, where a lieutenant spoke
Good English. Mackay said, "I will accept
Your surrender." A truck took him towards

116

Germany, he tried to escape and was
Beaten unconscious, and woke in an inn.

Now Frost had been taken prisoner with
The two hundred wounded from the cellars
Urgent relief was vital, but still no
1935 Breakout by Urquhart's troops was expected
And progress from the south was slow. Horrocks
Continued up the road dubbed Hell's Highway
And, having crossed the Maas at Grave bridge, he
Pressed on to Nijmegen, and, with Typhoons
1940 Attacking in the air and a thick smoke
Bombardment from a hundred guns, made an
Assault crossing of the Waal in boats near
Charlemagne's favourite imperial home
While Americans crossed westwards under
1945 Artillery fire and attacked east and
Cleared the railway and road bridges. As tanks
Rolled towards the road bridge, Harmel looked through
His binoculars and knew he was right
To put charges under the bridge despite
1950 Model's orders that it may be needed
For a counter-attack. Harmel did not
Intend to be shot in Berlin because
The bridges were now in enemy hands.
Two tanks appeared. He shouted, "Let it blow."
1955 An engineer pushed a box's plunger
But nothing happened, no bridge or tanks fell
Into the river. With heavy heart he
Knew his task now was to clear the Allies
From the Arnhem-Nijmegen area.
1960 It seemed the Allies would reach the Arnhem
Bridge that night, but Horrocks halted. Now SHAEF
Had moved from Granville to Versailles and with
Improved communications, realised
Market Garden had failed. Now Eisenhower
1965 Signalled to Montgomery SHAEF had not
Intended a broad-front advance, merely
A northern thrust – which was now a stalemate
With worn-out, wounded troops out of supplies.

A wet foggy day dawned. Without water
1970 Or food, Gough's men tried to break out northwards
From where they hid in the perimeter.
The Germans overran positions and

Forced men who had no ammunition left
To surrender. In ones and twos they now
1975 Emerged from cellars and heaps of rubble.
Some refused to give up or fought with knives.
The Germans lobbed grenades into windows.
Gough, trying to reach Urquhart, had made for
The waterworks building. While still outside
1980 He heard German voices and, crouching, hid,
Burrowed beneath a stack of logs, at bay
Like a fox before hunting hounds, then felt
His left foot being pulled, and found himself
In a group of grey-uniformed Germans.
1985 One by one the British were overwhelmed.
Wounded, exhausted, Frost's troops limped and crawled
Into captivity, their last stand done.
A man is not a fixed being and can,
In times of extreme danger and great fear,
1990 When pressed without, moved by a common cause
(Such as bringing war to an early end),
Find depths of strength and courage in himself,
Heroism, valour and dignity
He did not know he had, was not aware
1995 It is possible for a man to show,
And perform acts that surprise – amaze – him
Not once but consistently, so his view
Of his nature and what a man can do,
What a man is, his possibilities,
2000 Is changed for ever, redefined, revised.
Frost's stand will live for ever in men's minds
Like the three hundred Spartans' stand against
The invading Persians at the mountain
Pass of Thermopylae, and sacrifice.

2005 For three days and four nights they had held out,
And now the bridge was open. German tanks
Moved south, past rubble and a burnt pillbox,
Reconnaissance wreckage and a great mound
Of German dead near a roll of barbed wire;
2010 As Horrocks crossed the Nijmegen bridges
And attacked Arnhem bridge with Irish Guards
And halted at Elst under German fire.

In the Oosterbeek horseshoe Urquhart put
Hicks in charge of the west, Hackett the east.
2015 The Germans attacked from the west and took

The high ground, Westerbouwing hill above
The Heveadrop ferry, which was destroyed.
From there they could fire on river crossings.
They pushed the British back half a mile but
Could not wipe out the pocket. They then called
For surrender over loudspeakers while
German troops fired mortars and sniped. Urquhart,
Feeling like quarry for a beast of prey,
Made radio contact with Horrocks' corps in
Nijmegen, and called up artillery fire
On German troops north of the Lower Rhine,
While Model called in troops and Tiger tanks.
Polish paratroops took off from England.
Their forty Dakotas were attacked by
A hundred Luftwaffe fighters, but though
Some were lost, Sosabowski landed with
Seven hundred and fifty men at Driel.
The Germans pressing south saw their snow-shower
And, believing they would retake the bridge,
Harzer moved west off the Nijmegen road
To block their advance. Later an attempt
To resupply the pocket failed when ten
German fighters shot down over twenty
Transport planes and much-needed equipment.
Farther back, Dempsey pushed his HQ to
St. Oedenrode; Montgomery moved up
Just south of Eindhoven and demanded
That Eisenhower should halt Patton and send
Hodges' First US Army to relieve
The pocket under British command, while
Patton, with Bradley's support, arrived in
Versailles and asked Eisenhower for more troops
For his Third US Army's crossing of
The Rhine. Eisenhower called a conference
Of all his army commanders next day.

A misty morning and no supply planes.
At dawn Horrocks tried to relieve Urquhart,
Attacked north from Nijmegen towards Driel
And Elst, and armoured cars found a route through
The flat countryside to the Poles at Driel,
As fifty Poles crossed the Lower Rhine in
Four rubber boats on which the Germans fired,
And fifteen corpses were washed down river.
Now the Germans attacked Hell's Highway from

2060 Both and west and east and cut the road between
Uden and Grave. All round Nijmegen and
Arnhem, the Allies ruled the skies, and now
Typhoons thundered in and fired rockets at
The Germans along Hell's Highway. Dempsey's
2065 Chief of Staff tried to reach Horrocks by air
At Nijmegen, but was shot down. He lived.
All day the battle ebbed and flowed as when
A tide comes in, wave after wave breaks and
Withdraws and breaks again, further forward.
2070 The Germans reached Veghel by afternoon
And fired on the bridge, killing many men,
And Horrocks had to turn round and drive back
From Grave to Uden, clearing all Germans,
So supplies could cross the bridge at Veghel.

2075 Like huntsmen surrounding a deep thicket
The Germans attacked round the Oosterbeek
Pocket, and Urquhart signalled to Browning
That relief was vital, while Bittrich, von
Tettau and Harzer laid a German plan.
2080 Through the shell barrage roamed pitiful men,
Concussed, battle-fatigued, gravely wounded,
Bandaged, shell-shocked, morose. Among them strode
Major Lonsdale, arm in a bloodstained sling,
Bloodstained cloth round his head, with bandaged leg,
2085 Hobbling, urging his men to attack. Now
All troopers limped towards Oosterbeek church,
A square, buttressed bell-tower back off the road
Near the open polder by the river,
A ruin with no roof, and each shell crash
2090 Knocked plaster from the shattered walls. Here in
The broken pews, lolling against stones, sat
A broken army, tired, dishevelled, while
The din outside increased as each shell roared,
Each explosion, the whine of each mortar
2095 And confused shoutings. Lonsdale's steps rang out on
The stone floor; he climbed the pulpit, each hand
Bandaged, bleeding from every limb, and stared
At several hundred men with black faces,
At his grime-covered troops, and spoke fierce words:
2100 "You know a lot of bloody Germans are
Coming at us. We must fight for our lives.
Stick together. We've fought the Germans in
North Africa, Sicily, Italy.

They weren't good enough for us then, and they're
2105 Bloody well not good enough for us now!
They're up against the finest soldiers in
The world. You will now take up defensive
Positions north of the road, dig in well
And keep your weapons in good order. We
2110 Are short of ammo, so you shoot to kill.
Good luck to you all." Above him rafters
Hung loose, and out through the shattered windows
The sky was lit with fire. Men now wrung out
Their shirts and trousers, dressed and then filed out,
2115 Stirred and inspired, with new spirit to fight.

Eisenhower had now moved SHAEF's headquarters
To the Hotel Trianon in Versailles.
His office was too large, so he ordered
That it should be partitioned, and he gave
2120 The other half of the room to Kay and
The secretaries, who lived in a flat in
What were once Louis the Fifteenth's stables.
Eisenhower moved into a house in Saint-
Germain that had been vacated when von
2125 Rundstedt fled before the Allied advance.
He was tense, for Market Garden seemed doomed
To fail due to bad weather and German
Counter-attacks (ordered by von Rundstedt)
And Montgomery's inability
2130 To galvanise British Second Army.
It seemed that the Ruhr thrust would not happen.
Failure would at least demonstrate that one
Full-blooded thrust to Berlin was now out
Of the question, unrealistic, silly,
2135 And would vindicate his broad front approach.
He summoned twenty-three Generals, Admirals
And Air Marshals, the largest such meeting
Since before D-Day. Facing a setback
In Holland, Montgomery kept away,
2140 Sending de Guingand, refusing to be
Judged by scathing American Generals,
A straight snub. Eisenhower asserted his
Authority, and ordered an advance
To the Rhine by all armies, including
2145 The Canadians, who would open Antwerp;
The advance should be co-ordinated,
Not entrusted to one individual.

121

With keen intellect and sound compromise,
Giving each commander something, a part
2150 But not the whole, so no one was supreme,
Mindful of British sensitivities,
Eisenhower told Bradley to halt Patton,
Sent Hodges north to Aachen, and Corlett
To reinforce the British, who should now
2155 Wheel north-east towards Venlo and Kleve, not
Pass Arnhem. Montgomery could contact
Hodges, whose troops were still under Bradley.
Informed, Montgomery was dismissive,
But grasped the new direction could salvage
2160 What might otherwise be a clear defeat.
He went to Weert and explained the new plan
Throughout the Second British Army's ranks.

Now Arnhem was downgraded as a goal,
And though a bridgehead there might be useful
2165 The focus was humanitarian,
To extricate Urquhart from the pocket.
Now Urquhart had permission to withdraw,
Horrocks' role north of Grave was secondary.
Dempsey put 101 Airborne (Screaming
2170 Eagles) under O'Connor, in whose skill
Montgomery had trust and placed great hope.
In view of Horrocks' worrying signals
The previous day from the bridgehead, Dempsey
Told O'Connor's VIII Corps to keep open
2175 Horrocks' lines of communication. And
So VIII Corps did not drive eastward towards
The Ruhr at Wesel. If Horrocks did cross
The Lower Rhine and relieve First Airborne,
He would need an infantry division
2180 Which Dempsey was not able to provide.
He lacked the men to drive towards the Ruhr.

The next dawn broke through fog on the foxholes
And houses in the pocket. Skirmishes
Took place, but no German forces broke through.
2185 Angry, Model told Bittrich, "You have just
Twenty-four hours to wipe the British out."
He had blocked the drive to the Zuider Zee,
And now he gave command to von Zangen
And Student, planning to destroy Urquhart
2190 And Horrocks north of Nijmegen and hold

A line north of the Waal. While the Germans
Attacked Veghel, a thousand planes supplied
The Americans with three thousand troops
In gliders, and Polish paratroops dropped
2195 Near Grave, and Sosabowski, now supplied,
Sent two hundred men in assault boats to
Urquhart's pocket, across the Lower Rhine.
That night it rained, and next morning Urquhart
Received more air supplies and Horrocks gave
2200 Him artillery fire, and he held on.

A jeep drove through shelling with four wounded
Laid on the bonnet, among them Hackett,
Who had been hit by a mortar shell burst,
And reached St. Elizabeth's Hospital.
2205 Hackett was laid on the stone floor, and said:
"I've a hole through my leg and I feel sick."
The medical officer examined
His stomach. "A shell cap hit me over
The solar plexus," Hackett said. To which
2210 The officer rejoined, "There's no exit."
Hackett, wearing no badges of rank, pulled
A face and said, "Just do your best." He had
An anaesthetic. An SS doctor
Came by with an English surgeon, and looked
2215 And said, "Euthanasia's best for this one."
The surgeon said, "I think I'll have a go."
And the doctor said, "You're wasting your time."
Unconscious, Hackett had the cap removed
And turned back from death's tunnel towards life.

2220 Like Frost's heroes, Urquhart's brave fighting men
Were worn out and short of ammunition.
In a white-fronted house across the street
From Oosterbeek church, all windows blown out,
Kate ter Horst moved among three hundred men
2225 Who lay, wounded, in every space within
The hall, rooms, corridors, garden, attic,
Kitchen, boiler room, garage, stair cupboard.
In the ten-by-six cellar sheltered her
Five children and eleven civilians,
2230 And, an angel who had put on dank flesh,
Alone, for her husband had cycled out
Of the pocket to spy on the Germans
And could not now return, without sleep, calm,

123

She passed between her children and the sick,
2235 While one doctor knelt and tended to each.
And more kept limping, hobbling in, for word
Had spread round Arnhem of this "hospital";
And as men died, she prayed with them and read
Psalm 91, "Thou shalt not be afraid
2240 For the terror by night," then buried them
In her garden, fifty-seven in all,
In the torn earth under a ghastly sky
That was yellow, the eerie glow of war.
Snipers entered the pocket and now fired
2245 Into the rooms and corridors where men
Lay helpless on stretchers, and although two
Orderlies were killed she was unflustered
And certain of her ministry as if
Christ had appointed her to look after
2250 The dying as they lay on Nazi land.

A truce allowed seven hundred wounded
To be collected by the Germans, and
Driven to St. Elizabeth's Hospital.
With five hundred more wounded to join them,
2255 Urquhart now had just eighteen hundred troops
In groups to defend the pocket, and they
Had not slept for a week or had a rest.
Now thirty German Tiger tanks were sent
To Elst, and fifteen east of the pocket.
2260 After the two-hour truce Kate ter Horst heard,
From the cellar, a Tiger tank knocked out;
The shell burst with a shock that deafened her,
Cracking timbers, sending dust through all rooms,
Jamming the cellar door, her children still
2265 Beside her. Now, outside, men chipped with spades,
Tore up timbers, broke down the cellar door.
Fresh air choked their lungs like a mountain wind.
A corridor and room were open to
The sky where a house wall had been blown in.

2270 Horrocks looked across the Lower Rhine from
The steeple of Driel church with Thomas and
Sosabowski. Thomas believed Horrocks
Had ordered Urquhart's 1st British Airborne
To withdraw, and planned to cross the river
2275 And seize the Westerbouwing heights. Horrocks
Denied giving the order, while, informed,

Montgomery notified London and
Reported O'Connor would thrust north-east.
There were plans to airlift in belly tanks
2280 Full of supplies, but nothing came of these.
At nine p.m. Montgomery's new TAC
HQ at Eindhoven heard from Urquhart:
"All ranks exhausted. Lack of radios,
Water, ammunition and weapons with
2285 High officer casualty rate." Bad news.

In Rastenburg von Rundstedt told Hitler
That all German troops in Holland should fall
Back to the Maas (or Meuse) and Waal. Hitler
Emphatically refused and demanded
2290 Dawn attacks on Nijmegen and Veghel,
South of which Hell's Highway was cut. Horrocks
And Dempsey were cut off from their HQ,
And O'Connor was told to stay put though
The way was clear for an advance. That day
2295 The German counter-attack had begun.

At two Thomas crossed the Lower Rhine in
Rain and strong wind, noiseless as a burglar
Not wanting to awake a light-sleeping
Armed householder. The amphibious craft
2300 Made for Westerbouwing heights in the dark
And were fired on by the Germans, who killed
Thirty-five, and, after keeping the ridge,
Took a hundred and forty prisoners.
At eight that morning Urquhart signalled to
2305 Eindhoven that the evacuation
Must take place that night. Montgomery met
Dempsey at Eindhoven at eleven
And agreed that enough life had been lost
Across the Rhine. Soon Tiger tanks had thrust
2310 From the east into the pocket, and air
Support prevented full encirclement.
Horrocks met Browning and Thomas now feigned
A crossing at Renkum to help Urquhart
While Americans attacked Hoevering
2315 And re-opened Hell's Highway. O'Connor
Pursued the retreating Germans with zeal.

Limp, let down, tired, angry, feeling betrayed,
In the Hartenstein cellar Urquhart told

His officers of the withdrawal plan.
2320 Some, thinking of the men who had died, thought
The whole effort had been a great waste. Hicks
Muttered, "It's another Dunkirk." As at
Gallipoli, evacuation was
To be disguised with artillery fire
2325 Which would make it appear the pocket was
Still full of air, a blown-up paper bag,
As they poured through its seven-hundred metre
Gap to where Canadian Royal Engineers
Would hold boats till the pocket deflated.
2330 In drenching rain the bombardment began.
At nine the guns rained shells on the Germans.
In driving wind and rain, faces blackened,
Boots muffled, clutching the smock of the man
Ahead, in a human chain, hunched, the troops
2335 Tottered through the dark to the river bank.
Two thousand men passed near the Oosterbeek
Church where the gold cock on its weather-vane
Glinted in the glow of fires and burning
Buildings. At the Hartenstein Urquhart and
2340 His staff, the last to leave, knelt. The chaplain
Said the Lord's Prayer. Urquhart passed round a flask,
Went down to the cellar and said goodbye
To the wounded, and left for the river,
Where the Germans had seen the ferrying
2345 And lit it with flares. Mortars whined in and
Holed boats, which capsized. In the water men
Screamed. Some were swept away, some clung on to
Wreckage, wounded. Half the boats were destroyed.
But the ferrying went on. The Germans
2350 Took a hundred and seventy prisoners.
Once withdrawal north of the Hartenstein
Was finished, the British disabled their
Guns and blew up their ammunition, and
By dawn the ferrying had ceased. The men,
2355 Exhausted, almost asleep on their feet,
Wet, cold and hungry, and throbbing from wounds,
Marched from Driel to Nijmegen, where they changed
Into clean uniforms. Next afternoon
The Germans took the rest of the pocket,
2360 And made prisoners of the wounded. Across
The street from Oosterbeek church Kate ter Horst
Said goodbye to the wounded, who would now
Receive treatment as German prisoners,

And with her five children and a hand-cart
2365 She set out to walk to Apeldoorn with
Hundreds of refugees, leaving behind
A sky as scarlet as the Airborne's blood.

Ashen as glimmering dawn in defeat,
At Eindhoven Montgomery sat deep
2370 In thought, depressed. Williams consoled him: "You
Were very close to victory. The largest
Airborne landing in history, and the road
For our troops was wide open. Von Rundstedt
Wanted to withdraw all troops in Holland
2375 To the Meuse and Waal, till Hitler ordered
Him to counter-attack." Montgomery
Said philosophically: "The target was
Not Arnhem, but the Ruhr. Urquhart was to
Threaten to seize Arnhem while O'Connor's
2380 VIII Corps turned eastwards towards the Ruhr. We
Have advanced our Ruhr campaign. Here we are
Now in Eindhoven, we have a bridgehead
Across the Waal at Nijmegen, enough
Life was lost across the Neder Rijn. We
2385 Did the best we could, given the lack of
American support, which made it just
A British effort, given that Eisenhower
Reinstated equal priority
To the Saar. We tried to reach the V-2
2390 Rocket sites. There are many 'if onlys' –
Two German armoured divisions, the rain –
But we must put a brave face on Arnhem
And consider what we gained." But his stare
And sombre reverie belied his words.
2395 He who had been the highest of the high,
Overlord of the Normandy conquest,
Had been further humbled by the repulse.

Soaked and weary, Urquhart was taken to
Browning's headquarters near Nijmegen, where
2400 He refused to take off his wet clothes so
Browning could see him as they all had been.
Browning rose from his bed and put on his
Uniform, and now looked immaculate,
And Urquhart compared his dishevelled troops
2405 To the parade smartness of their command.
Still smarting at not having been relieved,

Indignant and sickened, he said simply,
"I'm sorry things did not turn out as well
As I had hoped." Browning said, "You did all
2410   You could," and offered him a drink, and then
Showed him the way to bed. But no sleep came
Like a waterfall of tranquillity
And cascaded through his weary senses
As he thought that three-quarters of his ten
2415   Thousand men were missing or killed – for what?
That night Browning gave a dinner party
For Horrocks, Thomas and Urquhart, who then
Went south to Montgomery's HQ at
Eindhoven. Montgomery did not show
2420   Any disappointment. Like a concerned
Father greeting his son, he said, "Good to
See you got back all right. Come and sit down
And let's talk it over." They sat in two
Canvas chairs outside his caravan, and
2425   Montgomery said: "You did all you could."
They had dinner in "A" mess tent, and then
Montgomery went as usual to bed.
21st Army Group now occupied
From Joe's Bridge up Hell's Highway to Driel.

2430   Market Garden ended. At Arnhem ten
Thousand fighting men had landed, of whom
A quarter were evacuated and
Sixteen hundred wounded were left behind.
Of those who dropped, six thousand had been killed.
2435   Montgomery advanced only sixty-
Five miles into the Netherlands and failed
To cross the Lower Rhine, at a huge cost:
In all there were over sixteen thousand
Allied casualties, eight thousand German.
2440   The Allies lost more men than at D-Day.

Now Shellburst was in the Trianon, Kay
Continued to breakfast with Eisenhower.
There were many visitors to see him,
Who took his time, groups of Congressmen and
2445   Politicians, after whose visits he
Would say to Kay "I never want to have
Anything to do with politics", and
VIPs, including Bernie Baruch,
Roosevelt's adviser to whom he'd written,

128

2450 And Prince Bernhard of the Netherlands. For
Sixteen hours a day he visited as
Many command posts and conferred with as
Many officers and men as he could,
And Kay drove him to Brussels, Luxembourg,
2455 Nancy and Aachen. Each time an advance
Was made by an American army
Eisenhower visited the new front and
Sometimes drove to meetings in three countries
In one day, and was driven home by Kay.

2460 In the Trianon, genial, ascendant,
His critic proved wrong, Eisenhower hosted
A conference for all Allied commanders.
To make sure Montgomery attended
He invited Brooke. He briefed the men on
2465 His three-step strategy: open Antwerp,
Clear the Rhine north and south of the Ruhr, then
Thrust towards Berlin. Admiral Ramsay spoke:
"We are an Allied force. I don't defend
Operations on national grounds. Arnhem
2470 Was a British undertaking. There could
Have been more American support, but
The plan was Field Marshal Montgomery's.
Any criticism he should accept.
I am concerned that he did not choose to
2475 Secure the approaches to and port of
Antwerp, rather than make this risky drop
Behind enemy lines." Montgomery
Replied thinly: "There were no orders from
The Supreme Commander to take the port
2480 Of Antwerp and its approaches. What does
The CIGS think?" He turned to Brooke,
His wise counsellor, hoping for support.
Brooke, put on the spot, uncomfortable, spoke:
"I have to say I feel that for once Field
2485 Marshal Montgomery's strategy was
At fault. Instead of advancing towards
Arnhem, he should have made sure of Antwerp.
I have been a supporter of the Field
Marshal, who won a brilliant victory in
2490 Normandy. But on Arnhem I have to
Agree with Admiral Ramsay. The port of
Antwerp first." Montgomery said nothing,
And sat depressed, while his failure was probed.

Now wise and generous conciliator,
2495 Eisenhower concluded with a noble
Speech: "We've had a reverse at Arnhem. For
This the blame is entirely mine as I
Approved Field Marshal Montgomery's plea
To operate an Allied Airborne drop
2500 At Arnhem. Any blame belongs to me
Alone, is my responsibility,
And no one else's. Now we need to get
On with the war, and our two thrusts into
The Ruhr and Saar against an enemy
2505 That is not as defeated as we thought
A month ago." There was considerable
Admiration for this speech. The conference
Broke up and Ramsay said to Brooke, "That was
Spoken like a military statesman."
2510 Brooke said, "Whatever his shortcomings as
A battlefield commander, he has great
Personal stature." Ramsay said: "He has
A sincere nobility I admire.
Montgomery has been marginalised."
2515 "He's the victim of an American
Coup," Brooke said. "But he has contributed
To his undoing and to some extent
Has marginalised himself. Now, after
Arnhem, and with only a quarter of
2520 The Allied troops, Britain has a junior
Role." Montgomery stood aloof, alone,
An isolated figure – who had been
Further humbled, his brave attempt to end
The war quickly in tatters. Eisenhower
2525 Seemed the victor, a military statesman
Whose stature now dwarfed the one outstanding
Battlefield commander of the war. Soon
The Allies would pay a strategic price
In the battlefields of the cold Ardennes.

~ BOOK 5 ~

THE JEWS REVOLT AND STOP
THE HOLOCAUST

O Dante, you who were born in Florence
Near the Duomo in this tall dark house of
The Alighieri in this narrow street,
With arched front door and barred windows, in twelve
Sixty-five, descendant of a Roman
Soldier who settled on the Arno and
Of the Guelfs who expelled the Ghibellines
From Florence at Benevento, and whose
Leader, Boniface the Eighth, blessed you in
A crowd; you who first met Beatrice, Folco
Portinari the banker's daughter, at
A party at Casa Portinari –
She lived in the sesto of San Piero –
Where, nearly eight, Bice (diminutive
For Beatrice) wore a bright scarlet dress, and
Who next met her down by the Arno near
The Ponte Vecchio when you were both
Seventeen, and she greeted you with charm,
Wearing pure white, walking with two ladies,
And you saw her as Love, the Virgin, and
Stood on summer evenings by this stone south
Of the Cathedral in this Piazza
Del Duomo, near twelve and thirteen, and, hurt,
Suffered the pain of seeing her marry
Simone de' Bardi – at the same time you
Married Gemma Donati, to whom you
Were betrothed six years – and then die in June
Twelve ninety, and had the idea of your
Divine Comedy beaten out of you
By grief for the loss of your first love, as
You, a Cathar Pure One, mourned the passing
Of Pure Love; you who then opposed the Pope,
An unscrupulous, imperial man
Dedicated to papal tyranny,
And led a White mission to Boniface,
Who detained you while Charles of Valois's
Black Guelfs re-entered Florence, and who then,
With fourteen other Whites, was condemned to

Be burned to death in March 1302
40 For bribery, as you heard in Siena,
And knew exile on "another man's stair",
Rueful that great poets are not read by
Philistine governments, who would suppress
Their truthful eye and universal voice
45 For ephemeral topicality,
And, travelling between noble houses
In North Italy, in Casentino,
Verona, Lunigiana, with Virgil
As your guide (the forerunner to Beatrice),
50 Described the souls of Hell and Purgatory
In terza rima, and soon left behind
Political crises that kept you from
Rising above the fallen world, and, in
Exile from your beloved Florence, found
55 A heavenly city through your Beatrice;
You who showed the damned in Hell – neutral souls,
Virtuous pagans, simoniac Popes,
Francesca da Rimini, Filipo
Argenti, Farinata Uberti,
60 Piero delle Vigne, Brunetto Latini,
Ugolino – and every cruelty,
Every conceivable torture, every
Harmful act humans are capable of,
Campaldino and Caprona battles,
65 Atrocities on Albigensians,
A million of whom the Pope massacred
(The clergy not "shepherds" but "assassins"),
The sad effects of Satan in human
History, and finished just before you died
70 In Ravenna; you who knew Hell on earth,
Reflected the savagery of your Age,
Temporal tortures in the eternal,
And gave them a divine significance,
You who, a Protestant before your time,
75 Were Cathar in turning against the Pope,
Were Supreme Pontiff of that defunct sect,
You who hoped the German Emperor, Henry,
Would overthrow the Pope and then restore
A purified Christianity, who
80 Wrote your *Divine Comedy* to exalt
Your faith in the Cathar religion (like
The House of Aragon, Counts of Toulouse)
And heap abuse on meddlesome Popes who

132

Persecuted the Albigensians
85 And intrigued your exile, so you consigned
    Odious Boniface the Eighth to the eighth
    Circle of Hell – help me now that I must
    Narrate the greatest evil of our time,
    Of our cruel century, and how it happened,
90 The extermination of a race in
    Death camps as desperate as your inferno,
    Premeditated killing in Auschwitz
    Where the Illuminati's guillotine
    (Malthusian Grand Orient's instrument)
95 Became gas chambers through inventiveness,
    Manned by the victims, under the SS,
    The Schutzstaffel or Protection Unit,
    Who, robot-like, always obeyed orders.
    Help me as I tell of the revolt that
100 Brought an end to gassing in one thousand
    Six hundred and thirty-four factory-like
    Concentration camps and to genocide.

    Tell, Muse, how the order for such evil
    Came to be given. In November nineteen
105 Eighteen Hitler, in Pasewalk hospital,
    Learned with dismay of the Bavarian
    Revolution (led by Kurt Eisner, Grand
    Orient Freemason Communist, a Jew),
    The naval mutiny at Kiel, and of
110 The Emperor's – Kaiser's – abdication, and,
    Blaming all these events on scheming Jews,
    Vowed to go into politics as now
    Germany could no more make pacts with Jews.
    The Protocols of the Elders of Sion
115 Produced by French Mizraim Freemasons
    (Who had merged with Memphis and Martinist
    Rosicrucians in eighteen seventy-five)
    Were taken from the Priory of Sion
    And the French Rosicrucian Masons (whose
120 Rose-like serpent, Satan, winds round a cross,
    Blasphemous red cross of Satan, not Christ)
    And, finding their way into the dark hands
    Of Rasputin (Grand Master of the Lodge
    From which the *Protocols* were first "stolen"),
125 Arrived at Nicholas the Second's court
    Where Rasputin urged pogroms, and were brought
    From Moscow to Munich by Rosenberg.

Believing the *Protocols* were Jewish,
Hitler believed that the Jews engineered
130   The Bolshevik Revolution, whereas
The Grand Orient Freemason Lenin used
Jews and then destroyed them, a Satanic
Anti-Semitic, anti-Christian plot
To destroy Jews' and Christians' religions.
135   Misunderstanding a Masonic coup
(Grand Orient against the 32nd
Degree Scottish Rite Mason Kerensky),
In August nineteen thirty-six, Hitler
Moved from the first, domestic phase of his
140   Programme to its second phase, aggression
And war, which he expressed in his Four Year
Plan, a memorandum that set the Reich's
Armed forces and economy on course
For war against "Jewish Bolshevism
145   In Moscow", holding, as in *Mein Kampf*, that
Now Lenin had gained them a Russian base
The Jews would prepare world insurrection
And pursue world domination. Hitler
Had thus prepared for war long before his
150   Conference of November the fifth, nineteen
Thirty-seven, when the agenda was
The swift conquest of both Austria and
Czechoslovakia. When Schacht resigned
As Minister of Economy, cruel
155   Hitler gave Göring the memorandum
And made him his Plenipotentiary
For the Four Year Plan with control over
All economic policies, and both
Göring and Himmler shared Hitler's plans for
160   The Jews when Hitler gave the National
Socialist movement the authority
To "solve" the Jewish problem through ghettos,
And by its systematic planning to
Expropriate the entire Jewish race.
165   In November nineteen thirty-eight vom
Rath, a third secretary in the German
Embassy in Paris, was attacked by
A Polish Jew. In retaliation
The Gestapo rounded up some fifty
170   Thousand Polish Jews living in the Reich
And took them to the Polish border, where,
Denied entry by Poland, they lived in

No-man's land. The Kristallnacht (night of glass)
Riots burned synagogues, destroyed Jewish
175   Businesses and Jews' homes. As vom Rath died
Goebbels unleashed the SA, whose pogrom
Set fire to Jewish businesses. Himmler
And Heydrich brought in the SS. Göring
Forbad Jews access to public places,
180   And on the twelfth of November nineteen
Thirty-eight he held a large conference
And announced he had received a letter,
Written on the orders of the Führer,
Requesting that "the Jewish question be
185   Now co-ordinated and solved one way
Or another." He urged that Jews should be
Removed from the German economy.
Heydrich sought forced emigration, and soon
Jews could not work, go to school or receive
190   State benefits. On the twenty-fourth of
January nineteen thirty-nine Göring
Put Jews at the mercy of the police
And SD, and gave Heydrich power to speed
Up the forced emigration of German
195   Jews and use the terror methods Eichmann
Used in Vienna, where the cruel SS
Rounded up thousands of Jews and sent them
To Dachau, Buchenwald and Mauthausen –
In six months forty-five thousand Jews left
200   Austria. The directive set up under
Heydrich a Reich Central Office for all
Jewish emigration. Three days before
Hitler told the Czech Foreign Minister,
"We're going to destroy the Jews. They will
205   Not get away with the Bavarian
Revolution, the vile overthrow of
The monarchy, their Weimar republic.
That event took me into politics.
The time of reckoning has come. If foul
210   International Jewish financiers plunge
The world into war, the consequence won't
Be the Bolshevisation of the world,
Victory for Jewry, but the destruction
Of the Jewish race in Europe." After
215   The grim outbreak of war, on September
The twenty-first, nineteen thirty-nine, hard
Heydrich held a conference for fifteen

SS officers including Eichmann
In Berlin, and issued a directive,
220   Which said a plan for annihilating
The Jews had been conceived: "the final aim",
Which Eichmann asserted meant "physical
Extermination". First the Jews must be
Expelled from areas to be taken
225   Into the German Reich (Danzig, Posen,
White Prussia and Upper Silesia),
With concentration of all Polish Jews
Into a few urban areas at rail
Junctions or along railway lines. Some thought
230   Heydrich referred to a final aim of
A Jewish reservation, but he meant
Extermination, first in Poland and
Then in Russia, where Hitler had always
Planned to wage war. In nineteen forty on
235   December the eighteenth Hitler issued
His directive for his Operation
Barbarossa "to crush Soviet Russia
In a rapid campaign", which planned to kill
Jews while conquering Russia.
240   Now a mage,
Like a garish spider in a web of
Secret occult societies and groups,
Framed by the anti-Semitic threads of
The Rosicrucian Order of the New
245   Temple and Thule Society (of Lanz,
Eckart and Gurdjieff) and by Sionist
Illuminati Satanism, and
Seeing the Bolshevik Revolution
As Jewish, not Masonic; cruel Hitler
250   Decided to exterminate the Jews
Before Himmler visited Auschwitz on
March the first and ordered Höss to expand
The camp to accommodate a hundred
Thousand prisoners-of-war (he meant Jews and
255   Bolsheviks) and thirty thousand "peace-time
Prisoners". In May nineteen forty-one, now
Receiver and transmitter of Hitler's
Orders for the Final Solution, its
Operational principal, Himmler
260   Summoned Höss to Berlin and told him that
"The Führer has given the order for

A Final Solution of the Jewish
Question, that it should now be solved once and
For all, and that we the SS must now
265   Carry out that order". He said Auschwitz
Was chosen because of its rail access,
Its isolation and concealment. In
Late summer Himmler told Heydrich's SD
Strike "special duty" Einsatzkommandos
270   Of the liquidation order and said,
"Responsibility is mine alone,
And the Führer's, as I have been ordered
To free the Eastern territories of Jews."
After the July invasion, Heydrich
275   Ordered "intolerable elements",
Soviet state or party officials and
Jews, to be removed from prisoner-of-war
Camps in Russia. Hitler now transmitted
Operational orders to Himmler
280   For the annihilation of the Jews;
Administrative orders to Göring,
As Plenipotentiary, head of state
Apparatus, who on July's last day
Assigned the task of co-ordinating
285   The Final Solution ("I commission
You to carry out all necessary
Preparations...for a total solution
Of the Jewish question") to Heydrich and
The RSHA's office IV B-4
290   Where Eichmann worked. Eichmann visited Höss
At Auschwitz a few weeks later and talked
About mass killing methods, including
Gassing while showering and gas-trucks. Höss,
Squeamish at shooting, preferred gas, which cruel
295   Hitler used for killing the mentally
"Degenerate", "racially valueless",
"Adult insane" from late nineteen thirty-
Nine in the Euthanasia programme
Controlled by Bouhler in the Chancellery
300   And based in a Brandenburg shower-room.
That summer Auschwitz was turned into an
Annihilation camp, and staff were taught
To handle Zyklon B. In September
The staff experimentally gassed eight
305   Hundred and fifty "Jews and Bolsheviks"

Whom Heydrich's Einsatzkommandos took from
The army's prisoner-of-war camps, in Block
Eleven's iron-barred cellars at Auschwitz.
During Eichmann's next visit Höss told him
310 About this use of Zyklon B, and they
Decided to employ it in the mass
Extermination operation, which
Began in the mortuary next door
To the crematorium at Auschwitz,
315 And the killing centre at Birkenau.
Death camps were functioning by December
At Chelmno, where mobile vans used exhaust
Gas; Belzec, near Lublin; and Sobibor,
Majdanek and Treblinka. Heydrich called
320 The Wannsee Conference in Berlin on
January the twentieth, nineteen
Forty-two, to co-ordinate thirteen
State agencies involved in working on
The Final Solution according to
325 Göring's directive of the thirty-first
Of July nineteen forty-one, copies
Of which were sent to the participants.
While Eichmann, who prepared the Conference,
Took the minutes, Heydrich spoke at length on
330 The "practical implementation" of
The Final Solution: the forcible
Evacuation of Jews to ghettos,
Thence farther east. The representative
Of Göring's Four Year Plan urged that all Jews
335 Essential to war industries should not
Be evacuated. Mass murder was
Now technical, beyond ideology,
And happened regardless of the state of
The war as a systematic end in
340 Itself: the liquidation of all Jews.
On July the nineteenth nineteen forty-
Two Himmler decreed that all Jews working
In war-industry shops should be moved to
Concentration camps. His directive said
345 That all Jews employed by the Wehrmacht in
Making arms should be replaced by Aryans.
Einsatzgruppen evacuated Jews
Eastward for mass murder by gassing and,
Enticed by offers of food, the hungry

350
    Jews of the Polish ghettos of Lublin
    And Lvov were resettled in Belzec, those
    Of Warsaw in Treblinka, those from France,
    Holland and Belgium in Auschwitz. All were
    Gassed. That summer Himmler went to Auschwitz
355
    And observed each stage of the death process,
    And ordered that all bodies buried in
    Mass graves should be exhumed and burned so there
    Would be no trace of extermination,
    And all the Sonderkommando Jews, or
360
    "Special Detachment" disposal squads, who
    Opened a mass grave and burned the corpses
    Should be shot and burned when their grave had been
    Cleared. Then in April nineteen forty-three
    The Warsaw ghetto was liquidated.
365
    Hitler's troops in Russia, Paulus's Sixth
    Army besieging Stalingrad had been
    Encircled by the Red Army, and though
    Trains were needed to evacuate them,
    In February Himmler had appealed for
370
    More trains to transport Jews, to prevent their
    Partisan ambushes. Now the Final
    Solution had priority over
    Military needs. The youngest, fittest Jews
    Arriving at Auschwitz, Belzec, Chelmno,
375
    Majdanek, Sobibor and Treblinka
    Were selected for work, while the other
    Ninety per cent undressed, had their hair cut,
    And were driven into gas chambers, one
    Person per square foot, standing. They were gassed,
380
    Squashed together like pillars of basalt,
    And after thirty minutes were thrown out
    Blue, wet with sweat and urine, legs covered
    With faeces and blood, and were burned on pyres
    That made the night sky turn red round Auschwitz.
385
    So Hitler's orders were carried out by
    Himmler and, through Göring, Heydrich – who served
    Under the supremo Himmler as one
    Of twelve SS-Obergruppenführers –
    As operational and technical
390
    Consequences of a systematic,
    Industrialised, factory policy of
    Death no one questioned, which opposed alleged
    Partisan attacks in territories

That Germany had recently annexed.
The SS under Himmler carried out
Hitler's order to exterminate Jews.

Tell, Muse, how Himmler controlled the SS
By creating (at Hitler's command) an
Order like the Teutonic Knights or like
King Arthur's Knights of the Round Table, that
Undertook genocide with loyalty
Unquestioning to their new cult of Death.
Tell of Himmler's castle at Wewelsburg,
Of the Round Table, the Realm of the Dead,
Shamanic underworld of dead spirits.
Tell, Muse, how Himmler kept his Knights loyal
To the SS's ideal with rituals.
Himmler had joined the Artamanen and
Thule Societies, which used occult hate
Rituals in which the swastika stood for
Darkness and the terrifying Goddess
Kali and her magical practices.
In nineteen thirty-three, a primary
Schoolteacher, strong in rational planning with
An imagination fed by occult
Gnosticism, Hermetic Alchemy,
Neo-Platonism and the Jewish
Kabbalah, Himmler met Karl Wiligut,
A poet like Eckart, Vienna-born,
Who, while serving in the Habsburg army
Published verse on Austrian-Moravian
Legends for List's publisher, Friedrich Schalk.
Round him formed an occult-volkish group, and,
Impressed at his clairvoyant knowledge of
The ancient Germanic past, his racial
Memory of the Aryan tradition
Over sixty thousand years old, Himmler
Put him in charge of prehistorical
Research in the SS. The sixty-six
Year old volkish occultist's role was to
Find the SS ideology's roots
By clairvoyant meditation. One of
The Illuminati who resurfaced
In Germany in eighteen eighty through
Leopold Engel – who was in touch with
Theosophical and Rosicrucian
Societies in England, both offshoots

Of the Illuminati, and co-founded
The Hermetic Order of the Golden
Dawn there, from which Crowley came (whose Ordo
Templi Orientis and Satanist,
Luciferian doctrine sought to destroy
Judeo-Christian culture) – Wiligut
Looked back to Weishaupt who served Lucifer,
Opposed Christian religion and states, and
For twenty years, till nineteen nine, had held
The rank of Knight in the Schlarraffia,
A semi-Masonic lodge at Görz, and
Had the rite-name Lobesam. Wiligut
Had a vision of diabolical
Black-uniformed elite troops who would be
The master race with purity of blood
And expand the Great German Reich abroad
Through a chivalrous rule of dread terror,
The method of the French Jacobins who
Ruled through the guillotine. Wiligut claimed
To end a line of Germanic sages,
A secret line of German kings with coats
Of arms and seals, the Uiligotis of
The Asa-Uana-Sippe, and with his
Ancestral, clairvoyant memory to
Recall the experiences of his tribe,
From which in nineteen eight he had written
Nine pagan commandments in the presence
Of Theodor Czepl of the Order
Of New Templars. In nineteen twenty von
Liebenfels sent Czepl to Wiligut,
Who said his crown was in the imperial
Palace in Goslar, his sword in a stone
Grave at Steinamanger. His description
Of the ancient Germans' old religion
Was like von List's, who described the Germans
As an ancient, heroic race of blond,
Blue-eyed warriors with the wisdom of
Pagan mages; he said his religion
Was Irminism, which opposed Odin
And Wotanism, and celebrates Krist,
A Germanic god, which the Christians stole:
The *Bible* was "written in Germany".
Christianity thus had Aryan roots.
He gave Czepl his poem, *German Faith*,
Which blended Teutonic archaic List

440

445

450

455

460

465

470

475

480

And Aryan Christian Lanz. History for him
Began two hundred and thirty thousand
485 Years back; his ancestors founded Goslar
Around seventy-eight thousand BC.
The Irminist religion of Krist was
Proclaimed about twelve thousand five hundred
BC; this universal German faith,
490 Whose main symbol showed the all-seeing eye
Of God revolving in a triangle,
Which became the Illuminati eye
Of Lucifer, was split by Wotanists
In nine thousand six hundred BC when
495 Baldur-Chrestos, Irminist prophet, was
Crucified by Wotanists at Goslar.
Wotanists destroyed Goslar's Irminist
Centre in twelve hundred BC, and then
The Irminists founded a new temple
500 In the jagged crags of Externsteine, near
Detmold, which new Wotanists captured in
Four sixty and Charlemagne sacked during
His drive against the pagan Saxons, when
He killed four thousand five hundred Saxons
505 At Verden. The Wiliguts escaped from
The Franks and fled to the Faroe Isles and
Central Russia, and founded Vilna. Then,
Persecuted by Catholics, they fled to
Hungary, and remained Irminist despite
510 Persecution by Catholics, Freemasons
And Jews, whom Wiligut blamed for the First
World War and the collapse of the Habsburg
Empire. Founding an anti-Semitic
League in Salzburg, he attacked Jews in his
515 Newspaper. Violent and deemed insane, he
Spent three years in an asylum, and then
Returned with his ancestral memory
To friends in the Order of New Templars
And Edda Society (both of which
520 Were Illuminati offshoots) and fled
To Munich, where he met rune occultists.
Next year, in January nineteen thirty-three
The Nazis came to power, and Anders of
The Order of New Templars, an SS
525 Officer, introduced Wiligut to
Himmler, who invited him to enter
The SS as Head of Pre- and Early

History in the Race and Settlement
Office in Munich. Under the name of
530 Weisthor he talked prehistory and racial
Ancestral memories, and soon had dark
Rasputin's hold over Himmler through runes,
Mythology, cosmology, epochs
Of prehistory and his nine pagan
535 Commandments. He had the conception of
An SS officers' college to train
Recruits in SS ideology.

Through his Illuminati past Weisthor
Knew the triangle with a capstone eye,
540 The Masonic eye of great God's wisdom
Upside down, not the infinite eye of
The great architect of the universe
But the finite eye of man – all-seeing
Eye of Satan within three points: spirit,
545 Energy, matter; worldly spying eye
Of man filled with Satan, become a god.
Weisthor told Himmler the SS college
Should be triangular. Himmler had passed
Through Westphalia in January during
550 The Nazi electoral campaign, and
Had driven through fog to Hermannsdenkmal,
The towering monument on a high hill,
Massive statue with raised sword to Hermann,
The Germanic Cherusker warrior
555 Arminius, warlord mightier than Rome,
Who defeated the Roman legions of
Brutal Varus in the Teutoburger
Wald in AD 9, whom Tacitus called
"The liberator of Germany"; and
560 Lodged at Grevenburg castle that dank night.
Wanting a castle for the SS home,
Himmler visited two castles that year.
Guided by Weisthor he found derelict,
Triangular Wewelsburg castle on
565 A hill overlooking the Westphalian
Plain and the river Alme on November
The third nineteen thirty-three, and chose it
That evening. Himmler rented the ruin
To convert it into an SS school
570 That was both Camelot and Monsalvat.
Wewelsburg, owned by Wewel von Büren,

Was a focus for Saxon resistance
During the time of the marauding Huns.
The SS took it over next July.
575 Weisthor was present. Several thousands of
Political prisoners (all Jehovah's
Witnesses as Jews were considered too
Unworthy to touch it) reconstructed
The lowering castle. Here Himmler summoned
580 The SS-Führers and told them, "We are
A Knightly Order, from which one cannot
Withdraw." He dreamt of Arthur, Perceval,
The Teutonic Knights who conquered Prussia
And, fearless, fought the Poles and Slavs, and of
585 Heinrich the First, but Weisthor's Order was,
Like Weishaupt's, modelled on the Jesuits
Who dominated the eighteenth century
Ingolstadt. In February nineteen
Thirty-five Himmler transferred it to his
590 Personal Staff, wanting to make it as
Marienburg was for the Teutonic
Knights. Weisthor pronounced, "This castle will be
A magical strongpoint in a coming
Conflict between Europe and Asia. In
595 Accordance with the shepherd's vision in
Battle at the Birchtree, a great army
From the east will be repulsed by the west."
Himmler, believing the SS would soon
Defend Europe against the east, was moved.
600 In Wewelsburg and in less completed
Castles at Sonthofen, Vogelsang and
Krössinsee, SS training colleges,
SS officers were taught to be cruel.
Stripped to the waist, they fought off snarling dogs
605 For twelve minutes, and all who fled were shot.
Each had to tear out the eyes of three cats
With his bare hands. Each was trained to be quite
Pitiless, indifferent to sorrow,
So each could walk among corpses unmoved.
610 Christian names were replaced with Teutonic,
Priests by local SS leaders, Christian
Beliefs by dark neo-paganism.
Weisthor introduced Himmler to Kirchhoff,
Who believed legends refer to actual
615 Prehistoric events, and traced ley-lines,
Energy-lines across landscapes. Kirchhoff

Claimed ancient Europe was ruled by Goslar's
Uiskunig, King Arthur of Stonehenge and
Ermanrich of Vilna, and with Weisthor
620 He surveyed the Black Forest during June
Nineteen thirty-six and found traces of
An Irminist religious complex in
Triangular landscape there depicting
The revolving eye of Lucifer. Now
625 Himmler founded a "Society for
The Promotion and Preservation of
German Cultural Monuments", which gave
Priority to the restoration
Of Teutonic Knights' castles or sites like
630 Sachsenhain bei Verden on the Aller,
Where four thousand five hundred Saxons were
Massacred by the Christian Charlemagne,
Whom Himmler called Charles the Frank, and where four
Thousand five hundred waist-high "archaic"
635 Stones were now laid in walls around the field
To commemorate the pagan heroes
In anti-Christian symbolism, where
SS rallies dipped flags in salute. Now
Himmler gave Teudt the task of reviving
640 Externsteine as a sacred monument
To the German spirit, as twelve hundred
Years before, with a lofty replica
Irminsul, the ancient sacred pillar
Of the Saxons on its highest point. Now
645 Himmler felt close to Heinrich the First, King
Of the Saxon dynasty, and German
Conqueror of the Slavs, whose bones he had
Carried into the Quedlinburg crypt and
Interred to show his hatred for the Poles
650 On the thousandth anniversary of
Heinrich's death, July the second nineteen
Thirty-six, and, sitting in the cold crypt,
Alone at midnight, communed with Heinrich's
Spirit, which came when he was half asleep
655 And softly gave him valuable advice.
Himmler harked back to days of the First Reich,
Which had been founded by Heinrich the First,
And swore that he would now complete Heinrich's
Bold anti-Slav mission in the east. Now
660 Weisthor made several trips to Wewelsburg –
In the south wing, above the dining-hall,

Were soon a library for twelve thousand
Books, a meeting-room and a court-room for
The highest SS court, and some guest-rooms –
665 And urged the commandant, von Knobelsdorff
To revive Irminist faith through SS
Rituals: pagan wedding ceremonies
For SS officers, at which Weisthor,
Priest-like, held a crosier carved with the runes,
670 And spring, harvest and solstice festivals
For the SS garrison and village.

Now Weisthor and Himmler gave Wewelsburg
A cult's rituals. List held that the Teutons
Practised a Gnostic religion in whose
675 Mysteries they were initiated:
Wotanism, the worship of the god
Of war and lord of dead heroes in his
Valhalla, Wotan or Odin, who in
Ritual self-torture hung on a windswept
680 Tree (the World Tree Yggdrasil) while pierced by
A spear, as a sacrifice ("myself given
To myself") to win a shaman's knowledge,
For nine nights without food or drink, and gained
Magical powers, mystical union
685 Of man and the universe, and a rare
Armanist gnosis of the Mysteries;
A one-eyed god, eye in a triangle,
Hanged man's tongue out, god of the gallows and
Of war, master of the dead from whom all
690 Occult knowledge is won, and so god of
Occult knowledge, Odin, full of deceit,
Cunning and treachery, but also god
Of ecstasy, sorcery and witchcraft,
Odin as Lucifer. In the large domed,
695 Circular twelve-pillared dining-hall of
The north tower hung coats-of-arms. Here Himmler
Met the Gruppenführers, and sat with his
Twelve Obergruppenführers at a round
Oak table on high-backed boar-skinned chairs, each
700 Bearing a name on silver plate, above
A black swastika inlaid in the floor
With twelve hooked feet. Each SS Knight slept in
A room decorated in the period
Style of a hero of Nordic legend –
705 Himmler's was called King Heinrich, and there were

Rooms named after Otto the Great, Frederick
Hohenstauffen, Philip of Swabia,
Henry the Lion, Vidukind, King Arthur
And Conrad the Fourth, all Kings and Emperors
710 Who had claimed Longinus's Spear or Lance –
And from their study-rooms, as in an old
Monastery, the Obergruppenführers
Assembled in the upper hall and sat
At the Round Table like King Arthur's Knights,
715 Twelve brave and noble Knights who defended
The Celtic creed against the invading
Dark Age Anglo-Saxons, and with closed eyes
Meditated on racial purity,
Contacted their ancestral memories
720 In a parody of the Last Supper,
In their Valhalla, Hall of the Slain, to
Which came all brave men who died in battle,
Chosen by the Valkyries to be slain,
A splendid palace roofed with shields of dead
725 Gruppenführers, and lived with Odin, god
Of the dead, ruler of the underworld,
Where heroes feast on the meat of a boar,
Where there was feasting among Odin's wolves
And ravens. Below the marble floor was
730 The holy of holies of the Order:
A secret Nazi temple, guarded by
SS elite, modern Knight-monastics;
Hel, the Realm of the Dead beneath the disc
Of the earth, guarded by the goddess Hel,
735 Where the Hound of Hel, Garm, howls and the wolf
Fenrir wanders unchained, its jaws stretched wide;
A stone crypt, round funereal room which
Was modelled on the Pantheon of the Kings
At the monastery of El Escorial
740 Near Madrid – Jesuit-planned burial-place
Of the Kings of Spain, where the dead would live,
Invoked in magic ceremonies – with
A shallow sunken well or stoup in which
Stood a hollowed-out stone pillar. When one
745 Of the twelve Obergruppenführers died,
His escutcheon was burned on the pillar,
And the smoke rose straight in a column as
In Aryan fire sacrifices made by
Iranian Indo-Europeans, due
750 To the ventilation of four air-shafts,

The arrangement of four vents in the dome.
The ashes were then placed in one of twelve
Cremation urns on niches round the wall,
Each one on a knee-high stone pedestal.

755 Here Himmler conjured and spoke with Heinrich –
A Führer from a thousand years ago,
The first Kaiser, who attacked the Christians
And effete Romans under Charlemagne –
And other spirits of men who had died

760 Hundreds of years before. Here spirits were
Summoned in a Black Mass to give guidance
In the black art of annihilation,
Their powers invoked in frequent séances.
Here was the capstone of the triangle,

765 Here in the Realm of the Dead was the eye
Of Satan, an oval eye (depressed stoup)
And eyeball (pillar). For one week each year
Himmler and his Knights of the Round Table
Meditated and did exercises

770 Of magic visualisation here
As a fine Aryan man was beheaded
And his severed head, like the Baphomet
Of the Templars, a head whose flesh Satan
Could occupy, was placed on the pillar

775 To link the Knights with Secret Masters in
The Caucasus, who flew into the head.
They descended to the Realm of the Dead
For a black ceremony to invoke
Lucifer, Lord of the Dead, the Death's Head,

780 Illuminati Lord. Each of the twelve
Stood by the niche which would bear the ashes
Of his burned coat-of-arms, honour in death,
Here in this beehive crypt with four window-
Like shafts for smoke, and when they whispered at

785 The wall, the sound travelled round the beehive
And could be heard clearly, though the same words
Spoken from the centre were indistinct.
It was rumoured Hitler would be buried
In this Hel, which was below Valhalla,

790 This Agharta in the earth's underworld,
Inhabited by supermen who were
Descended from people who lived in Thule,
Beneath the disc of the earth. Later, on
The black marble pillar stood an awesome

795   Object of occult power, a Christian cup
             Delivered to Satan's dark lair: the Grail.

             Tell, Muse, how the Grail was once Lucifer's,
             And what it looked like and its history,
             And how the Romance poet Wolfram von
800   Eschenbach knew where it was hidden and
             Named caves round Montségur in *Parzifal*.
             This silver-metal bowl was adorned with
             Three large stones and three gold bands or round plaques,
             And it fitted into a three-clawed base
805   Which seemed transparent emerald or jasper,
             So it became known as the Emerald Cup.
             This base was made from a great emerald which
             Had fallen from the crown of Lucifer,
             Satanael, elder son of God – once Light
810   And controller of the realm of Darkness,
             Prince of Angels who sought to overthrow
             The power of God and rule Heaven and earth –
             When Michael flung him into the abyss
             During the fall of the Angels, which left
815   God's second son supreme, Christ, now the Light.
             This emerald fell into the Kush mountains
             And, brought to Babylon, was made into
             The Cup of Abraham when his high priest,
             Salem, asked an Assyrian to make
820   A cup to catch the sacrificed ram's blood.
             He worked a lump of silver-like metal
             Found in the Zagros mountains of Persia,
             And shaped this emerald into a pale base
             Whose three feet showed an eagle's talons, grapes
825   And a lion's paw. The first band was engraved
             In cuneiform "This is the Cup of El –
             The One God – whose Name is Yahweh or I
             Am that I am" by King Melchizedek,
             High Priest of Jerusalem, who gave it
830   To Abraham. The second band proclaimed:
             "This is the Cup of Abraham, Chosen
             One and Friend of God. He speaks with God and
             Will be the Father of Many Nations."
             This Emerald Cup was placed in Ur's temple,
835   A ziqqurat to the One God, El, and
             It passed to Isaac, Jacob, then Levi,
             And down to Moses of the Levite tribe,

Who gave it to Aaron, the first high priest
Of Israel, who placed it beside the Ark
840   Of the Covenant, an acacia box
Overlaid with sheets of pure gold which housed
The stone tablets of the Ten Commandments,
In the Tabernacle. Later it passed
Down to David and Solomon, in whose
845   Temple it stood beside the Ark, until
It was hidden in the caverns beneath
The Stables in times of danger, as when
Sheshonk the First sacked Jerusalem. There
Sheshonk's grave-robbers found it and sold it
850   To Phoenician traders in Damascus,
Whence it found its way by boat to Marseilles,
Where Joseph of Arimathaea sailed
From Byblos via Carthage in 12 AD
With his twelve year old nephew Jesus, and
855   Found it in a Marseilles silversmith's shop
While seeking cups to sell to northern Celts.
The young Jesus gazed at the engravings.
The third band was inscribed: "This is the Cup
Of the Son. He who drinks from this Cup with
860   Him will become a branch of the vine and
He will never die, save what has withered."
Gazing at the silver, gold, jasper cup,
Jesus asked Joseph, "Uncle, will you keep
This for me? You will know when I need it."
865   Joseph bought it and they sailed to Britain –
St. Michael's Mount, Land's End, North Somerset –
And anchored at Burnham, at the mouth of
The Brue River near Glastonbury. Jesus
Spoke of a strange new God who protected
870   People from evil. Druids came to hear,
Who worshipped Du-w, "the one without darkness",
Whose three forms, shown by three gold rays of light,
Were Bel, Taran and Yesus: past, present
And future saviour, the coming Messiah.
875   Some Druids saw Jesus as their Yesus.
He spoke of Abraham, Moses, Joshua,
Saul, David and Solomon, and Joseph
Built a home of poles, mud and wattle by
The spring at the foot of Glastonbury Tor,
880   Where Jesus lived. In 16 AD, he
Worked as a tin-miner in Priddy and
Remained in England till 30 AD

When he returned to Palestine for his
Three-year ministry. At the Last Supper,
885 The last time Jesus ate or drank, within
Joseph of Arimathaea's house, in
The upper room, Joseph placed the Emerald
Cup, which he had kept, in the centre of
The table, remembering Jesus' words.
890 After the arrest in Gethsemane
Roman soldiers searched the upper guest-room
And found the Emerald Cup and presented
It to Pilate. After Longinus took
Pity on Jesus' suffering on the cross
895 And pierced his side with his spear to hasten
His death, so his legs would not be broken
At sundown, Joseph went to Pilate and
Asked for the body, which, once Longinus
Had certified death, Pilate granted and,
900 To please the "noble Decurion" and
Member of the Sanhedrin, handed back
The Cup and said, "I think this belongs to
You, take it." Joseph hurried to the cross,
Carrying the clawed Cup under his cloak.
905 Jesus had been dead an hour, and his wounds
Had ceased to bleed. He and Nicodemus
Took the body to the Garden Tomb and
Spiced it with myrrh and aloes, and the side
Began to bleed. Joseph took the Cup from
910 Under his cloak and caught the blood that oozed
From Christ's gashed side. They then wound the body
In linen and sealed the tomb with a stone,
Buried him like a king. Later Joseph
Was imprisoned, charged with body-snatching.
915 Released in 36 AD, he took
The Cup and sailed from Byblos to Marseilles
And then Britain, settled in Glastonbury,
Buried the Cup at the foot of the Tor,
Then lodged it in the underground chapel
920 Of the Celtic church near the Chalice Well,
Then passed it to his brother-in-law, Bron,
Who was known as the "Rich Fisher" because
He miraculously fed a great crowd
On one fish. Bron took it to his castle
925 On the coast of Somerset or Cornwall.
It stayed with his descendants, who were known
As the Fisher Kings, till 407,

When marauding Germanic warriors
Raided and sacked the Fisher King's fortress
930 And took the Emerald Cup to Normandy.
Next year Roman soldiers found these Saxons
Sheltering from a storm, and sent the Cup
To Stilicho, who passed it to the Pope.
When the Visigoth Alaric sacked Rome
935 He took the Cup to Carcassone in France
Along with the Treasure of Solomon –
The Ark, David's gold Harp, Aaron's Staff, gold
Urn with Manna, seven-branched candelabrum,
Which remained buried beneath the Stables
940 Till Titus dug them up in 70
And sent them to his father Vespasian –
And hid them in caves of the Pyrenees
Near what was to become the Cathars' fort
At Montségur, where the Cup was untouched
945 Till it passed to the Merovingian kings –
It had left Britain before Arthur's Knights
Sought it in vain in the sixth century –
And Dagobert the Second possessed it
When he married the Visigoth Princess,
950 Rich Giselle de Razes in 671,
And was murdered by a thrust of a lance
Into his sleeping eye. Four centuries on
Descendants of the Merovingian
Blood-line, Godfrey of Bouillon, who captured
955 Jerusalem from the Moslems in ten
Ninety-nine, and his brother Baudouin, were
Kings of Jerusalem, and took the Cup
As a secret symbol of their kingship.
To Godfrey came nine vagabonds, Hugues de
960 Tyre and his Knights Templar, who were given
A wing of Godfrey's palace that was built
Above Solomon's Temple and Stables,
Where for nine years they dug, seeking treasure –
Their main role was not to protect pilgrims
965 But to excavate – and shipped what they found
To North France and the Pyrenean caves
To join the treasure of the Visigoths.
The Cathars who began in Germany
(Hence Himmler's interest) spread into Flanders,
970 France and Italy, and with two million
Followers, now swept through Languedoc and
Inherited the Merovingian

Treasure hidden in caves round Montségur
And allied with the Templars, who also
975   Stored treasure in the caves. The Cup returned.
When Jerusalem fell to Saladin
In eleven eighty-seven Templars
Brought the Cup to France, to Chartres Cathedral,
Which had been built by Cistercian monks who
980   Taught the Children of Solomon, a guild
That was affiliated to Templars.
When the Cathedral was set on fire in
Eleven ninety-four, it was removed
By Templars; when, at Innocent the Third's
985   Request in 1209 the Cistercians
Ceased to preach peaceful conversion and turned
To war through a violent crusade against
The Albigensians, mobilising
North France against Provençal south, the Grail
990   Was passed by sympathetic Templars to
The dualistic Albigensian
Cathars in Montségur – Montsalvat was
A Cathar term – and used in their mystic
Feast, the "manisola", after the kiss
995   Of the "consolamentum", which passed on
The Light. There it served as a rallying
Point for Cathars, appearing on a cave
Wall in Ariège, and inspired the Grail
Legends which ceased around twelve twenty-five,
1000   Which the Church condemned as heretical,
And dignified the rituals of a sect
That denied sacraments, and regarded
This captured trophy of their enemy
As a palladium, which would repulse
1005   The besieging Crusaders. A million
Cathars were killed by Papal genocide
During the Albigensian Crusade
And in the massacre at Montségur
As Lucifer's armies besieged the fort,
1010   Demonising the Crusaders, and strove
To regain the jewel of Lucifer's crown.
There in twelve forty-four heretical
Cathars made their last stand against the might
Of the Catholic Albigensian Crusade
1015   And, according to tradition, the night
Before the final assault four Cathars
Descended on ropes with the regalia

Of the Merovingian King Dagobert
The Second, and a cup reputed to
Be the Holy Grail. After the sack of
Montségur and the cruel Field of the Stake,
Where five hundred Cathars would not abjure
Their faith and preferred to be burned alive –
Holding one final consolamentum,
Descending the hill, marching to the pyre,
Climbing ladders, threw themselves on the flames –
No treasure was found: it was in the caves.

Tell, Muse, how such treasure came to be at
Wewelsburg and how Himmler kept his Knights
Loyal with blood rituals of genocide.
In spring nineteen thirty-five Weisthor moved
From Munich to Berlin and worked within
The SS in the Adjutant's office
Of the Reichsführer-SS Personal Staff,
Re-establishing the old Irminist
Religion, restricting Christian priesthood,
Restoring ancient monuments, writing
Tribal mottoes and Germanic mantras
That awakened ancestral memory.
Himmler asked Weisthor to design a badge
Of membership in an Order which now
Demanded complete loyalty and strict
Obedience: the Death's Head badge and silver
Signet ring with its double sig-rune and
With swastika and hagall rune. The rings
Of all dead SS men were sent back to
A chest at Wewelsburg castle. Weisthor
Continued to shape Wewelsburg, and lived
In a villa at Kaspar Theyss Strasse,
Where he was visited by Himmler, von
Leers, Kiss, Schiller, Anders; and Otto Rahn,
Who studied Cathar and Grail legends and,
Like Parsifal, quested for the Grail and
Researched in Provence, working with Weisthor.
In nineteen thirty-one, scrambling through caves,
Backed by the Thule Society, Himmler
And Rosenberg, the treasure-hunting Rahn
Had made a long visit to Languedoc,
Seeking the Grail in hills for three whole months.
In September nineteen thirty-three Rahn
Had written *The Crusade for the Grail* which

Identified Montsalvat, Grail Mountain
Of Wolfram von Eschenbach's *Parzifal*,
As Montségur in the French Pyrenees
1065 Whose local grottos still bear Wolfram's names,
Sabarthez, Ornolac and Fontanet,
The Cathedral cave and the cavern with
The "Tomb of Hercules" stalagmite where
There was a hall for heretics to meet
1070 Among ancient stalagmites. Rahn studied
Mount Montségur's sacred geometry, and
Had found secret underground passages
Where he felt the treasure must be hidden,
On a geomantric point where it would
1075 Do good. He knew a priest at Rennes, Father
Sauniere, had found a coded parchment and
Lists of Grand Masters of Knights Templar and
The Priory of Sion and a history
Of the Merovingian bloodline in
1080 A pillar supporting the altar in
Eighteen ninety-six and placed a statue
Of Asmondeus in the church, hideous
Demon, guardian of treasure Lucifer
Has an interest in, and he knew the Lord
1085 Of the Underworld felt he was rightful
Owner of the Emerald Cup and jewel of
His crown. In September nineteen thirty-
Five, Rahn joined Weisthor's department, and that
December with Darré of "blood and soil",
1090 One of the Artamen self-reliant
Settlers on soil who armed against the Slavs,
Himmler set up the Ahnenerbe to
Research into German prehistory and
Archaeology. Next March Rahn entered
1095 The SS. His letters about the Grail
Were read only by Weisthor and Himmler,
Who kept Rahn's writings by his bedside, with
Wolfram von Eschenbach's great *Parzival*,
His *Wilhelmhaml* and his *Titurel*.
1100 And in nineteen thirty-seven Rahn wrote
On his discovery of a Cathar-
Gothic Gnosticism, a heresy
With German besides Cathar origins,
In *Lucifer's Servants*. The accurate
1105 Title was *Lucifer's Court in Europe*,
And the book saw the Pope as Lucifer:

Deceived by Satan, all the top Nazis
Saw the Church as Lucifer's black organ,
And their occult beliefs as close to God,
1110 Their name for their dark Lord. Rahn decided
That a race of pre-German supermen
Who attained ultimate knowledge inscribed
In runes on stone tablets the law of life,
An idea dear to the archaists of
1115 The Thule Society. To Aryans
The true Grail is this stone inscription of
Primordial knowledge, a secret book
Containing lost knowledge of First Masters
From Hyperborea ("White Isle") or Thule,
1120 The Manichaean "Graal" ("Gorr-al") meaning
"Precious engraved stone", Wolfram's "precious stone";
Aryan equivalent of the Jewish
Stone tablets of Moses. From Montségur
In the same year Rahn sent a consignment
1125 In a package to Himmler. This contained
What he had discovered, which he believed
Was the Christian Grail, the Emerald Cup,
Not the Aryan stone, the Nazi Grail
Which would make Hitler the Messiah of
1130 An ancient Aryan religion who
Would restore to the West its origins:
A secret Absolute knowledge. Himmler
Showed Hitler, who, having joined the anti-
Semitic Rosicrucian Order of
1135 The New Temple, was influenced – produced –
By the Priory of Sion and knew of
The regalia of the Merovingian
Kings of Jerusalem, the Grail and Lance.
With Sionist Hitler's blessing, Himmler
1140 Gave the vessel to Weisthor, who took it
To Schloss Wewelsburg and placed it upon
The black marble pedestal or altar
With silver SS runes in the Realm of
The Dead, beneath the Great Hall, where it stood
1145 For ceremonies. (At all other times
It was kept in the wall-safe.) Rahn then did
Four months' service with the SS inside
Dachau, and, being granted leave to write,
And, opposed to the coming war, being
1150 Ordered to die with honour or be tried,
Resigned from the SS in February

Nineteen thirty-nine, disillusioned that
The Holy Grail was now in evil hands,
And died while walking on the sacred peak
1155 Of the Kufstein mountain, bit cyanide.
So the occult repaid the service of
A Nazi who retained indignation.
Now twelve Obergruppenführers gathered
Like Arthur's Knights to descend into Hel
1160 And celebrate the Black Order's capture
Of the holiest Christian relic, now
A trophy within the eye of Satan
In the triangular castle, which turned
(They thought) the saving blood of Christ into
1165 The survival of pure blood, and reversed
The brotherhood of the Mass to slaughter
Of all racially impure blood, marking
The triumph of Death over Christian life
And the Jewish love of the Last Supper,
1170 And the triumph of Darkness over Light.
Now Wolff, Berger, Jüttner, Hildebrandt, von
Herff, Breithaupt, Heydrich, Daluege, Heissmeyer,
Pohl, Lorenz and Greifelt were the new twelve
Disciples round Himmler's Krist, Guardians
1175 Of the Grail, recipients of its power
Reversed by Satan, tied by chivalrous oath
And loyalty to the revolving eye
Of the triangular Irminist faith.
Where Christ and twelve disciples had sipped from
1180 The chalice at the first Mass, now Himmler
And twelve Obergruppenführers drank to
Their Black Order's massacring policy
Of extermination and genocide,
Manipulated subtle energies
1185 Still concentrated in the Emerald Cup,
The object of the quest of Parzifal.
The Grail remained in Wewelsburg until
On May the second, nineteen forty-five
An SS company took it inside
1190 A leaden casket to the Zillertal
Mountain pass in Austria and buried
It near the foot of the Schleigeiss Glacier,
In a ledge of snow by a precipice,
On the nine thousand foot high Hochfeiler,
1195 So it would now be safe from the Allies.
The moving glacier's frontal moraine,

Or debris carried down, could not disgorge
Its secrets until nineteen ninety-five.

Tell, Muse, about Himmler's Lance. Soon more Knights
1200   Joined the Wewelsburg rituals. In March
Nineteen thirty-eight the Anchluss added
Austria to Germany, and Hitler
Claimed the Holy Lance which had pierced Christ's side,
Which gave its owner the power of world rule.
1205   That same day as thousands of people cheered,
Tears in their eyes, and chanted "Heil Hitler!
Ein volk, ein Reich, ein Führer" ("Hail Hitler!
One folk, one empire, one leader"), Hitler
Went straight to the Schatzkammer (treasure room)
1210   Of the Hofburg and to the long glass case,
And gazed at what was now the "sacred Reich's
Lance" which would bring about the Third Reich's rise,
A grey metal barb wire-bound round a shaft
Forty-five Merovingian Emperors held
1215   From 752 to 1806 and
Which as a Rosicrucian he believed
Was central to the Grail mysteries of
The King of Jerusalem cult, in which
The holder of the Universal Throne
1220   In Europe must hold the titles "King of
Jerusalem", "Holy Roman Emperor",
And possess the Lance, making him the Lost
King of the Merovingians or Messiah,
A cult he would take over for Satan.
1225   Haushofer wrote the secret of the Lance
In runic code and told it to Heydrich
And no one else: "Who ever possesses
This Holy Lance and understands the power
It serves, holds in his hand the destiny
1230   Of the world, for good or for evil." Thus
If he who claimed the spear chose good, its power
Would spread world peace and its owner's empire,
But if he chose evil, and if the Lance
Came into evil use, then the great power
1235   Behind the Lance – the power of God – would turn
Against its owner, hurt and consume him,
Bring about his fall and his sudden death:
"Use it for good and the Lance will raise you.
Use it for ill and it will destroy you
1240   And be removed." Hitler did not know this,

He saw only possession and command.
Himmler and Heydrich were entrusted with
Transporting it from Vienna. Six months
Later Kaltenbrunner loaded it on
1245 A train bound for Nuremberg. Himmler had
It copied by a Japanese maker
Of samurai swords found by Haushofer.
Every speck and defect was reproduced.
This perfect copy, with a maker's mark
1250 Known only to the craftsman, Himmler and
Heydrich, was brought to Wewelsburg, where it
Had once been lodged by the Teutonic Knights,
Who brought it back from the Third Crusade, till
Around twelve forty-six they removed it
1255 To castle Trifels near Anweiler in
Germany's South Palatinate. Some said
Himmler retained the original and
Gave Hitler the copy, but all the Knights –
Himmler, Heydrich and "wizard" Haushofer –
1260 Took their oath to Hitler seriously and
Believed in Hitler's destiny and that
The possessor of the original
Would rule the world, and that to switch it for
A copy like a fake sceptre, besides
1265 Being an executable offence,
Would lose the war. It seems Himmler made sure
Hitler had the original, the power,
The Lance that Heinrich the First had carried
To battle, and Frederick Barbarossa;
1270 While *he* had the symbol. In deference
To Hitler's choice of cruel Heydrich as his
Future successor, Himmler made Heydrich
Custodian of the Lance, the only man
In the Third Reich allowed to invoke its
1275 Power in rituals (in which Hitler did not
Take part).
                    The Knights of the Holy Lance were,
Besides Himmler (Grand Master) and Heydrich,
Eicke, Sepp Dietrich, Peiper, Kaltenbrunner,
1280 Skorzeny, Gerbhardt, Pohl, Daluege, Jüttner
And Müller, who later guarded this Lance.
Haushofer and Weisthor advised the Knights,
And Hitler was an honorary member.
It was because Haushofer had told him
1285 Heydrich alone knew the Lance's secret

159

That Hitler announced Heydrich would be groomed
As his "Black Prince" (successor dressed in black)
Although Göring was still his number 2.
Only thirteen could sit round the table
1290   At any time. They wore the eleventh
Century regalia of the Order
Of the Teutonic Knights, red, white and black –
The black swastika on a white field with
Scarlet blood. The round oak table, carved with
1295   Runic symbols, was covered by a red
Velvet cloth and a white square banner with
Two runic signs, SS, "sig", on which, in
A glass case, stood the Holy Lance. Each chair
Of oak and boarskin bore a Knight's name, and
1300   Himmler sat before a huge red, white and
Black swastika flag and "Deutschland Erwache"
("Germany Awake") banner, Eckart's cry,
So that the lightning of the runes seemed to
Leap from him as power, and on his left sat
1305   Heydrich, the butcher of Prague, who alone
Understood the power of the Holy Lance.
On Himmler's right sat a Knight honoured for
Bravery or promotion. The other
Ten Knights sat in random order. From each
1310   Arch hung early Germanic arms and crossed
Swords, and flickering torchlight recaptured
The atmosphere of the Teutonic Knights
Of the Crusades. Behind each Knight hung his
Sword, dagger, lance and shield with coat-of-arms,
1315   Himmler's being a divided tree. In
Torchlight they began the ritual with
Meditation, with loyalty and thanks
For improvements in German fortunes. Then
Grand Master Himmler asked questions on books
1320   In the library they were asked to read,
Books on ancient heroes, Himmler's hero
Heinrich the Fowler, and Hitler's hero
Barbarossa, and other German kings.
Some recited their hunt for a wild boar
1325   In the Black Forest, the boar whose skin they
Now sat on. After each had taken his
Boar with a spear, leather shield and dagger,
And proved his courage, his skill and willpower
To conquer the brute force of enemies,
1330   He was admitted to the Circle by

Laying the boar's skin on his shield which was
On the table, and recounting details
Of the hunt. Some evenings Heydrich displayed
The power of the Holy Lance by going
1335   Into a trance-like state and then making
Contact with "astral light".
                       Like a high priest
With overweening ambition and will
To power, rising too high, butcher Heydrich,
1340   Nicknamed Hangman, "forgot" Haushofer's words;
Or rather, mirroring his cruel master,
The Führer, he deliberately used
The Lance for the "good" of the Third Reich and
Its champion Lucifer, who, opposing
1345   Jehovah's "evil" Jews, seemed "good"; and, with
Weishaupt's ruthlessness and with SS power,
Conjured Lucifer and received false light,
Dark light of Lucifer, not the true Light
Of God, and with his will (not selfless soul)
1350   By magic manipulated occult
Power to receive prophecy, clairvoyance,
And become a godlike Ubermensch, or
Superman: a man who would dethrone God
And through Lucifer attain all God's powers,
1355   The powers of the demiurge Jehovah,
A man become God, an overreacher.
Following Lucifer, the Circle of
The Knights of the Holy Lance saw the Lance
That pierced the side of Christ as the symbol
1360   Of the Antichrist, whose thrust they all served.
Hitler was the Antichrist, whose will was
Carried out by the Knights and the SS.
The Knights lived up to the brutality
Of the Lance. For Heydrich resettlement
1365   Meant extermination; he deported
And killed ninety thousand Czech Jews. Eicke had
Assassinated Röhm and been Dachau
Commandant. Dietrich had executed
Röhm's friends. Peiper ordered the Malmédy
1370   Massacre. Skorzeny with great daring
Rescued Mussolini from Italy.
Kaltenbrunner took over from Heydrich
And tortured all those who plotted against
Hitler's life. Gebhardt, more qualified than
1375   Mengele, performed experiments on

Human beings. Pohl built up the SS
And created a state within a state.
Daluege replaced Heydrich in Prague, and
Jüttner built up the SS counterpart
1380 To Army High Command. Also members
Were Wittmann, "Panzer" Meyer, Wolff, Bittrich,
Dirlewanger, Müller and a dozen
More, some of whom (for instance, Wolff) belonged
To a more secret group in the SS,
1385 The Knights of the Circle of Thor, who wore
Thor's hammer as their Germanic emblem,
Illuminist resurfacing for war.
Between nineteen forty and forty-two
Himmler drew plans to expand Wewelsburg,
1390 To relocate the village and to build
A semi-circular complex with halls
And turrets round the hillside and castle,
So Wewelsburg, an SS Vatican,
Would be the centre of the Irminist
1395 Religion revealed to Weisthor, and of
A thousand-year Greater Germanic Reich,
And then the centre of the post-war world.
Weisthor had now retired from the SS:
Wolff visited his wife in Salzburg and
1400 Learned he had once been certified insane,
And told Himmler, who in August nineteen
Thirty-nine took back his dagger and sword
And his Death's Head ring, which he had designed.
By now all SS warriors were led,
1405 Commanded, by a group of supreme Knights
Of the Black Order and Knights of the Blood,
Who lived in a Black Camelot and formed
The Allgemeine-SS, black-uniformed
Or Black Order-SS, as opposed to
1410 The Waffen-SS or Armed-SS, and
Guarded the Flag of Blood stained with gore from
The Beer Hall putsch of November the ninth
Nineteen twenty-three, and guarded the Grail,
Once symbol of the pure blood of Christ which
1415 Was caught from the wound made by the Lance as
He hung on the cross and now symbol of
The pure blood of the Reich, to achieve which
The Black Order exterminated Jews,
Had lanced millions, and the Lance which had pierced
1420 The side of Christ thus also symbolised

162

The purification of all Reich blood
Through concentration camp and Holocaust.
Like Adam Weishaupt's Illuminati,
The SS was structured in the same way
1425 As was the Society of Jesus:
The inner Black Order of high priests was
Divided from lay brothers like Jesuits.
"Priests" conjured spirits of dead Nazis just
As at a "lay" parade Hitler walked down
1430 A wide pathway in silence, and stood at
A sacred fire in an urn, then walked back
In silence: act of mass ritual magic.
Now the SS's role in the Thousand
Year Reich would be like the Jesuits' in
1435 The Catholic Holy Roman Empire, and
The Gestapo were the Inquisition.
Each Nazi Knight was the new superman
Just as Arthur's Knights aspired to be Christ,
The higher man. The Nazi SS, like
1440 The medieval chivalrous orders,
Imposed a feudal system on the serfs
And carved out feudal domains in the east,
The Ordensstaat of the Teutonic Knights
Who suppressed non-Germanic nations in
1445 The east and forbad Jews to settle in
Their Ordensstaat. Like the Teutonic Knights
The SS excluded Jews and sought to
Exterminate local populations,
Reduce the survivors to slavery
1450 To leave a vacuum for demonic
Powers which ruled Wewelsburg and the Third Reich.
By now Himmler had bound together all
Black Order Obergruppenführers and
Knights of the Holy Lance into a new
1455 Religious sect-cult as disciples of
A reincarnated god-man: himself.
Himmler blended all legends and all faiths.
He was at once Christ with his disciples,
Krist and his Irminist priests, Odin and
1460 His warriors, the sun with his zodiac,
Arthur with his Grail Knights, Cathar leader
And his "Perfects", Templar Grand Master with
His Templar Knights, Teutonic Grand Master
With his Teutonic Knights, Thor with his men,
1465 But all as Lucifer with his demons –

163

Perverse, reverse Universalism –
Not seeing that the Lance was the symbol
Of the Cosmic Christ's redeeming blood which
Converted the centurion Longinus,
1470   That transmitted the power of God for good,
Not perverse, reverse Satan's for evil.
So Himmler controlled them. Each of the twelve
Spread downwards, below them were Ancestral
Heritage, Waffen-SS, Gestapo,
1475   RSHA, Resettlement, Einsatz-
Gruppen, concentration camps and many
Other agencies, all dependent on
The twelve controlling Knights and policy,
A scheme that may be imitated by
1480   Aspiring world government leaders with
A population reduction programme.
So in March nineteen forty-one Himmler
Gathered all the Gruppenführers – Heydrich,
Wolff, Daluege, Berger and the rest, who
1485   Would be commanding Einsatzgruppen, and
Told them of the coming invasion of
Russia, initiated them into
The secret plan. He told them the Führer
Would strike a great blow to smash the Soviet
1490   System of the Jewish Bolsheviks, and
Reduce the Slav population by some
Thirty million. Famine would kill tens of
Millions when foodstuffs were diverted to
The Reich. The twelve assisted Himmler in
1495   Securing the silence and the assent
Of all to this plan.
                         Next year Heydrich died.
Himmler, Heydrich's senior, wanted him dead,
He feared Heydrich was plotting to oust him,
1500   Seeing that the secret of the world Lance
And the position of Custodian
Had made him too powerful, brought him too close
To Hitler as his Black Prince. When Hitler
Received a message, "Heydrich mortally
1505   Injured by partisans near small village
Of Lidice," he telephoned Himmler,
Who said, "I am shocked, stunned, dumbfounded, and
Unable to speak." Hitler said, "Do not
Let one of those responsible escape."
1510   To cover up his own involvement (though

British secret agents had held the guns)
Himmler resolved that Lidice village
Should be smashed, then flew there and "learned" Heydrich
Was attacked in Prague while riding in an
1515 Open touring car without an escort.
He was in Bulkova Hospital and,
Having just had an exploratory
Operation, developed a fever,
Which Gebhardt treated with sulphonamide.
1520 The power of the Third Reich at its high tide,
Began to ebb from that moment as if
The wound to the Custodian of the Lance
Had affected his tenure of the land –
Stalingrad, North Africa – so he no
1525 Longer held the destiny of the world.
As Heydrich's infected spleen grew worse, he
Knew he would die from his wound, and that he
Must replace himself as Custodian
Of the Lance and as one of the five-strong
1530 H powers of Germany: Hitler, Himmler,
Haushofer, Hess and Heydrich. Now he wrote
Furiously, then sent for Müller on June
The second nineteen forty-two, and three
Other SS officers, and gave each
1535 Officer a letter: one to Hitler
Recommending Colonel Hartmann, Bormann's
Aide who Hitler often spoke with, as his
Successor; one to Hess; one to a Swiss
Bank. Müller had a package to give to
1540 Haushofer, containing a bronze box which
He should bury in the Bavarian Alps,
At the foot of the Schleigeiss Glacier.
Haushofer did this and then took his life,
Sad that his son was executed as
1545 A bomb-plotter, and Müller also died.
Himmler phoned hourly and then flew to Prague
And sat by Heydrich's bed and talked at length
Of fate and death, and Heydrich hinted at
The secret of the Lance: "My father's fourth
1550 Opera, *Amen*, has these words: 'The world is
Just a barrel-organ which the Lord God
Turns Himself. We all dance to the tune which
Is already on the drum.' The Führer
Has misused the power of the Lance, and so
1555 This has happened to me, in consequence.

You will see in due course, the war is lost."
He died on June the fourth, with Daluege
And Frank outside his door, and lay in state
In Hradcany castle.
1560   Now Hitler was
Inconsolable that his heir had gone,
Devastated, and asked that ten thousand
Czechs should be shot as a reprisal. Three
Thousand Czech Jews were sent to death camps. All
1565   Inhabitants of Lidice near Prague
Were surrounded by police, and all two
Hundred men were shot in groups of ten and
Thrown into a mass grave. Many children
Were taken off and killed. Women were sent
1570   To Ravensbruck, Auschwitz and Mauthausen,
And the village of Lidice was burned,
Dynamited and then bulldozed, so that
Only rubble remained. That was carted
Away or buried, and all traces of
1575   Lidice vanished under the ground. Corn
Grew and Lidice simply disappeared.
Next, Lezaky was levelled. There was no
Link between the victims and the killing
Except in Hitler's mind and his orders.
1580   Hitler now ordered that thirty thousand
Czechs should be shot as a reprisal. Whole
Families were executed. This preyed
On the minds of the seven assassins
Who waited guiltily to be betrayed.
1585   For a million marks, Karel Curda told
The Gestapo that they were hiding in
A Prague church crypt, which the SS attacked.
The seven fought till, out of ammunition,
They shot themselves. The SS then displayed
1590   Their bodies, their eyes unclosed, and two heads
Were severed and removed by Gestapo.
Himmler had given the funeral address –
Hitler was overcome and merely said
His protégé was "irreplaceable" –
1595   And at Wewelsburg in the circular
Lower chamber, lit by an eternal
Flame, in the round stoup, the arms of Hangman
Heydrich were cremated, smoke rising in
Aryan style, like a pillar due to
1600   The four ventilation shafts. The only

166

Knight who knew the full secret of the Lance
Was the first to die.
                    Now Heydrich was gone,
Himmler lost interest in the Holy Lance,
1605   Whose power had not protected stern Heydrich,
And the Knights' rituals declined and ceased,
As did the fortunes of Hitler's Third Reich.
But the SS continued to act as
A secret society, a state in
1610   A state with its own laws, and to control
And exact "cadaver obedience"
Through its Order's cult fanaticism.
Over its evil Himmler presided,
The Grand Master of the Mysteries of war,
1615   Opposite of the peaceful Mysteries of
Eleusis which celebrated rural
Dionysos and Demeter, the vine
And agricultural calm, into which
Were initiated Socrates and
1620   Plato; which came from Egyptian Mysteries
Of Osiris and Isis, into which
Was initiated Orpheus, King of
Thrace, who then founded the Greek Mysteries at
Eleusis, whose ban on animal food
1625   Was followed by the Pythagorean
Brotherhood. There were seven Eleusinian
Degrees, progressive initiations
For spiritual development (the fifth
Being a-physical love, Christian-like
1630   Love), each held secret; for truth has divine
Origin and is revealed to the few
Who make the necessary effort to
Get close to it, and should not be freely
Communicated to those who do not
1635   Desire to make the effort. Demeter's
Agriculture had spiritual meaning:
From a "life of thorns" (echoed by Christ's crown
Of thorns), the savage, painful, warlike life
Of barbarian ancestors, there was
1640   Progression to the lived reaped ear of corn
(The seventh degree), and a "ground-life" in which,
Having grown ripe ears of corn for grinding,
Humans distribute the goods of the earth
Without fighting each other, an upward
1645   Progression, pacifist ennoblement

167

That led Alcibiades to enact
A profane mockery of the Mysteries
Of Eleusis at his house before he
Set sail for Sicily at the head of
1650   The great Athenian fleet and armies.
Himmler's SS Mysteries reversed those of
Eleusis, leading initiates to war.

Hitler approved of the SS's strict
And ruthless adherence to his orders,
1655   But he opposed Himmler's revival of
Nordic cults and neo-paganism,
A "return of medievalism",
"Worse than the Church". He opposed the worship
Of Odin and arrested Odinists
1660   Such as von Sebbottendorf and banned von
Liebenfels, Ebertin and Issberner-
Haldane. Nordic-Aryan man, Rosenberg
Believed, should not fight for Odin but for
The Aryan Ahura Mazda, god of
1665   The Aryans who moved from India to
Iran (he meant for dark Ahriman), and
For the Manichaean heresy which
Taught that the Devil was equal in power
And status to God. The Manichaean,
1670   And later Cathar, belief, strengthened by
Kabbalistic writings, held the Devil
Was the creator of the world as Rex
Mundi, King of the World and ruler of
Matter and all things worldly, and Satan,
1675   Enemy of Christ. Hitler agreed with
This outlook. Yet when Rosenberg took charge
Of Third Reich education in nineteen
Thirty-four, and all Nazis were urged to
Leave the Church, a hundred thousand resigned
1680   From the Catholic Church three years later,
Including Himmler. But Hitler, Göring
And Goebbels, seeking to revive the grand
Old Catholic Holy Roman Empire,
Remained Catholics in name until they died.
1685   (Hitler had been Catholic since his schooldays
At the Benedictine Lambach Abbey.)
To consolidate his reign as Emperor
Of Europe, like Napoleon the First,
Hitler took the sacred regalia

1690 Of Kingship from each place he overran:
      From Vienna the regalia of
      The Holy Roman Empire, Conrad's crown;
      From Prague that of the Bohemian kings;
      From Warsaw the Polish royal treasures.
1695 All came to Germany, Hitler believed
      The magical powers of rulership in
      The sacred symbols would transfer to him.
      Hitler, an occultist, feared the occult,
      And the Gestapo's spies infiltrated
1700 All occult groups which might challenge his power
      And unseat him with witchcraft and black arts;
      Jehovah's Witnesses and Jesuits,
      Astrologers, Rosicrucians, Masons –
      Whose myths were based on Solomon's Temple
1705 And referred to the Jewish Jehovah –
      Were investigated and imprisoned.
      And still the SS shot and gassed the Jews,
      A brutal, effective killing-machine.

      In Hungary three Zionists had formed
1710 Waadah, the Jewish Rescue Committee,
      To help all Jews escape from Germany,
      Poland and Slovakia to Hungary
      And thence to Palestine. Brand and Kastner
      First contacted Wisliceny, Eichmann's
1715 Executioner in Slovakia,
      And on getting nowhere, via the Abwehr
      And Clages of the SD, his channel,
      In April spoke with Himmler, who wanted
      War materials, weapons and equipment
1720 To expand the SS without Hitler's
      Knowledge, and to form a secret peace link
      With Washington. Himmler ordered Eichmann
      To see Brand and propose Hungarian
      Jews should be exempt from the death programme.
1725 With some unease, Eichmann summoned Brand to
      Budapest and told him the contract price
      That World Jewry must pay: ten thousand trucks,
      And huge amounts of soap, tea and coffee;
      But deportations of Hungarian Jews
1730 To Auschwitz would begin, and continue
      Until World Jewry paid. Brand agreed but
      Asked for a sample train of refugees
      To show German goodwill. The seventeenth

Of May Brand left Hungary. The next two weeks
Eichmann cleared the ghetto into trains bound
For Auschwitz, where gassings rose from just eight
Thousand in April to two hundred and
Twenty-eight thousand in May. Brand vanished,
Arrested in Syria by the British.
Eichmann refused to send the sample train,
And now the deportations continued.

Höss, Commandant at Auschwitz, had been given
Orders by Himmler to build a new camp
For a hundred thousand prisoners, and to
Enlarge the old camp so it took thirty
Thousand, and earmark ten thousand prisoners
For the synthetic rubber factory,
But he had no authority to buy
Materials such as barbed wire or posts,
Or wood for huts or plumbing for toilets,
And had to filch them, using staff who had
Little initiative and let him down.
He turned inward and would not socialise,
Became suspicious, grew a hard veneer,
Turned into a withdrawn man who just thought
Of work and drank to drown his ill-humour,
Shut out his wife, who drew away from him.
Once the building was done and the prisoners
Arrived by train for gassing as Eichmann
Had commanded, he had to keep order,
And watched with loathing as his SS staff
Set up a regime using the prisoners
As guards, Kapos. He soon discovered that
A prisoner is stripped of all his pretence
And stands, naked, as he really is,
Selfish instinct for self-preservation:
Ruthless towards the wretches they preyed on,
Kapos like Eschen enticed Jews into
Violent acts and threatened to report them;
The guards derived a Satanic pleasure
From watching prisoners torment each other.
Teleprinter messages from the Reich
Main Security Office gave a list
Of prisoners to be shot as "hostages",
Or hanged. Höss gave an order, and those on
The list were taken from their work or called
Out at roll-call and shot by firing-squad

Or hanged. Kattowitz military court trials
Took place every four to six weeks in Block
1780 Eleven, where inmates admitted their
Actions freely and firmly, and died with
Calm resignation and fervent belief
That they were sacrificing themselves for
Poland. The prisoners who paraded past
1785 Escapees or "hostages" who had been
Shot or hanged showed horror, terror, fear that
It might happen to them, sympathy with
The victim and a resolve to avenge.
The large numbers of Russian prisoners-
1790 Of-war meant the Germans could not feed them.
They squatted in the camps, eating roots or
Potatoes raw. In Birkenau some beat
A prisoner to death for food, ripped open
The body, tore out the liver and ate
1795 It raw like famished Stone Age cannibals.
They were no longer human beings but
Had become animals who sought for food,
And killed to take another's food bucket.
Soon the prisoners became hopeless and quite
1800 Indifferent to their surroundings. Once their
Mind collapsed, their body died. State of mind
Was as much a cause of death as hard work,
Poor food, overcrowding, and they became
Stumbling corpses without wills, and gave up.
1805 But not the Jehovah's Witnesses, who
Worked as female servants in the homes of
SS men, and worked well unsupervised,
For such was the will of their Jehovah.
By suffering in captivity for
1810 Jehovah's sake, they hoped for positions
In the Kingdom. They felt it was right that
Many Jews should suffer and die now, as
Their forefathers had betrayed Jehovah.

Höss, ex-Commandant who had returned to
1815 Birkenau from Berlin for "Aktion Höss",
The mass murder of Hungarian Jews,
Watched with the new Commandant, Kramer, as
A new trainload arrived. All luggage was
Left on the ramp; after the selection,
1820 Men separated from women, husbands
From wives, mothers from sons, ten thousand walked

171

To the crematoria and the first batch
Of women were herded by SS guards
Into the dressing-room, where the Jewish
1825   Sonderkommando calmly told them they
Would be bathed and deloused, that they must leave
Their clothes neatly piled up so they could find
Them quickly later on, reassured them
As they helped them undress, pacified those
1830   Who were suspicious, did all they could to
Deceive them, and, half-trusting their own race,
Half-believing their lies, the condemned went
Into rooms fitted with showers and water-
Pipes, with the Sonders and an SS guard.
1835   One woman, terror in her eyes, joked with
Her children. One shrieked and tore at her hair.
She was taken behind the building and
Shot, by a Jewish Sonderkommando
Who considerately hid the muzzle,
1840   In the back of her neck with a soundless
Small-calibre weapon. One said to Höss,
"How can you bring yourself to kill children?
Have you no heart at all?" An old woman
Hissed, "Germany will do heavy penance
1845   For this mass murder of the Jews." She walked
Calmly into the gas chamber. A young
Woman who had run about, busily
Helping young children and old women to
Undress, encouraging them to enter
1850   The gas chamber, now stood in the doorway
And, naked, like an angel, said to Höss:
"I knew all the time we were being brought
To Auschwitz to be gassed. I avoided
Being selected as able-bodied
1855   Because I wanted to look after these
Children and go through it, fully conscious
Of what was happening. I hope it will
Be quick. Goodbye." Two children were absorbed
In a game just outside the gas chamber.
1860   The mother, naked in the doorway, looked
At Höss with pleading eyes. Full of pity,
Stifling his emotion, Höss nodded and
The NCO on duty picked them up
And carried them struggling and screaming at
1865   The interruption of their game into
The gas chamber, pushed them inside as if

Into an overcrowded underground
Rush hour carriage. Quickly the Sonders left.
As the doors closed on naked girls the young
1870 Mother tried to throw the two children out,
Weeping, "At least let my children live." With
Reproachful looks at Höss, the calm "angel"
Tenderly restrained her. The gas-proof doors
Were screwed up, while all stood naked, squashed up
1875 Together, knowing this was not a shower.
Looking through the peep-hole in a door, Höss
Saw the gas pour through the roof-vents, killing
A third at once. There was a bellowing
As the squashed, trapped prisoners hurled themselves at
1880 The doors, piled on those who had already
Fallen, and gave a choking, smothered cry.
There were no convulsions because Prussic
Acid paralysed the lungs, and death came
Swiftly, unlike carbon monoxide or
1885 Oxygen deficiency which both caused
Convulsions. The remainder staggered till
Their screaming and gasping became a death-
Rattle. In a few minutes all twitched, still.
In twenty minutes there was no movement.
1890 After half an hour the doors were opened
And ventilators switched on to extract
The gas. Sonders began to drag bodies.
There was no discoloration, little
Soiling through opening of the bowels
1895 Now the gassing technique had been improved.
The Sonders extracted gold teeth and cut
Off hair as Himmler had ordered, and then
Dragged the corpses to the crematorium,
Smoking and sometimes eating with callous
1900 Indifference, as though it was all part of
An ordinary day's work.
                                    One Sonder was
Dragging a corpse with one hand and eating
An apple with his other hand. One stood
1905 Still over a body. Höss called, "What's up?"
To a Kapo, who said, "It's the Jew's wife."
Höss watched him, fascinated but detached.
Now he continued to drag her with his
Colleague, there was nothing exceptional
1910 In his behaviour; quite expressionless,
He carried on dragging corpses as though

Nothing untoward had happened. Höss said
To Kramer, "I wonder if he's hiding
His emotions, or is too brutalised
1915   To care even about his own wife's death."
Kramer did not reply and walked away.
The Kapo asked, "Is it necessary
To do all this?" Höss, wondering the same,
But having to appear indifferent,
1920   Said coldly: "It is the Führer's order,
The extermination of Jewry has
To be so, so posterity will be
Freed for ever from our adversaries."
He did not say, "It's the Fehme against Jews."
1925   Höss had always done the Führer's will, as
A member of the Fehme or Vehme, thousand
Year old medieval blood tribunal
Which Hitler, allying with the Prusso-
Teutonic tradition that began with
1930   The Order of Teutonic Knights, revived,
And which was now active in Germany.
In just three and a half years from nineteen
Nineteen, over three hundred and fifty
Political assassinations took
1935   Place, including Eisner's – some said the Thule
Had revived the Fehmemord and killed him – and
A victim, Gareis, a Deputy in
The Bavarian Landtag, spoke of the Fehme
As a "thousand year old conspiracy"
1940   And was assassinated a few days
Later by the forces he was about
To expose: a secret society
Whose members acted as both judges and
Executioners, carrying out each
1945   Sentence at once, hanging victims on trees
Like Odin. Many Comthurs, regional
Commanders of the ancient Order of
Teutonic Knights, were members of the Fehme
And the Grand Master, who did nothing when
1950   Two Knights were hanged from an oak-tree, was thought
To be leader. Very few punishments
Were meted out. One of these was to Höss,
Who had met Hitler in nineteen twenty-
Two and joined his Party and shot Kadow
1955   In such a Fehmemord or vengeance killing
Next year and received ten years in prison.

Hitler's assassinations were Fehme-like,
He killed Röhm and Strasser to reassure
His secret Prusso-Teutonic allies,
1960 Who were concerned at their leftward drift. Now
Hitler became the Fehme, and the SS
The Fehme's executioners; and chief of
These was Höss. And just as (after blandly
Accusing Palitzsch of an affair with
1965 A Birkenau prisoner) he kept silent
About his own affair with Eleonore
Hodys, an Italian woman prisoner
Who worked at his house, whom he made pregnant
And put in Block 11's cellars, in
1970 A standing cell, condemned to starvation,
So he kept silent on how his Auschwitz
Embodied the much-feared Teutonic Fehme
Used by the Knights to clear Poland of Jews.

Eichmann sent a hundred and seventy
1975 Thousand to Auschwitz in June. In despair
Kastner turned to Eichmann's rival, Becher,
Who was in charge of finding equipment
For the Waffen-SS. While looking for
Twenty thousand horses, Becher had bought
1980 The Weiss works and let forty-eight members
Of the family leave for Portugal,
Which Eichmann saw as threatening Himmler's
Final Solution programme. Had Himmler
Gone soft on the Jewish problem? Kastner
1985 Made contact with Becher, who, in late June,
Flew to Himmler and won authority
To deal with Waadah in place of Eichmann,
And authorised a sample train of one
Thousand seven hundred Jews at a thousand
1990 Dollars a head. The train left on the last
Day of June. Enraged, Eichmann diverted
The train to Belsen camp and now threatened
To send it on to Auschwitz unless World
Jewry paid. Kastner went to Becher, who
1995 Refused to help as Himmler chopped and changed
To Eichmann's side. Clages of the SD
Asked Brand's cousin Biss to draft a memo
Of financial proposals, which he sent
To Himmler. On July the twenty-seventh
2000 He told Biss, "My memo has been received

Favourably in Berlin, and Himmler has
Given instructions for deportations
From Hungary to cease till further notice."
Becher now flew to Himmler and secured
2005 Permission for a sample train to leave
With five hundred Jews on board. He was to
Discuss payment for more with the Jewish-
American Aid Organisation,
The American Joint Distribution
2010 Committee in Switzerland, which Himmler
Believed was linked with President Roosevelt,
An idea that Waadah encouraged. Now
The SS leaders pressed Waadah to start
Peace negotiations. The Jewish sought
2015 More than trucks-for-Jews; they wanted an end
To extermination and the release
Of all Jews on the Belsen sample train
As Mayer, a Swiss banker, requested.
Becher, hoping for a separate peace, took
2020 Waadah's side. At the end of September
Roosevelt dispatched a Quaker, McClellan,
To assist the talks between the SS
And the Joint Distribution Committee.

Himmler's ruthlessness in Warsaw was known
2025 To the Jewish resistance in Auschwitz.
Polish resistance forces had challenged
The German occupation as Soviet
Forces approached the Vistula's east bank,
Seeking to hasten the departure of
2030 The demoralised Germans who, they thought,
Could not resist the Red Army, and to
Announce Polish control before Soviet
Forces arrived. Hitler acted swiftly
To crush the uprising. Reinforcements
2035 Were moved in from the Baltic and France, and
The SS Panzer Korps counter-attacked
Russian forces outside Warsaw, forcing
Them into a defensive posture. Bór
And his underground army of forty
2040 Thousand men, on their own, attacked German
Controls and strongpoints, and they were joined by
A thousand Jews, some of whom they released
From Gesiowka camp. Guderian applied
To Hitler to have Warsaw placed under

176

The Wehrmacht, who had units there, so that
The Army could put down the revolt. But
Himmler went to see the Führer at once
And, with Heinrich the Fowler in his mind,
Told him: "The time is disagreeable
But seen historically it's a blessing
The Poles are doing this. After six weeks
We shall leave, but Warsaw, the capital,
The head, intelligence of this former
Seventeen million Polish people will
Be extinguished, this Volk that has blocked us
In the east for seven hundred years and
Has stood in our way ever since the first
Battle of Tannenberg. Then the Polish
Problem will no longer be a large one
Historically for those who succeed us."
Hitler asked Himmler and the SS to
Put the uprising down. In an address,
Himmler ordered Army officers to
Raze Warsaw to the ground: "You may think I
Am a frightful barbarian. I am,
I may say, if I have no other choice."

It was as when the Warsaw ghetto rose
Under Mordechai Anielewicz, who
Had been alarmed by reports that, after
Himmler's policy of starving the Jews
Had not worked, sixty thousand Jews rounded
Up for "labour service" in Treblinka
Had been killed. In January, SS guards
Herding – deporting – Jews were shot. Enraged
That "sub-humans" should resist the master
Race, Himmler ordered the entire ghetto
Should be cleared of Jews and every building
Razed to the ground. He entrusted the task
To SS Brigadeführer Stroop, who toured
The ghetto in disguise. On Passover,
April the nineteenth 1943,
Two SS battalions, two thousand men,
Led by a tank (which was soon set on fire),
Three armoured cars and three canons, and armed
With flame-throwers and field guns, burst into
The ghetto at 6 a.m., to be met
By ferocious resistance from some twelve
Hundred Jews armed with just two machine-guns,

Seventeen rifles, five hundred pistols
2090 And several thousand hand-grenades. SS
Brigadeführer Stroop had hoped to present
The extinction of the ghetto's Jews to
Hitler as a birthday present the next
Day, but the Jews held out, contesting each
2095 House though the ghetto was on fire, fighting
Through smoke and flames, thundering guns and whole
Families leaping from the windows of
Burning houses, and everywhere a stench
Of singed bodies, until May the eighth, when
2100 Handsome Anielewicz was killed during
The grim battle for the bunker beneath
18 Mila Street, and the uprising
Ended on May the fifteenth. Of the Jews
Seven thousand had been killed in the fighting
2105 And seven thousand were shot at once. Perhaps
As many as forty thousand were sent
To Treblinka. Todt slave-workers using
Explosives, employed by Kammler, SS
Obergruppenführer, razed the ghetto;
2110 A Warsaw district of four by two and
A half kilometres was levelled. There
Was so much rubble left that seventeen
Kilometres of narrow gauge railway
Were laid to carry it away. Knightly
2115 Stroop reported to his superiors,
"The previous Jewish residential
Quarter of Warsaw no longer exists,"
And was rewarded with the Iron Cross.

Now with the ghetto still in mind, Himmler
2120 Put von dem Bach-Zelewski in charge with
Help from Dirlewanger's Brigade of cruel
Criminals, Kaminski's Ukrainians,
Reinefahrt's Posen police units and some
SS-cavalry. Von dem Bach was given
2125 Heavy artillery, flame-throwers, gas-
Machines for sewers, and miniature tanks,
And was ordered to kill all Poles out of
Hand. The Germans systematically
Cleared blocks of houses, which were set on fire,
2130 Herded their occupants into public
Squares, parks or cemeteries and mowed them down
With machine-guns or ripped them with fragments

Of lobbed grenades. Their bodies were burned on
Mass pyres. Some had to tear planks from fences
2135 And hold them against their bodies as they
Were shot so they could be readily burned.
All Poles caught were killed, women, babies and
Hospital patients. Nurses and nuns were
Raped, then killed. So shocking were the brutal
2140 Excesses that both Guderian and
Fegelein protested to the Führer,
Accused Dirlewanger and Kaminski.
The Home Army fought from sewers, sniping
At officers and hurling Molotov
2145 Cocktails, fighting to the last man or girl,
Knowing that if they were caught they would be
Shot or placed before rolling tanks and crushed
(Symbol of the crushing of the revolt),
Or sprayed with petrol and then set on fire.
2150 The RAF dropped supplies in August,
But the Russians continued their stand-off.
By September Warsaw, Bór reported,
Was a "city of ruins", and the dead
Were "buried inside the ruins or else
2155 Alongside them".
              Anglo-American
Indignation at Russia's inaction,
Which, Himmler declared, would split the Allies,
Stirred Stalin to order the Red Army
2160 To bombard the Germans; and Soviet Poles
To reach the Vistula (token gesture).
The Germans blew up the bridges, and then
The Soviet Poles exceeded their orders
And crossed in amphibious assaults in
2165 Mid-September, but, due to the lack of
Russian support, had to return. Towards
The end of September Hitler granted
The Home Army combatant status, and
Bór's survivors emerged from the ruins
2170 With their weapons and red and white armbands
And marched proudly, between ranks of Germans
Who lined the streets, in surrender. Fifteen
Thousand Home Army men and two hundred
Thousand Polish civilians had been killed,
2175 Against ten thousand of the Germans' troops.
Kaminski was executed because
Of his troops' debauchery – actually,

Because he was "a dangerous witness"
(Guderian's words). Dirlewanger received
2180 The Knight's Cross. Von dem Bach and Reinefahrt were
Promoted. All remaining civilians
Were evacuated from Warsaw as
Forced labour. Those too weak to work were sent
To camps or gas chambers. Now Raümungs, or
2185 Clearance Kommandos, looted valuables,
And teams with flame-throwers and explosives
Completely razed Warsaw, and only two
Houses were left standing in the rubble.

Excited, wanting peace, Himmler brooded
2190 In Bratislava as he directed
The suppressal of the Soviet-controlled
Free Slovakia movement of rebels
By Dirlewanger and his criminals,
The smoke of Warsaw still in their nostrils,
2195 Whom he had assured "You can be certain
I will never reprove you for excess"
As SS Panzer units advanced past
Burning homes, mass graves, refugees, marches
Towards internment and forced labour camps.
2200 Soviet forces in the Carpathians
Were closing in on Poland; Auschwitz and
Other extermination camps were now
Vulnerable to a Russian advance,
All trace of gassing and burning should be
2205 Removed from the extermination camps,
Slave labour was needed for anti-tank
Ditches – the East Wall – in central and west
Germany to hold back the Red Army
Before the Reich. If he now put an end
2210 To gassing in Auschwitz, the US might
Talk peace with him as Führer, not kill him.
Meanwhile men would march across Germany
And dig, he would have labour. And if he
Bartered Jews for foreign exchange to fund
2215 The war task, Hitler and Bormann could not
Complain. He would not incur Hitler's wrath.
Hitler still sought to exterminate all
Jews. Himmler sent a message to Waadah:
He had authorised the suspension of
2220 The "actions" in Auschwitz (a lie, and it
Was anyway threatened by advancing

Soviet forces), and would allow part of
The sample train to leave for Switzerland.
It seemed the US might respond to this.

2225 On his way back to his field headquarters
In Eastern Prussia Himmler visited
His mistress (formerly his personal
Secretary) Hedwig or "Häschen" Potthast
And his second family at their home
2230 On the Obersalzberg: a two year old
Boy, Helge, and a baby girl. The day
He legalised his paternity, he
Wondered if the Church still had room for him,
And now he spent a whole day playing with
2235 The two children, hanging pictures, doing
House chores, and not taking phone calls. He gazed
As Helge wheeled his blue wheelbarrow in
The garden under huge mountains, Häschen
Smiling happily at his side. Auschwitz
2240 And the extermination ovens seemed
A long way away from domestic bliss.

Jozef Dorebus (alias Warszawski),
Sitting beside Jankiel Handelsman, who
Had emigrated from Poland with him
2245 To France and also joined the Resistance
And been arrested by the Gestapo
And sent to Auschwitz a long year before,
Had been appalled at the huge numbers of
Hungarian Jews sent by cruel Eichmann for
2250 Gassing at Auschwitz-Birkenau: over
Four hundred thousand during May and June.
Long trains brought ten thousand people each day.
With Christ nearby sending him energy
(Christ did not reveal himself to a Jew
2255 At this stage), Dorebus as leader spoke
To other resistance organisers:
"What is beginning is the genocide
Of a whole race, the Hungarian Jews.
The world is full of races. Its forests
2260 Are full of trees of different kinds, and to
Exterminate one kind, uproot all beech
To leave oaks, yews and pines, is not the way
To live in acceptance of God's great world.
All races are shades of one race just as

181

2265 All kinds of trees are variations of
One tree replicated in the woodland
Of universal Nature. It is wrong
To single out Jews, Slavs and gipsies for
Extermination when they were made in
2270 The image of the Creator as much
As Aryans. We must oppose this wrong,
This evil policy of factory death."
Like Stauffenberg, Dorebus hoped to stop
The killing and save the lives of millions.

2275 The Polish underground had full details
Of Auschwitz-Birkenau from escapees:
Tabeau, who wrote a report for the West,
And Cieliczko; then in April Wetzler
And Vrba ("Walter Rosenberg"), who trekked
2280 To Slovakia and wrote about the camp;
In June, Galinski and his friend Mala
Zimetbaum, who wore SS uniforms
But were captured and then hanged in public;
In July, Bielecki and Cybulska,
2285 Who also disguised themselves as SS.
From the prisoners, the underground received
A flow of information: blueprints of
The ovens and gas chambers, and photos
Of mass killings, gassings and corpse-burnings.

2290 Dorebus and the resistance leaders
At grim Birkenau and nearby Auschwitz
Smuggled a secret letter from the camp –
Cyrankiewicz and Klodzinski sent out
Photographs of gassing and corpse-burning –
2295 To the Polish underground. It said that
The SS authorities were planning
To liquidate Auschwitz-Birkenau camp
And murder all witnesses to the foul
Atrocities committed there. And first
2300 They wished to get rid of several hundred
Of those who knew the most about their deeds.
At Birkenau the hundreds of men of
The twelfth Sonderkommando ("Special Squad")
Prisoners who worked in the gas chambers for
2305 Privileges, their own barracks with warm
Blankets and food, dragged the bodies of Jews
Who had been gassed into one of the four

182

Crematoria, burnt them in ovens
And then scattered their ashes on the paths
2310 Or the ponds. Just as they had cremated
(For being privy to SS secrets)
Their predecessors of the eleventh
Kommando, so they would themselves be killed
After four months and be cremated by
2315 The thirteenth so their memories would be
Obliterated. Now, angry with fear,
They all knew it was their turn to be killed
And unlike the eleventh Kommando
They were not in favour of submitting,
2320 They wanted to live to tell the world what
They had seen, and, awaiting their SS
Executioners, they plotted revolt.

Dorebus knew there would be no mercy
For anyone caught helping escapees.
2325 Over a year before in the roll-call
Square in Auschwitz, from an iron rail on two
Posts, were hanged twelve Polish political
Prisoners, who were suspected of helping
Three escapees and contacting Poles who
2330 Lived near the camp. As all stood for roll call,
The twelve stood on stools, which were kicked away
From under their feet. The drop was too short,
The men writhed for several minutes. SS
Hauptsturmführer Aumeier said, "Let them
2335 Kick for a while," and then, losing patience,
"Jump on them, hang on them." Hesitantly,
Guards hugged their knees and swung on them and pulled
To hasten strangulation in each noose.
Horror turned to disgust. As the prisoners
2340 Standing nearby clenched their fists, the torment
Of the dying men brought tears to their eyes.

The Polish underground were active, and
A secret radio station broadcast news
Of the SS's plan to London on
2345 September the twenty-third. The Polish
Government-in-Exile contacted the
US and British foreign ministries,
Who conferred and agreed that they would have
A common stance and broadcast a warning.
2350 The underground also sought to protect

The lives of the Sonderkommando, who
Knew the SS's crimes. They planned to steal
And smuggle into barbed-wired Birkenau
Explosives from a munitions factory.

2355   Dorebus knew of two other death camp
Uprisings which had led to mass break-outs.
More than a year before in Treblinka
The last thousand prisoners in the camp who
Had not been gassed had to exhume and burn
2360   The bodies of the Jews of the ghettos
Of Warsaw and Bialystok, which had
Been buried in shallow pits. Then they would
Be killed. The barber Rajchman in the clothes
Sorting camp had found his sister's dress. He
2365   Had to open mass graves and pulverise
The bones, including his sister's remains.
Inspired by the Warsaw ghetto revolt,
The prisoners filched some weapons from the camp
Arsenal and planned to destroy the huts
2370   And the gas chambers. They armed themselves with
Picks, shovels, grenades and petrol. A shot
Rang out, the signal to rise up. It came
Half an hour early, took all by surprise.
The garages and warehouse were on fire,
2375   Then guards began shooting. Many were killed.
Two hundred prisoners escaped, half were caught.
In Sobibor death camp that October
A Soviet Jew, Sasha Pechersky, and
Underground leader Leon Feldhendler
2380   Killed an SS man with an axe and soon
Set the camp on fire, and with guns aimed at
Guard towers, by dark more than half the prisoners
Escaped. A third were caught, the rest spent harsh
Winter nights hiding in the surrounding
2385   Forests, and slowly died of exposure.
Dorebus had discussed what had gone wrong –
The too early signal, the wintry deaths –
And vowed he would not repeat such mistakes.

At the Weichsel-Union factory, between
2390   Birkenau and Auschwitz main camp, thousands
Of gaunt prisoners made fuses for V-2
Rockets and grenades as slave-labourers,
Working around the clock in three long shifts.

184

Roza Robota, a Polish Jew from

2395 Upper Silesia, born in Ciechanow,
Who was twenty and from a Zionist
Youth organisation, worked in the grim
Personal effects camp or clothing store
Which stood beside Crematorium Three,

2400 Making neat piles of good clothes for Germans.
The previous November she saw her own
Family and all Jews from Ciechanow
Herded with sticks into the gas chambers
Like a flock of sheep into a slaughter-

2405 House, and she vowed revenge. Across the fence,
And during deliveries of clothes worn
By the dead, discarded before gassing,
She had met Wrobel, a Sonder, and had
Loved him through the barbed wire. Wrobel had said:

2410 "You are sent stuff from the Union factory.
Ask for some explosives. The resistance
Want them to make primitive grenades. I
Will hide them in the crematorium.
If the SS try to blow up the camp

2415 To destroy evidence of gas chambers,
We Sonders can wipe out the SS in
A partial or general camp uprising."
Roza talked to her friend at the factory,
Ella Gartner, when she brought effects, clothes

2420 Of skeletonic girls who had died, from
The Union works, and said, "We must all help
The Sonders destroy the gas chambers and
Crematoria, and help them escape
Before they are killed." Soon a few Jewish

2425 Girls repeatedly stole minute amounts
Of gunpowder and wheels of dynamite
That looked like buttons, which the women hid
In their bosoms or sewed into their hems,
Or wrapped in sachets and kept in pockets

2430 They sewed on the inside of their aprons,
And which they could empty if they were searched,
The gunpowder trickling out through a hole.
Girls collected explosives and gave them
To Ella Gartner, and two girls known as

2435 Toszka and Regina carried them out
Of the Union factory in the pockets
Of their camp aprons and in a food-tray
Which had been fitted with a false bottom

185

And into Birkenau to brave Roza
2440 Robota, who hid them in the handcarts
On which the corpses of those who had died
At night in the barracks were taken to
The crematoria. By this bold means
She managed to pass them on to Wrobel
2445 And the bold Sonderkommando, of whom
There were a hundred and sixty-nine at
Each of Crematoria One, Two and
Three (counting those at Birkenau only,
The second camp, excluding the one at
2450 Auschwitz), and a hundred and fifty-six
In Crematorium Four. Half manned the day-
Shift, half manned the night-shift when the ovens
Lit lines of corpses furnace-red. In all
There were six hundred and sixty-three men.

2455 In the small hours of an October day
A shot rang out from one of the watch-towers
And a Russian prisoner-of-war fell in
The forbidden zone between lines of guards.
He was probably trying to escape.
2460 Doctor Mengele examined him. Had
He been Jewish, he would have been taken
To one of the crematoria. As
He was a Russian officer, there was
An autopsy in the dissecting-room.
2465 In the nearby incineration-room
Of Crematorium One, near SS guards,
Several hundred bodies were stacked before
The ovens. The workers whispered in groups.
The Polish camp resistance movement had
2470 Told the leader of the international
Auschwitz Combat Group the camp management
Planned to liquidate all present members
Of the twelfth Special Squad, starting with three
Hundred who worked in Crematoria
2475 Three and Four. The Combat Group was in touch
With Soviet forces and was preparing
An uprising that would keep prisoners safe
When the Allied armies approached Auschwitz.
In their living quarters the night-shift of
2480 Crematoria Three and Four was now
Still up, wearing sweaters and boots despite
The warm October sun, and men now packed

Suitcases, huddling and whispering.

In
2485 A small room the Kommando chief sat with
The night-shift leaders – chief of gas, furnace
Engineer, mechanic – drinking cumin
Brandy, eau-de-vie. Here their brave leader,
Dorebus, sitting beside Handelsman
2490 And other resistance organisers
Who planned an uprising – Deresinski,
Gradowski, Kalniak, Langfus and Panusz –
Said: "The evidence suggests that we will
All be liquidated by tomorrow,
2495 All six hundred and sixty-three members
Of the twelfth Kommando. We'll not accept
This without a fight. We have often talked
Of a break-out, but many have been tied
To this camp through good food or through a girl
2500 And chose to stay here. Plans have been made for
All members to force their way out of this
Camp tonight. We will head for the loop of
The Vistula just two kilometres
Away. We will ford it and reach the vast
2505 Forests eight kilometres on, which stretch
To the Polish border. We'll live for months
Under their trees, and may meet partisans.
We will be safe. A hundred boxes of
High explosives, which the Germans use for
2510 Blowing up railway lines, have reached us from
The Union factory where Polish Jews work.
We have five machine-guns and twenty hand-
Grenades." Another said, "We can disarm
The guards with revolvers." Their leader said:
2515 "The signal to attack will be flashlights
From Crematorium One to Two, from
Crem Two to Three, and from Crem Three to Four.
Only One is working, and as you know,
There are only three SS guards for each
2520 Crematorium. We will escape and
Carry news of the Nazi cruelty
To the outside world, to Eisenhower, who
Will then know he must bomb the SS here.
By reaching Eisenhower, one of us will
2525 Strike a blow against this dire Nazi rule,
And, if we can expose Himmler's role in
The gas chambers and crematoria,

We can force Himmler to change his mind and
Cancel all gassings in all one thousand
2530   Six hundred camps, and save the Jewish race.
As we save our lives and inform the world
We will act for the prisoners in all camps.
The fight back against the SS starts here."
Like Stauffenberg, Dorebus stood against
2535   The deaths of millions, whom he sought to save.
That day of disquiet in the oven room
Men worked slowly, and at lunch time, outside
In the crematorium courtyard in
The slanting rays of the autumn sun, no
2540   SS guards could be seen. They could have been
In their rooms, or, some prisoners wondered,
Were they organising liquidation?

Eisenhower left his car, his ears ringing,
His head buzzing with the latest request
2545   From the Polish Government-in-Exile
To the US War Department to bomb
Auschwitz ("In all Polish concentration
Camps the Germans are now increasing their
Extermination activities") and
2550   The risk of bombing extermination
Chambers and German barracks flat without
Killing prisoners, musing on his reply
That the Polish Government-in-Exile
Should organise an uprising to stop
2555   The extermination in Oswiecim;
And stood in calm near woods with browning leaves
And hedgerows and saw a harvest of nuts:
Beechnuts, acorns from oaks, conkers from horse
Chestnuts. A sycamore wing spiralled down
2560   Like a helicopter. Toadstools poked from
Tree-roots, feeding from decay. He saw two
Puffballs and a fairy ring. A missel-
Thrush pecked berries. He heard the "cha cha cha
Chak" of a fieldfare and saw a starling,
2565   A crow, a jackdaw and in the distance
Rooks round a rookery. A squirrel ran
Down a tree and bounded towards a nut
And sat on its tail, cupping the shell. Near
His feet were yarrow and corn marigold.
2570   A yellowhammer flitted. He recalled
How Bob Davis had taught him about woods

188

In Abilene, how to fish and trap and
Handle toads without acquiring warts, and
The ringing in his ears had subsided
2575   As he warmed to the eternal smile that
Beams from sunlit countryside despite war.

That October Saturday, the senior
Kommando at Crematorium Three
Was told to list three hundred Squad men for
2580   Crematoria Three and Four, who would
Be "evacuated" at noon. Fearing
They'd be driven in lorries once round the camp,
And then gassed, he refused. Now a truckload
Of political SS screeched and stopped
2585   At one, aware from an informer that
There would be resistance. As SS Squad
Leader Buch pedalled his bicycle to
Crematorium Three, Max, his German
Orderly ran and stopped him and told him
2590   He had surprised the whole Combat Group in
Conference during the mid-day break in
Crematorium Three. At once Buch turned
And cycled back to the camp and informed
The block leadership. Observed, Max was now
2595   Surrounded and killed by the Combat Group
With hammers, axes and stones. The SS
Ordered a roll-call. The Jews stood in lines
And the SS commander spoke: "You have
Worked here long enough. By orders from my
2600   Superiors, you will in a convoy
Be sent to a rest-camp. There you will be
Given good clothes, plenty to eat, and your
Life will be easier. Those whose tattoo
Number I call, step forward and line up.
2605   You go by train to work at camp Gleiwitz."
The SS commander now called numbers,
First a hundred Hungarians who were
Marched off without protest to a barracks,
Then Greeks, then Poles who grumbled. Their protests
2610   Swelled to a roar. The SS man threatened
The Polish Jews. The SS officer
Called a number. Silence. He raised his head
And frowned. On parade, Chaim Neuhof, a Jew
From Sosnowiec, stepped forward. He walked up
2615   To the SS man, gesticulating,

189

And, as the SS man reached for his gun,
Shouted "Hurrah", the password, and hit him
On the head with a hammer, felling him
As a woodsman fells a rotten fruit-tree
2620 With a single blow. As prisoners shouted
"Hurrah", a Pole threw a large bottle of
Mineral water filled with explosive, which
Fell among guards and exploded, stunning
Or wounding seven SS. They then attacked
2625 The guards with hammers and axes, wounding
Them, and, shouting, pelted them with camp stones.
The Jews pursued the SS with crowbars,
Axes and picks, and several fell, wounded.
Some men fell to the ground and bled. Some ran
2630 To the barbed-wire fence, shooting at the Jews
With pistols. Outside the dissecting-room's
Front door machine-gun fire broke out, and now
The plotters were not sure if they had been
Betrayed or if partisans had attacked
2635 The camp. Sirens wailed in both Auschwitz and
Birkenau. Louder explosions came from
The crematorium, the rattle of
Machine-guns became more urgent. Into
This uproar on motorbikes rode dozens
2640 Of SS men from the SS barracks
Inside Birkenau, armed with machine-guns.
There were two machine-guns for each prisoner.

In battle formation the SS guards
Fired on the rioters, who retreated
2645 Into Crematorium Three, and they
Threw explosive-filled bottles from windows
Into the courtyard, where the Greeks were still
Lined up. There was a burst of machine-gun
Fire and most of the Greeks fell. A few tried
2650 To escape but were shot as they ran to
The gate. The SS, firing, moved towards
The crematorium entrance. Bottles
Fell all round them and exploded. Just then
A tremendous explosion rocked the walls,
2655 Felling SS. The crematorium
Roof blew off, beams and red tiles flying in
All directions. Flames leapt, smoke billowed up.
Four drums of gasoline had exploded,
Had been dynamited in a fire-bomb.

In the barracks where, unusually,
They had been herded at midday, confined
By the Germans who had been informed to
Expect trouble, the prisoners heard a crash
Like thunder and saw dense black smoke that did

Not smell of burnt human flesh, and they thought
An air raid had bombed Birkenau's chimneys.
The crematorium was now rubble,
The Sonderkommando buried inside.
A few who escaped were machine-gunned. Some

Staggered out with their hands up and were shot.
As fire raged through the building, men preferred
To face a hail of bullets in battle
Rather than to be burned alive (a fate
Akin to cremating corpses just gassed).

The hundred Hungarians were brought back
To the courtyard and machine-gunned at once.
All who had axes, hammers, picks or bars
And all who had set fire to the roof of
Crematorium Three were machine-gunned.

The thunderous explosion was heard at once,
The blazing roof of Crematorium Three
Was seen by the Kommando who were in
Crematorium One, the only one
That was working that day. They saw the flames

As a signal to revolt, as when a
Beacon is lit on a dark hill, and all
See a chain of revolt across the land.
Soviet prisoners-of-war working ovens,
They were all tense, waiting to be put down.

They left their posts and gathered at one end
Of the long incineration building.
The SS guards stood at the other end.
A German Kapo (or inmate in charge
Of other prisoners, "trusty"), Karl Konvoent

Overheard talk of the planned rebellion,
And he approached and asked, "Tell me, who has
Given you permission to stop work and
Leave the ovens?" Not satisfied with what
He heard, he gave the Jew in charge a blow

On his head with the curved end of his cane
And threatened to betray the planned revolt.
The work boss, his head split open, staggered,
Blood pouring down his face, drew a knife from

His boot and stabbed him in his chest. He fell,
2705 And two workers quickly opened the door
Of the nearest oven, dragged him and shoved
Him head first, still alive, into the fierce
Flames of the hot furnace. Seeing the crowd,
An SS guard hurried across and saw
2710 The oven door close on the booted feet.
He advanced to learn if the man had been
Sonder or SS. A fist hit his jaw,
He fell and was lifted and pushed head first
Into the red-hot oven, where his warm
2715 Flesh fused with burning coke. Then they turned on
Another SS man who hurried up
And beat him to death with the cane, leaving
His brains spilled on the stone floor. Now there was
No return, the revolt was on.
2720   The Jews
Handed out guns and grenades and opened
Hidden boxes of dynamite. Firing
Broke out between groups at the room's two ends.
A grenade thrown at the SS killed one
2725 And wounded more. Several Kommando died.
More SS fell and twenty Kommando
Ran to the crematorium door and
Were joined by reinforcements from outside.
At that moment a hundred trucks drew up.
2730 Half a company jumped out and stood in
Front of the barbed-wire fences in battle
Formation. The workers returned inside
And all fortified the building, and fired
From every window, and several SS
2735 Men dropped, wounded or stunned. The fierce fighting
Lasted about ten minutes. The SS
Brought up fifty police dogs and unleashed
Them on the Sonderkommando. The dogs
Refused to move and cowered. They had been trained
2740 To terrorise weak men in striped burlap
Who were not armed, and they were not used to
The smell of powder and scorched flesh, the noise
Of battle. Now the SS hauled up two
Howitzers. Seeing the unequal odds,
2745 Some gave out tools and cut the electrified
Barbed wire behind the crematorium.
Firing, the Jews rushed out of the back gate
And, after shooting at SS corporals,

Fled into the surrounding countryside,
2750 Some two hundred and fifty prisoners, free,
Headed for the loop of the Vistula
To hide in the fields and farmsteads between
Bleak Birkenau and the river Sola.
As a flock of small birds fly together,
2755 Alight on grass, then fly again, wheeling
Now left, now right, as if all obey one
Will of one mind, members of a group soul,
So ran the prisoners, together though free.
Without arms or grenades, some sought a route
2760 To freedom through the living quarters of
The Cleaning Installations Kommando.
SS men machine-gunned from the watch-tower.
Many dead were strewn on the ground, some crawled
Through a hole in the barbed-wire fence into
2765 The women's camp. The sirens wailed alarm.
More trucks brought SS men with dogs, who searched
The countryside for all who had escaped.

Leaving the two howitzers still unfired,
The SS men in front of the now quiet
2770 Crematorium advanced with bayonets
Fixed and searched all rooms. More SS entered
The dissecting-room, surrounded doctors
And drove them with blows to the courtyard and
Made them lie face down. The SS rounded
2775 Up two hundred Sonderkommando and
Made them lie face down on the ground, shouting
With fearful force, "Anyone who moves or
Raises his head will get a bullet in
The back of his neck." Guards walked among them,
2780 Kicking and beating them with clubs on heads,
Shoulders and backs till blood trickled down their
Cheeks. Dizzy, with ringing ears, they lay for
Half an hour, waiting for the bullet that,
Fired point-blank, would blow their head off and smash
2785 Their skull into fragments. Nearby a fire-
Fighting squad from Auschwitz fought the fire in
Crematorium Three. A car whined up.
Doctor Mengele got out and spoke to
Three political SS. One called out,
2790 "Doctors, on your feet." Four men stood and moved
Towards Mengele, who asked, "What part did
You play in this?" One said, "No part. We were

193

Dissecting the body of the Russian
Officer when the explosion happened.
2795 We did not leave our posts." Mengele said,
"Go, wash and return to your work." Without
Looking round, the four walked twenty paces,
Stiff with bruises and aches. Behind them came
A burst of machine-gun fire, and a third
2800 Of the twelfth Sonderkommando were dead.

In the countryside round Birkenau camp
The SS dogs found escapees, who were
Shot on the spot by the SS. Many –
Including their brave leader Dorebus –
2805 Ran into a barn at Rajsko not far
From Birkenau, which the SS now set
On fire. Dorebus spoke to his fellow
Uprising leaders as the timbers caught:
"My friends, comrades, the fire has taken hold.
2810 We have a choice. We can remain inside
And be burnt alive, but we who have worked
The ovens and burnt piles of dead bodies
Will never consent to become ashes
As long as we have breath. We can walk out,
2815 Free men. The pitiless Germans will shoot
Us, but we will retain our dignity
And our freedom. We can walk out with heads
Held high, for our action has struck a blow
Against those who perpetrate genocide.
2820 We have drawn the attention of the world
To unacceptable death processes.
Our stand against extermination has
Doomed us, but may – who knows – have saved countless
Millions of suffering prisoners in
2825 The sixteen hundred camps like this that swelled
Like boils on Greater Germany's pocked face.
My friends, I am proud of your sacrifice.
For our uprising will have shocked Himmler
And when publicity about it spreads
2830 He will be forced to close the gas chambers
And let the fires go out in the ovens.
My friends, that is your achievement. Who will
Now walk with me out of the flames, to be
Fêted by men and honoured in Heaven,
2835 And be admired for all eternity?"
So saying, brave Dorebus in the fire

Embraced each of his comrades, the last two
Being Zalmen Gradowski and Josef
Deresinski, his co-leaders, then strode
2840 To the door. With upright bearing, and with
A scornful look and a defiant air,
He walked out of the barn and stood. Guns cracked,
He fell. Now all the fugitives emerged
In like fashion, and were felled by flashes
2845 From rifles as the barn blazed bright-red like
A pyre. Their dead souls rose like glowing sparks
Into the blackness, and many shone like
Bright stars. Two hundred and fifty brave men
Were shot outside the wire; just one, Isaac
2850 Venezia from Salonica, broke
Back into the main camp; and only twelve
Of those who dashed for freedom were alive.

Union factory explosives had been stored
In the barracks of Kommando who worked
2855 In Crematorium Two, the other
Side of the ramp from One, in the quarters
Of the prisoners. The SS surrounded
Crematorium Two, and the prisoners
Moved the hidden explosives and poured them
2860 Down the latrine. The SS entered and
Locked all prisoners in one room and then searched
The barracks for explosives, but they found
Nothing. The men were marched across the ramp
To Crematorium One, where six hundred
2865 Corpses still lay in the gas chamber. They
Were ordered to burn them. So life went on,
With relief workers manning the ovens
And burning the backlog of gassed corpses,
Until they would be shot and join the pile.

2870 The SS had received firm orders to
Liquidate the Sonderkommando that
Day, and when the twelfth would not line up for
"Roll call", the revolt provided them with
A pretext for extermination that,
2875 They thought, justified their actions. Now all
Dead Sonderkommando were loaded on
Pushcarts and brought to Crematorium
Two, which was manned by thirty hastily
Recruited, new Sonderkommando, and

Laid naked in long rows near the ovens
On the stark, cold, unfriendly concrete floor
Of the incineration factory room,
All dead from Crematoria One, Two
And Three, and from the blood-spattered courtyard:
2885 Several hundred corpses like butchers' joints.
Now work resumed in Crematoria
One, Two and Four with fewer men per shift.
By midnight all had been cremated and
The thirty new Sonder men sat or lay
2890 In silence on the beds of the Sonders
Who had been killed, whose bodies they had burned.

In the barracks rumours of the revolt
Spread and were listened to in disbelief
By inmates conditioned and reduced to
2895 Non-thinking, non-feeling cowed sub-humans
Who shuffled obediently, with no will
To plan or make decisions, or to act
Like human beings. At first they were all
Joyful that men had risked their bodies to
2900 Remain human amid starvation and
Torture and retain their rebelliousness
In their twilight world. Then all were afraid
And waited apprehensively for some
Appalling collective punishment, some
2905 Communal retaliation: gassing.

That night the twelve fugitives were found in
A house across the Vistula, worn out.
The owner betrayed them to the SS
Detachment that was combing the district.
2910 The SS patrol brought the fugitives
Back to the crematorium courtyard.
Unarmed, using their fists, the twelve now tried
To seize their guards' weapons, and in the fight
Two SS men's faces were streaked with blood.
2915 There was a burst of machine-gun fire and
The twelve fell dead, their bid for freedom lost,
Their efforts to tell the world of the Hell
In Birkenau thwarted; though news seeped out
As prisoners told civilians who worked with
2920 Them, and SS men talked outside the camp.
So ended the revolt, the first one since
The camp was founded. Three SS corporals

And four hundred and fifty-one prisoners
Had been killed. In the crematoria
2925 Small groups were left. Crematorium Three was
Burned down and Four damaged. A quarter of
The ovens at Birkenau were now closed.
By their heroism, these brave men had
Reduced their factory's productivity:
2930 The disposal of stacks of gassed bodies.

The SS were stunned by the revolt and
Alarmed lest it should spread to other camps
And impede extermination inside
The death factories. Kramer and Höss were shocked
2935 And felt responsible. Their spirits rose
When, the revolt crushed, Iron Crosses were
Awarded to five SS guards, and Baer,
Commandant of Auschwitz, in a speech, said
This was the first time troops in a camp had
2940 Been decorated by the Reichsführer
For heroic conduct in suppressing
A mass outbreak. SS Brigadier-
General Dirlewanger, the most brutal
Of SS commanders, suggested to
2945 Himmler that German prisoners, inmates who
Were ex-criminals and anti-Nazis
Who wished to demonstrate their own inner
Transformation, should be enlisted in
The SS and report on prisoners so
2950 That no more revolts like this could happen.
Himmler agreed. The Birkenau revolt
Had convinced him that the camps were seething
With unrest. The Sonderkommando had
Risen because they knew they would be gassed.
2955 Publicity had leaked, and the Allies
Threatened him with death, and the war was lost.
If he stopped the gassing, peace could return.

News of the revolt reached the Council for
Rescuing the Jewish Population
2960 In Poland, whom Dorebus contacted
During the break-out. The Council knew that
The revolt had been caused by the increased
German gassing of Jewish prisoners and
Sonders, and, keeping quiet on the rising
2965 To protect survivors still in the camps,

It renewed its earlier appeal to
The two principal Allied governments
To do everything possible to stop
The Germans' plans for the mass murder of
2970 "All persons imprisoned" at Auschwitz and
Birkenau, and the "annihilation"
Of all remaining Polish Jews. Again
The Polish Government-in-Exile took
The plea to London's Foreign Office and
2975 The State Department in Washington, and
Their joint warning was broadcast, saying that
The Germans planned mass executions at
Oswiecim and Brzezinky, and that if
The plan was carried out, or any like
2980 It, the Allies would "bring the guilty to
Justice". Berlin stated that the reports
Were false, but the killings went on as if
The joint warning had been ignored. The same
Day, eight hundred gipsy children were gassed,
2985 And two days later three thousand women
Were gassed in Crematorium One, while
Next day three thousand Jewish women were
Gassed, and nearly fourteen hundred arrived
From Theresienstadt. Two thousand unfit
2990 Workers from I. G. Farben were gassed next,
Making eighteen thousand gassings during
The week after the joint Allied warning.
The next day three thousand three hundred Jews
From Slovakia and Budapest were gassed,
2995 And the Polish Government-in-Exile
Announced the Germans had begun "the mass
Murder of Poles" (still no mention of Jews)
"In gas chambers at Auschwitz". The next day
Professor Fraser broadcast in German
3000 Seven names of camp personnel, including
Auschwitz's political chief, Hauptschar-
Führer (Sergeant-Major) Palitzsch, and warned
Their atrocities were capital crimes.

Auschwitz answered the broadcast the next day.
3005 Six hundred and fifty boys had been locked
In two barracks since the revolt two weeks
Before, most thin teenage Hungarians
Who shivered in long striped clothes and old clogs.
One boy, Salmanovitch, climbed a pole to

3010   Escape from a roof window, but a guard
    Stopped him. Now all were taken to a hall
    Where an SS man selected fifty
    To unload potatoes from trains. He asked
    Salmanovitch, "How old are you?" Cheeky
3015   Salmanovitch said, "Nearly a hundred."
    The SS man yelled, "Is that the way you
    Speak to me? Go back in." The remaining
    Six hundred were taken by twenty-five
    SS through bright sunlight to a large square,
3020   And told to undress. Some saw a chimney
    With smoke and ran in terror round the square.
    The SS beat them with clubs. Now afraid,
    The naked boys huddled together. Some
    Ran to Sonderkommando, begged for help,
3025   Then sobbed and wailed in lamentation till
    The SS drove them into the bunker,
    Herding them with blows from clubs and truncheons,
    Looking from a distance like time-conscious
    Schoolmasters urging laggard boys with canes
3030   Into an end of term school assembly,
    And slammed the door on all, including short,
    Cheeky Salmanovitch. With smiles and beams
    The SS waited like teachers outside
    An assembly hall while the boys were gassed –
3035   A few more bits of flesh to be added
    To the millions of carcasses now gone.

    Policies are confirmed by deeds, not words.
    The gassings continued till the end of
    October. During that month some thirty
3040   Thousand Jews were gassed despite Himmler's firm
    Assurance to Waadah at the end of
    September that he had authorised all
    "Actions" in Auschwitz to be suspended.
    However, after the Allied broadcasts,
3045   The SS had to abandon the plan
    To kill the Auschwitz-Birkenau prisoners.

    The Allied threats after Dorebus's
    Revolt at last changed Himmler's attitude
    To extermination and genocide.
3050   SS-Brigadeführer Schellenberg, Head
    Of the Ausland-SD, had urged Himmler
    To end the war. He spoke to the Sternbuch

Brothers in Montreux and now met Doctor
Musy, President of the Swiss Altbund,
3055 Who wished to rescue Jews. In October
Musy met Himmler in Vienna, where,
With Schellenberg present, Himmler declared,
After some initial hesitation:
"I am now ready to release all Jews
3060 In German custody gradually, and
Allow them to travel to Switzerland."
It seems he said the same to Becher, who
Claimed that he ended the death factories when
In his presence Himmler dictated an
3065 Instruction to Kaltenbrunner to spare
The lives of all Jews who were still held in
Concentration camps: "By this order, which
Has immediate effect, I forbid all
Extermination of Jews and order
3070 That on the contrary care should be given
To weak and sick persons." By sparing Jews,
Himmler was now in conflict with Hitler
And had ignored Hitler's directive that
The Final Solution of the Jewish
3075 Question was to be pursued regardless
Of the war and its impact on men's lives.
The Jews' revolt had stopped the Holocaust.

President Roosevelt's representative,
McClellan, met Himmler's emissary,
3080 Becher, in Zurich, November the fifth,
In breach of the Teheran Agreement
In which the Allies agreed with Stalin
To boycott the Third Reich, and to press for
Unconditional surrender. Himmler
3085 Now recalled Eichmann from Hungary, but though
In December the sample train arrived
In Switzerland, the Jewish Committee
Refused to pay Himmler in cash or kind.

Struggles to save Hungarian Jews went on.
3090 A Swedish diplomat, Wallenberg, who
Was descended from one of the first Jews
To settle in Sweden, reached Budapest
After the deportations had stopped with
A list of six hundred and thirty Jews
3095 From Hungary who could have Swedish visas.

200

He represented the American
World Jewish Congress, Joint Distribution
Committee, State Department and the War
Refugee Board, four agencies, and his
3100 Jews were guarded in protected houses.
In October deportations began
Again. He worked with a Swiss diplomat,
Lutz, who sheltered twenty-five thousand Jews
In seventy-six buildings under Swiss
3105 Diplomatic protection. Wallenberg
Had five thousand protective passports, and
Four thousand more on the way from Sweden.
As a hundred thousand Jews were marched to
The Austrian border, tens of thousands
3110 Died of exposure and mass shooting, and,
Stirred, in November Wallenberg hosted
A meeting for all trying to save Jews
From deportation. He was successful.
In January when the Soviet forces
3115 Rolled into Budapest some hundred and
Twenty thousand Jews were safe. Wallenberg
Was summoned to Soviet military
Headquarters and given his reward: he
Was seized and questioned, and then disappeared,
3120 A victim of anti-Semite Sion
Through Martinist Rosicrucian agents.

An informant told the SS from where
The explosives had come: Weichsel-Union.
In the munitions factory the next day
3125 The SS arrested the three Jewish
Women who had stolen the explosives:
Ella Gartner, Estera Wajsblum and
Regina Safir, a Belgian and two
Poles. The next day they arrested two more
3130 Women in the Birkenau women's camp,
The Poles Toszka and Roza Robota,
And rounded up from Birkenau's Sonders
Wrobel and thirteen more Sonder men who
Worked in Crematoria Three and Five,
3135 Including Jankiel Handelsman, friend of
Dorebus, co-leader of the revolt.
All were taken to Auschwitz and locked up
In the cellars, then known as "the bunker",
Of Block Eleven, the Death Block. In this

Bunker in September nineteen forty-
One, six hundred Soviet civilians and
About two hundred and fifty Poles were
Crammed into cells behind iron-barred doors,
Their hands and legs smarting from flailing rods,
Locked in, and, in a test massacre, gassed
With Zyklon B, the first time gas was used
(Rather than bullets or exhaust fumes) in
The Holocaust. The bodies of the gassed –
Skin falling off in strips, faces twisted
In pain, nostrils bulging, hands scratched – were then
Taken out at night in eighty carts to
The Auschwitz crematorium ovens
And burned. From this same bunker the leaders
Of the revolt were fetched by day and were
Now interrogated under torture
For several weeks at the Political
Department in Camp Gestapo next to
The gas chamber and crematorium
At Auschwitz. There they met the sadistic
Gestapo chief, Palitzsch, the most brutal
Torturer. It was Palitzsch who had first
Used Zyklon B in Block Eleven, and,
Wearing a gas mask, found some prisoners were
Still alive. Palitzsch was the indifferent
Executioner who had dispatched two
Hundred and six prisoners who, having lain
On their front for weeks before machine-guns,
Forbidden to change their position or
They would be shot, were stood in the Auschwitz
Crematorium and were led into
The mortuary in groups of ten. Palitzsch
Shot each in the back of the head. All those
Waiting could hear the shots and thud of heads
On the concrete floor. Ten more were taken
And lined up near the groaning bodies, made
To stand with feet in puddles of their blood.
At the end Dr. Mildner, ruler of
Upper Silesia, who had been watching,
Raised his arm and saluted Palitzsch with
Respect, smiling jovially, stepping on
Corpses as he left, fresh blood trickling down
Walls.
        In Camp Gestapo the ringleaders
Of the revolt were all pushed to the floor

3185 And beaten with rubber truncheons and whips,
Hit in the face and kicked so mouths and eyes
Were swollen shut, and if they did not talk,
Were beaten till they blacked out. Each of them
Was put on a "swing". Palitzsch took the men,
3190 Women guards the women. All had to sit
On the floor, draw up their knees, cross their wrists,
Which were handcuffed. An iron bar
Was placed between their elbows and their knees
And each was suspended head down between
3195 Two hurdles a metre apart. Palitzsch
Then beat each one's naked buttocks and bare
Soles with bull-hide whips and riding crops, so
Violently that each rotated wheel-like,
And when their cries became too loud, gas masks
3200 Were put on their heads. Every so often
A mask was taken off and one was asked,
"Are you ready to confess?" Blood dripping
To the floor, too faint to talk, each one was
Allowed to hang head down, and hot water
3205 Was dripped inside each nose, which brought more screams.
Palitzsch beat Handelsman senseless and till
He died. Through such punitive "questioning"
All died except four of the five women,
Who did not talk but, swollen-faced, survived
3210 As their treatment by the women guards was
Slightly less severe than that of the men.
No one could match Palitzsch in cruelty.
The corpses were carried on wood stretchers
Into the crematorium nearby
3215 And burned to cinders in the ovens there.

It was in the bunker of Block Eleven
The SS and Palitzsch had suffered their
Greatest defeat three years before in cell
Eighteen, the starvation cell, where Father
3220 Kolbe, Polish Franciscan, was martyred.
Wailing camp sirens announced the escape
Of three prisoners, for whom ten men must die
As retaliation. All stood in line
All day till Gestapo chief Palitzsch and
3225 Fritzsch walked between ranks. Fritzsch pointed and an
SS man pushed a victim out of line.
Fritzsch selected the ninth man, who cried out,
"My wife, my children, I shall never see

Them again." And then a man with wire-frame
Spectacles stepped forward and volunteered
To take his place, a total stranger's place.
Fritzsch gasped to this sub-human, "Who are you?"
"A Catholic priest," came the reply. Kolbe
Removed his cap, showed his tattooed number,
16670. Palitzsch accepted,
Not grasping that his world of violence was
Lost to this saintly act of brotherhood
Which overcame the greatest cruelty.
Palitzsch ordered the ten condemned men to
Remove their rags and be buried alive.
Kolbe was flung naked on the cell's floor
In gloom, grating window and wrought-iron door,
And lay like St. Francis, who asked a friar
To lay him naked on the bare earth to
Die. Kolbe's act had shown that man is not
Dehumanised; he challenged the SS
View of prisoners as having no value,
He transcended personal agony.
As he starved, Kolbe said prayers and sang hymns,
Helping the other condemned men to die
As human beings. He made cell eighteen
Into a church, he led with prayers, the rest
Responded. SS guards opened the doors.
Feebly the condemned begged water and food.
One was kicked to the concrete floor and killed,
One shot. The prayers became feebler, and then
A mere whisper. Kolbe did not complain
Or ask for water. When all lay like heaps
Of rags, he sat propped against a wall and
Looked calmly at them. The SS shouted,
"Lower your eyes, don't look at us like that."
After two weeks just four were still alive.
Only Kolbe was conscious. The SS,
Wanting the bunker for more prisoners, lost
Patience and ordered a criminal called
Bock to inject the four with carbolic
Acid. Propped against the wall, lips moving
In prayer, Kolbe held out his left arm for
The injection. Later grim Borgowiec,
The jailer, found him still sitting, eyes wide
Open, serene, radiant, as if seeing,
As if in ecstasy, embodying
The deepest meaning of humanity.

It was August the fourteenth, the feast of
3275 The Virgin's assumption into Heaven.
Soon his body was scattered ashes, grains
Of Auschwitz soil. His triumphant spirit
Which had defied the might of the SS
Was cheered into Heaven by Christ's Angels.
3280 Yet even he could not take on himself
All the effects of evil meted out
And another man's destiny to grieve.
Franciszek Gajowniczek, the man whose place
Kolbe took as he had a family,
3285 Returned home to learn that in the war's last
Few days, his two young sons had been killed by
Russian shells. Through his sacrifice, Kolbe
Had saved him from starvation and the pain
Of not seeing his young children again,
3290 But not from the anguish of bereavement.
No man can take away another's fate,
But by his gesture he left Gajowniczek
An example of how to endure pain,
Of love's power to embrace the worst evil,
3295 Of making friends with Death and conquering him:
The truth which Kolbe embodied, that love
Is stronger than hatred and can forgive.

In life as well as camps such as Auschwitz
Individuals achieve the greatest fame
3300 Or notoriety when position
Lifts them above anonymous faces.
Roza, the organiser of the theft,
Was now as famous as the camp hangman:
Jakob Kozelczuk, who, having arrived
3305 From East Poland over a year before,
Was now the bunker's attendant, jailer,
Who kept the cells in order and led out
(When they had undressed in the lavatory
And their name in indelible pencil
3310 Was written on their naked bodies, to
Facilitate identification
Before the crematorium ovens)
The victims to the Black Wall, named from its
Black cork insulating plates, in the yard
3315 Between blocks Ten and Eleven, where, before
Grabner, the Political Head, they were
Shot in the back of the head in pairs. He

Grabbed each pair of skeletons by their arms
And at the double hurried them over
3320 To the Wall of Death and stood between them,
Still gripping each at the scrawny elbow,
And made each kneel on one knee, then one rise,
Head to the Wall, not looking to one side,
Unable to stand upright after months
3325 Of crouching, famished, in a stinking cell.
As a pied wagtail on a sea-wall bobs
And dips its tail and bobs again and then,
Running, dapper, wags its tail up and down,
So, to and fro fussed dapper Kozelczuk.
3330 Nearby a prisoner stood, holding a spade
And, strutting slowly like a carrion crow
In black plummage, in black above his prey,
With short air pistol or small-calibre
Rifle so no sound carried to those who
3335 Lived on the main road just beyond the Wall,
The executioner, generally
Gestapo chief Palitzsch, menacing with
His gun behind his back, shot each in turn
In the back of the neck where the spinal
3340 Cord enters the skull. When each had fallen
With a groan, as blood ran in a thin stream
The executioner put a boot on
His forehead, pulled up an eyelid to see
If the eye was motionless, and if there
3345 Was a gurgle, shot him again in his
Eye or temple. The corpse-carriers, with
Fear in their alert eyes, and with speed, then
Loaded the corpses on wooden stretchers,
Ran them to the other end of the yard
3350 And threw them, blood still trickling down their heads
And backs, on a mounting pile of corpses
By a far wall where a swarm of flies buzzed.
The spade-holder shovelled sand on the blood.
Kozelczuk fetched and led out the next pair.
3355 Most guards saw men as vile material that
Could be stilled with one shot and in an hour
Reduced to its component atoms and
Returned to the earth mixed with clinker and
Ash.
3360   Not Kozelczuk, he was a caring
Man. He had a room in the bunker Block
And was given food, drink and privileges.

He was jailer to Mala Zimetbaum
And Edek Galinski when they were caught
3365 After their bold escape in SS clothes,
And without anyone knowing he had
Allowed them to meet and converse at night.
As hangman who assisted at roll-call
Hangings, he had helped them to the gallows.
3370 By the noose at roll call, inmates watching,
Mala cut her wrists with a razor-blade
Edek had given her, and with bleeding
Hand had hit an SS guard in his face.
He helped Alina Brewda, and he now
3375 Helped Roza Robota. He had brought her
News of her boy-friend Wrobel. He told her
When Wrobel died in the course of extreme
Interrogation, merciless beatings.
And, her tears shed, he now took the risk and
3380 Secretly admitted a male friend of
Roza's from the youth organisation
At night. Her face was so swollen that he
Hardly recognised her. Roza clung to
Him and whispered in his ear: "Those who helped
3385 Me smuggle the explosives have nothing
To fear from me. I have not talked, will not.
During my interrogation I blamed
Everything on Wrobel once I knew he's
Dead." On a scrap of paper she bade her
3390 Comrades farewell in the words of greeting
Of her youth organisation: "'Hazak
V'ematz', 'be brave and strong'. I shall not talk,
I know what is ahead for me, but no
Others will be involved." Inspired, her friend
3395 Embraced her for the last time and crept out
As a grey dawn broke round the dark Death Block.

Christ loitered in the bunker passageway,
Peering into the cells through wrought-iron doors,
Being with the condemned in their anguish
3400 In the gloom of a cold January noon.
Near the snowlit wall of cell twenty-one
And a scratched outline cross and a scraped Christ,
Arms stretched and nailed, with a thin, starved, ribbed waist,
And rays of Light streaming onto his heart
3405 From a dark cloud, a Polish prisoner priest,
Kneeling, alone, said Mass for the condemned –

A chair an altar, glass the gold chalice,
Handkerchief the communion cloth, water
Become wine, morsel of bread Host – and with
3410 Heart pounding with joy, with heavenly bliss
Behind his closed eyes like a lit candle,
Held a votive Mass to the Sacred Heart,
A thanksgiving to Jesus for caring
For Kolbe, who forgave his captors, and
3415 For seventy priests in the camp, and for
Roza Robota and all condemned souls
Whether of Christian or of Jewish faith;
Not praying only for Christians, but like
Kolbe concerned in a Polish Jew's fate,
3420 Forgiving all SS, all hangmen and
All executioners like Palitzsch, and
At one with all men's heads on the Black Wall
And with all women's necks within the noose,
Accepting Christ crucified in this hour,
3425 Confident that the spirit goes to Heaven
After its last ghastly ordeal and pain,
And felt Christ's presence through the barred iron door.

A cold early January evening,
And a cold hanging at the women's camp
3430 In Birkenau, as four Jewish women,
Roza Robota and Ella Gartner,
Then Regina Safir and Estera
Wajsblum, were brought to two floodlit gallows,
Crunching across the sparkling frozen snow
3435 In the bleak snow-covered assembly square.
The first two were hanged during roll call in
The presence of all prisoners who worked in
The night-shift at the Weichsel-Union
Factory, male as well as female prisoners,
3440 Their breaths like mists above the crisp deep snow.
Roza and Ella were led to wooden
Gallows – post, bar, crossbeam, hook and white noose
Above a platform with a trapdoor. All
Were silent as sentence was read out by
3445 First Protective Custody Commander
Hössler, who screamed: "These women assisted
In the October seventh uprising
By stealing and providing explosives
To the Special Squad. All traitors will be
3450 Destroyed in this manner. Hangman, proceed."

Jakob Kozelczuk looped nooses round necks
With gentleness hidden from the Nazis.
Shivering from the cold as much as fear,
Roza called out, "Vengeance will come," and her
Organisation's words, "Be brave and strong,"
As the trap fell. She hung, eyes closed, floodlit,
Neck askew, limp, turning to left and right,
Her last breath floating in the floodlit frost
As Ella, with a haughty look, followed
Her to a more friendly world where being
Floats like a cloud of breath, beyond all cold.
The night-shift left to work, silent, each man
In his thoughts, each woman indignant as
The slack bodies were thrown into a cart.
The day-shift returned for roll call, and then
The second pair were led to the gallows
To end the last public execution
Before the evacuation of Auschwitz.

Where the Warsaw ghetto once stood now see
A monument (in slabs of grey-black stone
Hitler ordered for a victory salute
To the battles of the Third Reich) which stood
In the rubble from nineteen forty-eight,
Ruins since cleared into a spacious square –
An artist's tribute to the Holocaust:
A dozen bowed humans trudge to be gassed,
Two women with shawls over their bent heads
Hold children; behind them: soldiers, bayonets.
One woman has her hands over wet eyes,
One head held back, elbows out, is aghast.
In the centre a bearded rabbi holds
The Torah, looks up, draws strength from above.
One woman looks back to the future as
Does one child, but all else is lack of hope.
In the Warsaw ghetto Christ blinked back tears
For the fate of five million such as these,
Whose frail bodies would soon be cinders, cold
As the stone in the nine-foot ghetto walls.

God, Fire, from which all forms at first emerged,
Transcendent One and immanent Light, is
Like both the silence in a timeless cave,
Eternal stillness in whose sea we are
Like white wave-crests, with which we are at one,

As in Capri's Blue Grotto's blue-white light,
3495   And the loving tide in which we all live,
With crabs and shrimps, starfish and all creatures;
The current that carries us through our time,
Gently pushing us to warmer waters,
Sad that some men are predators who hunt
3500   And devour their brothers in great numbers
As sharks kill shoals whose souls dwell with the Light,
But, ever moving history forwards, glad
That men as brave as Dorebus resist,
Fight back for universal peace and right.
3505   "Why did God allow Auschwitz?" you ask. So
Evil energy could be neutralised
And souls made pure by suffering could crowd
Into Heaven's tiered amphitheatre and,
Released from the fierce gladiator's sword,
3510   By their endurance end Europe's discord,
Express hidden harmony in one choir.

~ BOOK 6 ~

HITLER STRIKES BACK

O Homer, you who, though blind, wrote the first
Western literature about your hero
Odysseus, King of Ithaca, who won
The ten-year long Trojan War by a trick
And who then journeyed home for ten more years
And killed the usurpers in his palace,
So many places claim your birth – besides
Ithaca, Smyrna (now Izmir), Chios,
Colophon, Pylos, Argos and Athens,
Salamina in Cyprus, Rhodes, Kymi –
From 800 to 550 BC,
And learned men assert that you were just
An oral tradition, not a person.
Yet I intuitively sense that you
Grew up here in Ithaca in the eighth
Century and absorbed your local legend,
Odysseus, and detailed geography
Of the island you first knew as a boy:
The Cave of the Nymphs with a round hole in
Its roof for nymphs and gods to enter, and
Just a slit for mortals, where Odysseus
Hid Alcinous' treasure; and the Hill
Of Hermes, Pitikali, where his great
Palace was, from which three seas can be seen –
The Ionian, Tyrrhenian and Gulf
Of Patras – by an ancient round stone church,
And, across Polis Bay, Asteris isle,
Daskalio, where the suitors sought to lure
Telemachos. I feel you visited
Troy for local detail and sat where I
Sit now on this hot July afternoon,
Wind in my hair from the Scamander plain
Where Achilles once camped and heroes fought,
By the altar of Alexander's late
Temple of Athena, and looked back as
I do at the east gate where the Greek Horse
Was brought to the approach and dragged inside,
Barely big enough for a few men to
Hide in, then up the steps to the royal

Palace where it stood as a wheeled trophy;
And, before you went blind, while you could see,
Gazed as I do now back at house VI E,
Paris's well-walled house ten yards down steps,
Where Helen lived, the prize for whom all fought.

From this vantage point, then a stone terrace,
Where I sit now, your Helen sat and watched –
Content with Paris, flattered and troubled
Just ten yards up the steps from her front door –
A thousand ships gathering to rescue

Their kidnapped queen and take her back to Greece.
You too wanted to show war is absurd,
That thousands died so Helen could go home,
A war that Zeus wanted so he could curb
The overpopulation of the earth;

You admired their exploits and bravery,
Not the futility of ten years' war.
You showed how wily Odysseus, King of
The Kephallonians, whose capital
Was Ithaca, tried not to take part in

The war against Troy, but unable to
Refuse because of his oath to Helen's
Father (who, to avoid trouble from her
Many suitors, made all swear that if one
Took Helen away from Menelaos,

The rest would unite to win her back by
Armed force), followed the Greeks and took twelve ships
And won the Trojan War by devising
The trick of the Trojan Horse, a victor's
Trophy, and then, when the Trojans had been

Massacred, took Hecabe, Priam's Queen,
Whose treasure Schliemann found by Troy II's ramp,
As booty, till the Cicones killed her,
And after ten years' wanderings came home,
Landing, ever wily, at Phorkys cove,

Stowing Alcinous' souvenirs in
The Cave of the Nymphs, then seeking out old
Eumaos in his farm by the Fountain
Of Arethusa, and found what Paris
Had done to Menelaos, Greeks had done

To him, that his own people were suitors
In his own palace. Helen, Hecabe
And Penelope were equally wronged,
You were saying, and Paris, Odysseus
And the suitors were all at fault. So war

Over Helen was senseless. I find you
Not far from Didyma's oracle where
A priestess went into trance by the well
And uttered words which priests took down and made
Into hexameters, your line, in the
Cresmographeion or oracle room,
And delivered them to the suppliant who
Waited patiently in the pronaos –
In Izmir, writing your *Iliad* in
730, and its sequel thirty
Years later, in a cave by six springs which
Flowed to the sea, a cave cool in summer
With its own water supply (like the cave
Of Eumaos), in what later became
The baths of Diana, now in the grounds
Of Izmir Water Board. I see you in
A Greek-speaking Ionian settlement
(Which claimed you were born in nearby Bayrakh),
In Asia Minor, sympathetic to
Both sides, admiring Odysseus, your own
Island's hero, but sad for Priam and
Hector and the slaughtered Trojans. Did you
Return to Ithaca and teach pupils
In the "School of Homer" by Meliandros
Spring, high above Odysseus' palace and
Regain your sight through its healing waters
As Stavros locals say, just as Shakespeare
Retired to Stratford after his great works?
And did you then go to Ios and die?
There are reports your Ios tomb proclaimed:
"Here the earth covers the sacred head of
The dean of heroes, the divine Homer."
O Homer, you who were so wise on war
And understood its folly, how brute force
By one side is matched by its opponents,
Whose stance was neutral between Greece and Troy,
And who understood how deviousness
Wins wars, as I sit on a stone and gaze
Across the plain to the distant blue sea,
My tongue parched at the end of a hot day,
July sun warm on my left cheek, the wind
Whipping from the sea and drying my sweat,
Sparrows chirping, cicadas sh-sh-ing,
A tractor cutting an early harvest,
And wonder how the Greeks found wood from dry

130 Olive trees and made a Trojan Horse on
That dusty plain, and see your Troy VI and
VII A, blanking out the rest, and dream –
Help me now that I tell of Hitler's trick,
How he deviously hid an attack
135 Behind a feigned defensive "Wacht am Rhein"
To stun the Allies into surrender;
And tell how the Germans were stopped and held
On Elsenborn ridge, and then round St. Vith;
Tell how the encircled Bastogne was freed;
140 And tell how Eisenhower blocked the advance
Of the German armies towards the Meuse.
Tell, Muse, of the greatest American
Battle and the largest American
Surrender in the entire Second World War.

145 Convalescing from Stauffenberg's attack
In his East Prussian headquarters, Wolf's Lair,
Confined to bed with jaundice, sallow-skinned,
Pale and listless, reading philosophy
(Mainly Schopenhauer, Nietzsche and Hegel),
150 Hitler stared at reverses on his map:
D-Day, the Normandy defeat, his haste
To reinforce the West Wall, pressure in
North Italy, loss of North Africa,
The abandonment of Greece, the Allied
155 Bombing in the Reich. He was in gloom at
The delay of his secret war-winning
Reprisal weapon, V-2. The attempt
On his life had damaged his health, leaving
Him with stomach pains, insomnia and
160 Nervous twitching. There was now total war
And more adversity. Friendless except
For Hungary and Japan, Germany had
Suffered demoralising casualties
(Four and a half million in five war years,
165 Half a million in August) and the might
Of the "sub-human" Soviets who had
Five hundred and fifty-five divisions,
With whom peace talks were out of the question.
The front was collapsing, and the Allies
170 (Thanks to Montgomery's pressure for one
Thrust to the Ruhr, and Eisenhower's decree)
Were closing on the Rhine by attacking
On both sides of the forested Ardennes.

Two days before the Falaise Gap was closed
175 He had known that an attack on the east
Might wipe out twenty Russian divisions
Whereas attacking the west, where there were
No more than sixty divisions in all,
Two-thirds American, could turn the tide
180 With just thirty or forty divisions.
Now he studied maps and found a weak point
In the American front line. The Ardennes!
Where Manstein and he struck in May nineteen
Forty on news supplied by the Duke of
185 Windsor. The Americans had three weak
Divisions there. If all went well, he could
Annihilate some twenty or thirty
Divisions and drive back the enemy.
With sound intuition, he saw the brash
190 Allies would halt and wait for their supplies.
With great effrontery, he had held all
Fronts and prepared by assembling units
And holding them in reserve for a blow,
A counterstroke, an offensive that would
195 Destroy the Allies' flimsy coalition.
He would amass twenty-eight divisions,
He had two Panzer armies, six hundred
Thousand men who were coiled and could soon strike.
As Frederick the Great had continued
200 The Seven Years War against all advice
And had outlasted the coalition
That opposed him, so with this offensive
He would split the Allies and Germany
Would not be conquered. At a stroke he would
205 Reverse the flow of war and turn retreat
Into pursuit, all the way to Antwerp,
The supply base for the Allied forces,
Which would be the goal of his great onslaught.
Sitting in bed, he shared his brainwave with
210 Jodl, head of the OKW,
The Armed Forces' High Command who always
Concurred. He gabbled: "My Panzers will cross
The Meuse and take Antwerp and drive a wedge
Between the British and Canadians, and
215 The Americans. The British are worn
Out, the Americans will collapse. It
Will be another Dunkirk. We'll defeat
The enemy in the west, then turn our

Forces east to the Vistula, attack
220   The Red Army."
                        The Americans reached
        Bastogne in early September and crossed
        The West Wall into Germany, to be
        Driven out by Panzers. On the sixteenth,
225   The day before the Allies' Arnhem drop,
        Hitler attended a briefing at his
        OKW headquarters, and heard
        A report on "the successful counter-
        Attack by Panzers in the Ardennes". He
230   Leapt to his feet and said: "I have just made
        A momentous decision. I shall go
        Over to the counter-attack, out of
        The Ardennes to Antwerp." All were too stunned
        To speak at first, knowing that Germany
235   Was on the run. Incredulously, they
        Listened. "Such a massive thrust will sever
        The American and British armies
        And cause another Dunkirk. The attack
        Will take place in bad weather and so will
240   Neutralise Allied air supremacy.
        The Allied response will be slow while they
        Co-ordinate their plans, and our tanks will
        Reach the Meuse before their reserves arrive.
        The American soldier is not tough.
245   A surprise blitzkrieg assault will soon spread
        Confusion and terror, and crack their line.
        We must be daring. Fate often preserves
        The man of courage. The gods love and bless
        All those who strive for the impossible.
250   A big reverse will knock the Americans
        Out of the war, bring Britain to her knees.
        Like Frederick the Great, with a great blow
        I will split the Allied coalition.
        The Ardennes will be my Rossbach and Leuthen,
255   And throw the enemy from our homeland."
        Now aloof from his Prussian officers
        Following the Wehrmacht's attack on him,
        Disregarding his staff's doubts, he ordered
        Jodl and his circle to make a plan,
260   And in October combined two of their
        Five options to implement in the flesh
        The flash of his initial conception,
        Or "divine intuition" as he called

His demonic intention: an attack
265 Towards Antwerp through the Ardennes (now held
By just four US divisions), crossing
The Meuse on both sides of Liège, to be
Codenamed "Wacht am Rhein", or "Watch on the Rhine",
Which would suggest a defensive posture –
270 Guarding the Rhine round Dusseldorf, Cologne,
Where a bogus Twenty-Fifth Army was
Invented to deceive the Allied might –
Rather than an advance from Monschau to
Losheim, and from Echternach to Gemünd
275 With no more than twenty-eight divisions.

Tell, Muse, how Allied conflict on Antwerp
Encouraged Hitler to capture the port.
In October Eisenhower was again
Frustrated at Montgomery's lack of
280 Progress. The Germans had a defensive
Line from the North Sea to the Swiss border,
The West Wall, and had rebuilt divisions
And brought in new ones, and now outnumbered
The Allies. Montgomery was sunk in
285 Gloom. He knew he could have ended the war
In three weeks from his Normandy victory,
Which left him invincible in the minds
Of the Germans but not the minds of SHAEF.
Now he felt that, without his single thrust,
290 He had been defeated by the Germans
At Arnhem and by the Americans.
He was scornful of "useless" Eisenhower
And Bradley who wanted to show the world
American power and blundered in their
295 Decisions, dispersing the Allied effort
On too wide a front. They had created
A shambles, and so the war would last through
Winter till next spring. He was now stuck at
Eindhoven while his men saw mistresses
300 In Brussels; he turned a blind eye. Nothing
Much happened. It was cold and damp. Dawnay
Brought back his winter wear – thick vests and pants,
Woollen pyjamas and his dressing-gown –
From Phyllis Reynolds in England. Bradley
305 And Hodges brought General Marshall, Chief of
Staff, US Army and Eisenhower's boss,
To Eindhoven. At once Montgomery

Said, "General, could you spare me just a few
Moments in my office caravan? Would
310   You mind, Generals?" Marshall looked at Bradley
And Hodges and, shrugging, wary, followed
Montgomery into his caravan,
Where Montgomery made a strong complaint
Against Eisenhower: "I feel you should know
315   That since the Supreme Commander assumed
Personal command of the land battle
As well as forces on sea and in air,
The Armies have become separated
Nationally, not geographically.
320   There is a lack of grip and a lack of
Operational direction and control.
Our operations have become ragged,
Disjointed, and we have now got ourselves
Into a real mess." Marshall said, "Field
325   Marshal, I have listened. There is more than
One view in such complex matters." With eyes
Darting, Montgomery said, "I can see
That you entirely disagree." Marshall
Rejoined: "There has to be a balance of
330   National effort. General Eisenhower is
The Supreme Commander." And with that he
Nodded and turned and left the caravan.
Montgomery had paid Eisenhower back
For his complaint about him to Churchill
335   And Brooke.
                    Marshall at once briefed Eisenhower,
And next day Eisenhower, irritated
That Montgomery should have tried to go
Over his head to his boss about him,
340   And receiving Admiral Ramsay's report
That the Canadians could do nothing due
To lack of ammunition, signalled that
Montgomery should take Antwerp or else
All Allies operations would now reach
345   A standstill. Irked, Montgomery replied
That the Canadians had ammunition
And were attacking, that Ramsay was wrong.
He said that at Versailles Eisenhower had
Made attack in Holland the main effort.
350   Eisenhower replied it was now Antwerp.
Smith rang and demanded when there would be
Action, threatened Montgomery would lose

218

His supplies. Montgomery wrote blaming
The failure at Arnhem on a lack of
Co-ordination between Bradley's troops
And his. He asked to be given sole control
Of the land battle. Exasperated,
Eisenhower lost patience and wrote bluntly:
"The Antwerp operation does not involve
The question of command in the slightest
Degree. If after reading the SHAEF plan
Of campaign you still characterise it
As unsatisfactory, then indeed
We have an issue that must be settled
Soon in the interests of efficiency.
If you as the Senior Commander in
This Theater of one of the great Allies,
Feel that my conceptions and directives
Are such as to endanger the success
Of my operations, then it is our
Duty to refer the matter to higher
Authority for any action they
May choose to take, however drastic." He
Threatened to go to the Combined Chiefs of
Staff, and Montgomery knew that they would
Support Eisenhower and perhaps seek his
Own dismissal. He knew that he had pushed
Eisenhower as far as he could. He wrote
Promising a hundred per cent support
("You will hear no more on command from me")
And giving Antwerp top priority –
When he could wind down his search for V-2
Sites in Holland, which took a few more days.

In Germany the terror continued
Like an epidemic, a spreading plague,
And hundreds had died on the gallows at
Plötzensee prison. In the Rastenburg
Bunker Bormann told Hitler: "My Führer,
I have a report on Rommel. Speidel
Testified on October the fourth that
Hofacker spoke of the plot against you
And passed the information to Rommel.
On your orders, Keitel summoned Rommel
Here but he pleaded his head injury.
Now the Gestapo report that he has
Recovered from the crash and goes for walks

'Leaning on his son', and I have reports
From local Party officials who say
He is still making mutinous remarks.
He should be told to see you if he is
Innocent, or face the People's Court, or
Behave like a true Prussian officer."
Hitler stared and said, "I feel wounded by
His betrayal. I esteemed Rommel highly,
But he took part in the conspiracy."
Bormann interrupted: "Goerdeler said
He was to be President of the Reich."
Hitler nodded tiredly, recalling how
At Soissons Rommel tried to end the war.
"Tell Keitel to send Burgdorf and his chief
Law officer to Rommel's villa with
Such a request, to do what you have said.
The German people should remain without
Knowledge of his high treason as he is
A popular Field Marshal and hero."

The terror descended on Herrlingen
At midday on October the fourteenth.
Rommel's son, Manfred, had arrived home on
Leave from his anti-aircraft battery
At seven, and Rommel walked with him and said,
"I am expecting a visit from two
Generals about my future employment.
I'm not sure if that is the true purpose
Of their visit." Rommel had told Loistl,
His soldier-servant, to leave the garden
Gate open so his visitors could drive
To the house. Loistl was surprised to see
The car, with a Waffen-SS driver,
And a grey car behind it, remain in
The road. Loistl took the coats of Burgdorf
And Maisel and showed them into the house,
Where Rommel asked Manfred to leave the main
Living room. There they produced a copy
Of Speidel's and Hofacker's statements and
Made it clear that the Führer knew. Burgdorf
Said: "If you do not go to Rastenburg
To contest this evidence, you are to
Accept arrest by me and trial for
High treason by the People's Court and then
Execution." Maisel added, "And then

220

Sequestration of your house." Burgdorf said:
"Or you can take the officer's way, in
Which case you will have a state funeral with
Full honours, and your family will not
445 Be penalised. Your death will be proclaimed
As natural, you will have died of your wounds,
Your injuries, your reputation will
Be intact, no one will know, and there will
Be a guarantee of safety for your
450 Family, which will be revoked if you
Choose the People's Court." Rommel instantly
Decided. He said, "How?" "Not pistol. Quick-
Acting poison. Three seconds. I have it
Here." Composed, Rommel said, "It is 'die now'
455 And save my family, or 'die later'
And put it at risk." Burgdorf nodded and
Said, "We will wait in the garden." He and
Maisel paced up and down while Rommel told
Loistl, "Send Manfred now, and Aldinger
460 After half an hour." He lingered, he had
Been awaiting this day for three months. There
Was no real choice. Disgrace and poverty
For his family, or a quick end and
His family would keep the villa he
465 Had mustered. He had known of the plot and
Was shocked and would not join, but he wanted
German surrender and honourable peace.
He knew Speidel had tried to save himself.
He was innocent, but as a Prussian
470 Officer would not stoop to plead or beg
For mercy.
                    He went upstairs and found his
Wife Lucy, held her and said, "My dearest,
You must be strong and look after Manfred.
475 I have to say goodbye. I shall very
Shortly be dead. I have been given a choice
By Hitler's order, to appear before
A People's Court or suicide. Burgdorf
And Maisel have the means, a quick-acting
480 Poison. I have been implicated in
The events of July the twentieth.
Stülpnagel, Speidel and Hofacker have
Accused me, I suspect under torture,
And Goerdeler whom I have never met
485 Or spoken with, has said I was to be

President of the Reich in Hitler's place."
Frightened, Lucy said, "But it isn't true,
You can deny it." He said gently, "There
Is no truth in the accusation, which
490   Is unbelievable. I'm not afraid
To face a People's Court. I can defend
Every action honestly, openly.
But it will be execution, and you
And Manfred will lose everything. Besides,
495   I do not think I would ever appear
In court, I would disappear. Talk of my
'Future employment', which Burgdorf mentioned
On the telephone, was a deception,
They have planned my extinction and will have
500   It anyway. This is the end. I must
Say goodbye. They are waiting for my Field
Marshal's cap and baton." Lucy whimpered,
"I love you." Manfred came in, bewildered.
Rommel said, "You must be strong. I have to
505   Say goodbye." He again outlined his choice
And the so-called "evidence". He said, "My
Family will not suffer provided
I make this choice. I love you both. My first
Thoughts are of you, of the life you will have.
510   Remember me as an honourable man,
An officer who fought well but could not
Stand the casualties and when he knew we
Had lost the war sought peace and pulled the front
Line further and further back – but not as
515   A conspirator or traitor." Manfred,
Wet-eyed at his father's self-sacrifice,
Held one hand, Lucy, eyes glistening, held
The other. Captain Aldinger, an old
Staff officer of Rommel's who was then
520   Staying with him as amanuensis
And aide, came in and Rommel said goodbye.
There were now several cars outside the house.
Completely calm, Rommel kissed Lucy and
Manfred, put on his greatcoat and cap, and,
525   Carrying his Field Marshal's baton, walked
With Aldinger and Manfred to one of
The waiting cars where Burgdorf and Maisel
Saluted him with the greeting which had
Been compulsory since Stauffenberg's bomb:
530   "Heil Hitler." Rommel climbed into the back

Of the car, which drove off. The desert fox
Who had escaped Montgomery's pursuit
Was now cornered by hounds under Hitler's
Command. Fifteen minutes later the phone
535 Rang at the Herrlingen house. The reserve
Hospital in Ulm reported Rommel
Had been brought there by two Generals. He seemed
To have had a heart attack and was dead.
Rumours that the terror had reached Rommel
540 Swept like a shudder through Hitler's Generals
Who, fearful for their own safety, were now
Less inclined to dispute the Ardennes plan.

Learning the plan in early November,
Both Rundstedt, who was in charge of German
545 Forces in the west, and Model, who led
Army Group B peering through monocle,
Thought so few troops could not reach Antwerp. All
Generals knew Germany was under siege.
Hitler pursued a scorched earth policy.
550 Any land conquered should be reduced to
A desert, and no German wheat should feed
The invaders. All industrial plant and
Supplies should be blown up. Goebbels was now
Cutting food rations, the youth were digging
555 Trenches. Himmler set up the People's Storm,
So each active male could be drafted to
Defend the Fatherland. Hitler ordered
Hochtief company to build a bombproof
Bunker beneath the Chancellery, and all
560 Generals knew he would move back to Berlin
When it was ready. But terror prevailed,
It was useless to protest to Hitler,
Who needed a great victory to reverse
The tide of war, make the Americans
565 Evacuate Europe and Britain sue
For peace. "A great blow like a thunderclap,"
He prophesied in a very certain voice,
"A winter battle in a dark forest,
Will destroy the coalition between
570 A dying empire, an ex-colony
That is waiting to inherit its lands,
And a Marxist state that loathes capital.
This is a turning-point, like Ludendorff's
Advance on Amiens. We must stake all

On one throw." He deluded himself with
Wishes and hopes, not realistic aims,
And the commanders of the Fifth and Sixth
Armies, von Manteuffel and Sepp Dietrich,
Could not change Hitler's mind towards the end
Of November. In early December
The Generals argued against Hitler's plan.
Von Rundstedt stayed away, and sent Westphal.
The Führer insisted on Wacht am Rhein.
Model said, "If it succeeds, it will be
A miracle." Divisions arrived from
All over Hitler's empire, a secret
Build-up not on Enigma, that Ultra
Therefore could not penetrate and decode.

Driving to Maastricht, where he was hosting
A conference of commanders, Eisenhower,
His knee still uncomfortable, noted
How thinly spread Middleton's troops were in
The Ardennes, the one place where the Allies
Were not attacking, and he asked Bradley
Before the conference, "Is that sector of
The front vulnerable?" Bradley said: "I
Cannot strengthen the Ardennes area
Without weakening Patton's and Hodges'
Offensives. If the Germans advance in
The Ardennes we can hit them in either
Flank and stop them before they reach the Meuse.
As a precaution I've not put any
Major supply depots in the Ardennes."
Satisfied with his reply, Eisenhower
Opened the conference. Soon Montgomery
Was complaining: "First Army is struggling
Forward, but there are no reserves at all.
Everyone is attacking everywhere
With no reserves anywhere. I propose
Patton's Third Army should be moved north for
The Ruhr offensive, and that Brad should be
Commander-in-Chief of Land Forces, as
General Eisenhower's simply not doing
The job. Or at least, that Brad should command
All Allied forces north of the Ardennes,
So the Allies can fight with one effort,
Under one unified command." Before
Eisenhower could say anything, Bradley

Said: "That is not a good idea. There should
620 Be separate national Armies, with me
As Commander of the American
Forces, and they should fight in separate
Places." Montgomery asked awkwardly,
"Then how do we deal with the Sixth SS
625 Panzer Army, which is now strengthening
The Germans' lines according to reports?"
Bradley said confidently, "Those Panzers
Are to plug holes, gaps that will be made when
Hodges and Patton attack the Ruhr and
630 Saar. Patton's new drive will start December
Nineteen." Montgomery said, "So although
The present plan has failed, we must believe
It has not failed and stick with it?" Bradley
Said, "The present plan has not failed," and beamed
635 To himself, having won a tournament.
Eisenhower sat back, content with SHAEF's plan.

Hitler needed bad weather – overcast
Skies and mists – to give his tanks cover that
The Luftwaffe could not. Divisions moved
640 By rail, as did artillery shells and
Ammunition, tanks and guns. One thousand
Five hundred trains unloaded secretly
A quarter of a million men and seven
Hundred tanks four miles from the enemy,
645 All camouflaged. Hitler came from Berlin
To Ziegenberg castle sixty miles east
Of the brimming Rhine near Bad Nauheim, his
Headquarters in the west, the Adlerhorst
Or Eagle's Nest, deceptive title for
650 It was no high eyrie in a shaman's
Sky World but underground near dead spirits,
A group of drab rooms in the underworld
Close to Satan's nether chthonic kingdom,
Deep concrete bunkers in the Taunus hills.
655 Rundstedt's and Model's headquarters were near.
Here Hitler summoned his commanders who
Were stripped of arms and briefcases and led
Between two rows of SS troops into
A deep bunker where Hitler stood, pale, sick,
660 Before a map. They sat at the table.
SS guards stood behind them, menacing
As all stood arms out and swore on their lives

225

To keep secret what they were now to hear,
Bound by the oath of the Teutonic Knights,
665 The Fahneneid, to serve him to the death,
To break which oath violated the Fehme.
Hitler spoke, their Commander by the map:
"These are the details of Operation
Wacht am Rhein. On December the sixteenth
670 At O5.30 three powerful armies
Under the command of Model will launch
An attack to break through the Ardennes front
From Monschau in the north to Echternach
In the south. The Sixth Panzer Army will
675 Strike first in the north under Sepp Dietrich,
From Monschau to the Losheim Gap across
Elsenborn hills, and thence across the Meuse
To Antwerp. The Fifth Panzer Army in
The centre, under Manteuffel, will strike
680 The Schnee Eifel and St. Vith, at Eifel
And Luxembourg. The Seventh Army in
The south, under Brandenberger, will seize
The Vianden-Echternach area
And protect Manteuffel's left. Von der Heydte's
685 Paratroops will drop on Baraque Michel
And block reinforcements from the north, and
Skorzeny's English-speaking commandos,
Disguised as Americans, will then seize
The bridges at Huy and Amay, and sow
690 Confusion. Our objectives are the Meuse
Bridges and Antwerp, the large port which feeds
The Allies. The offensive will decide
Our fate, determine if we live or die.
If it succeeds, victory is the Generals';
695 If it fails, I alone am blameworthy.
I want all my troops to fight hard, without
Pity. The battle must be fought with great
Brutality, and all resistance must
Be broken by a wave of terror. Know
700 The enemy must be broken now, or
Never! So will our Germany survive."
Hitler spoke for nearly two hours, full of
Mistrust for his Generals. Then wrinkled
Rundstedt, recalling his oath, spoke: "We are
705 Staking all on our last throw. We can't fail."

Like a monastic monk shuffling in cell,

Later, alone in his private room in
The depths of the bunker deep underground,
Hitler lit candles and, as Eckart taught,
710 Invoked the "good" Lucifer to his aid,
Summoned the "equal" of Jehovah's power,
Of "evil" Adonai Christians revere.
Tell, Muse, how he could think Lucifer good
And believe with the Priory of Sion
715 And the Templars (who were influenced from
Iran during the Crusades) that Satan
Is a "spiritual" god of good battling
With a material god of evil,
And worship Lucifer and not Jesus.
720 Satan appears in one of his three forms.
Just as God is three in the Trinity –
Father, the source of all creative power,
Who is perceived both as force and Yahweh,
Jehovah, later known as Adonai;
725 Son, the suffering Christ, illumined soul,
God's shining embodiment in the world,
Incarnation of Light and perfect will,
The King of Heaven in a crown of thorns;
And Holy Ghost or Spirit, Divine Light,
730 The Providential power of all goodness –
And is source, Light and lit soul (or, the One,
Life-bringing power and manifestation),
And God is present in Christ through the Light;
So Satan, three-headed as in Dante
735 ("Three-headed Beelzebub", form of Baal),
Was, in counterbalancing symmetry,
A Trinity of dark and evil power –
Father, the source of evil energy,
Naked force of darkness and Ahriman,
740 Also known as Baal, the evil Satan,
Lord of the Underworld and King of Hell,
Spirit of Evil, Creator of Crime;
Son, the darkness in the soul and the world,
The Devil posing as benevolent,
745 As Lucifer, deceptive power of
Evil, which persuades men that it is good,
Teaches that all men can become a god
And recreate their own morality,
Power that asserts that it is really God,
750 Not evil Adonai or Jehovah
Who makes man subservient to his will,

Deceiving flush that took Hitler beyond
All good and evil to a godlike state,
Lucifer, who seems to set a value
On illumination (his hate) as if
He favoured his followers according
To the level of their openness to
The mystic Light of God's glory, so that
Satan can steal the souls of all good men
Who are not wary, and control the world;
And the dark Power of the Antichrist,
The current of evil that can possess
A soul open to it, like Hitler's soul,
That thinks it sleepwalks to a divine will,
The power of disharmony and conflict.
Satan admits he is evil but as
His mask Lucifer, he pretends to be
Good, an Angel who never really fell.
With lies, deception, boasting and false claims,
Lucifer pretends he is really God,
The equal of Adonai, God of Light
And Good, not god of Darkness and Evil.
Satan appeared in his deceptive form
As a beautiful antlered Beast-man with
A stag's head, surrounded by his elite,
Attendant demons, as in the horn dance
Which Morris dancers sedately trot in
Abbots Bromley, or each June in Thaxted
Near whose churchyard and silent crowd a lone
Violinist plays, raising dead spirits
For Cernunnos, Lord of the Underworld,
A presence in his absence, a dark shape
Descended from phallic Dionysos,
The horned one hiding under stag's antlers,
The Antichrist who would destroy the world.
In dread silence six priests process and show
Six sets of antlers, a hermaphrodite
And fool follow, a horseman and archer –
Herne the Hunter doomed to hunt for ever
After meeting a stranger (the Devil),
To ride at night in Windsor Great Park in
Phantom imitation of Cernunnos;
Attendants on their pagan god, they dance
The mysteries of the Devil's magic power,
The Devil's Dance returns to the churchyard
To claim the spirits of the restless dead

228

And take them down into the underworld
While, uncomprehending, the throng applaud.
So Satan, the Devil, Lucifer and
800 All his manifestations in each race
And culture, stood with his attendants, who,
Demons, carried antlers in his train, just
As an Archbishop's priests carry candles.
Impressed, awestruck, mighty Hitler bowed down
805 Before the temporal power of Antichrist,
The horned image of "good god" Lucifer
Who opposed the "bad god" Adonai or
Jehovah, mere equal in power to him,
Dualistic Manichaean-Cathar
810 Opponent in an eternal struggle.

The arch-deceiver had disguised himself
As one of Nature's gentle creatures so
It would seem natural for Hitler to ask
The question he knew Hitler wished to put.
815 "Hitler," he said, "you know I am with you
And oppose the impostor Jehovah
And his evil deceptions. You know I
Have many forms, and though I may appear
(To show just one of the faces I wear,
820 For all power is mine, I am Protean)
Celtic – from the La Tène culture which you
Know covered ancient Germany some two
Thousand five hundred years ago – as one
Of my incarnations, Cernunnos, who
825 Is identified with Esus, whose name
Was plagiarised by the deceptive man,
Mere man, the Christians worship, I also
Am Odin in the Nordic culture and
Now stand at the entrance to Valhalla,
830 The hall of heroes lined with shields that you
Have venerated, naming headquarters
After the sacred beasts that adorn them,
The eagle and the wolf. You honour me
As Lord of the Underworld – your bunkers
835 Are shrines to me – but, most of all, prefer
Me to oppose Jehovah, the Jews' god."
Hitler breathed: "It's true. I knew at once it
Was you. I relate to you in the form
Eckart taught me to follow: Lucifer,
840 Scourge of Jehovah, unequal partner,

229

The evil god whose power you exceed.
Not long ago I begged you to scatter
The Allies at Falaise, pledged you my soul.
You said events would further your Empire.
845 I understand, *I* judge by *my* Empire.
Now that I am poised in the Ardennes, I
Again invoke the pact I made with you.
You know I am about to strike a blow
At Christians who have streamed across Europe.
850 I need a week of bad weather: fogs, mists,
Low cloud so that the Allies' planes cannot
Have air superiority. Please send
Me weather that will cloak my purpose and
Disguise my aim, help me achieve surprise."
855 Wanting to believe that the Falaise rout
Was a blessing in disguise that had lured
The Allies into his Ardennes trap, where
He could surround them, cripple them and end
The war, he trusted his pact, not seeing
860 That Satan only gives enough to keep
His victims' hopes up; not knowing Satan
Has less power than he claims, and that though he
Can create misty weather from the murk
In his energies – can form conditions
865 For hiding and dissembling – he cannot
Create the conditions of openness,
Not clear weather, bright sun and cloudless skies.
Satan, as Lucifer, inclined his stag's
Head, his aura shimmering with false light,
870 In a gracious, dignified, noble nod.
Dazzled, deceived, self-deceiving Hitler
Knew his request had been granted. A haze
Rose from the stag, a cloud now filled the room,
A mist, a fog that enveloped the group,
875 A fetid murk that had slowly risen
From the crannies and crevices of his
Foul, outwardly beautiful shape, and when
It cleared, snuffing the candles, Hitler stood
Alone, smirking, but wondering if he dreamt.

880 In the thick snow-white woods of the Ardennes
Men huddled in foxholes, distant salvos
Barely disturbed the thin Allied front line.
After the setback at Arnhem, in which
Montgomery's single thrust near wiped out

230

1st British Airborne, Eisenhower, convinced
Of the need for a broad front, now placed three
Army groups on the German border: in
The north, brave Montgomery's 21st
Army Group to capture Antwerp; in the
Centre, Bradley's 12th Army Group, US
First and Third Armies; in the south, Devers'
6th Army Group. After the battles at
Aachen, the Hürtgen Forest and Lorraine
The Allies had suffered huge losses in
Cruel static war on the German border
Like the battles of the First World War: one
Hundred and thirty thousand casualties
Since September in US First, Third and
Ninth Armies, and many losses of troops
Fatigued and suffering from disease or
Exposure. There were no replacements and
Bradley spread troops in a thin line across
Belgium and Luxembourg, where the terrain
Was not suited to winter war. There were
Thrusts at the Ruhr and Saar, but the Ardennes
Was only lightly defended, and quiet:
A foggy still in peaceful, sleepy woods.
As sheared sheep in a white field at dusk baaa
To each other as the evening shadows
Creep longer, and, fleeces snow-white, shiver
At the impending night and chew long grass
That pokes through a late fall of frozen snow,
So wrapped troops in the field bent over holes
And called to each other, to keep up their
Spirits as they dug new foxholes and looked
Through the twilight at the bleak snow-white sky
And wondered how they would keep warm till dawn.

In the last hours before the offensive
Hitler urged Model to control Dietrich,
The Bavarian butcher's son who was
His chauffeur-bodyguard in the street days,
Commander of his praetorian guard,
Chief executioner on the Night of
Long Knives, and when six Germans died, butcher
Of four thousand Russians at Taganrog.
Of his trusted commander Hitler spoke:
"He must bypass Liège and not wheel north
Too early, and a great victory is

885

890

895

900

905

910

915

920

925

Assured." German soldiers advanced through mud
930 And snow, not realising why they were
In their positions. When they were told, they
Were full of enthusiasm. Morale
Rose. Rundstedt sent them a message from his
Bunker near Ziegenberg castle: "Soldiers
935 Of the western front! Your great hour has come.
Large armies are attacking the Anglo-
Americans. We gamble everything!
Achieve things beyond possibility
For our Fatherland and our brave Führer.".

940 In murky pre-dawn fog and darkness, shells
And rockets roared down round American
Positions along an eighty-five mile
Front. Gun barrels thundered, the sky flared and
Vibrated, hailing steel, and then burned red
945 As farm buildings went up in flames and smoke.
Above buzz-bombs droned up towards Liège
As Dietrich's troops advanced in what they called
Offensive Von Rundstedt. The Americans
Reeled. The opening barrage took place on
950 The slopes of the Elsenborn ridge, round the
Gloomy pine forest before Rocherath
And Krinkelt, and overcame all but one
American platoon, which held out though
Three hundred men were lost. The Americans
955 Were taken by surprise. The Germans were
Repulsed nearby with machine-gun, mortar
And artillery fire; by traffic jams,
By mines and blown bridges. But Joachim
Peiper, commander of the Panzer thrust,
960 Holder of the Knight's Cross of the Iron Cross
For bravery, was ruthless. He had burned
The Soviet village Pekartschina to
The ground to help an advance, and had killed
Two thousand five hundred Russians in one
965 Savage tank battle on the eastern front
And had taken only three prisoners.
Scorning superiors, he led the charge
Against the Losheim Gap. Hungry and cold
In freezing snow, the Americans stood firm,
970 But the Germans attacked their positions,
Battered and pounded them. Half a mile south
Of Wirtzfeld Lieutenant McDermott fired

Tank destroyers at the first of Peiper's
Tanks to cross the ridge, halting them. Dismayed
975 At the billowing smoke, Peiper gave up
His northern thrust at Wirtzfeld and headed
For the Meuse, ending the most dangerous
German threat to Elsenborn from the south.
His platoon had turned back a vast army,
980 A decisive feat which earned McDermott
A glorious Silver Star. Twenty-five miles
South, wearing a long leather coat, saying,
"Our Fatherland is encircled, and our
Comrades fighting at the front now expect
985 Each one of us to perform his duty,"
Slim, small, elegant and noble Prussian,
Master of the rapid armoured attack,
Von Manteuffel attacked across the Our
Before dawn with a short bombardment and
990 Searchlights that bounced off the clouds. In lit fog
Assault troops infiltrated quietly,
And shells burst on Hosingen's long ridge road.
An assault force of Panzer tanks rolled up,
But the Americans held the town till dark.
995 Panzers attacked Marnach, then by-passed it.
Bridges were built at Gemünd and Dasburg.
Now from Clervaux Colonel Fuller ordered
Road-blocks, and held all but three positions
Till nightfall. Brandenberger's thrust had not
1000 Broken through the line from Vianden to
Echternach.
                    The Germans only broke through
In one place: the seven-mile wide Losheim
Gap, through which the Germans had invaded
1005 In eighteen seventy, nineteen fourteen
And nineteen forty and which was held by
Nine hundred US troops with poor command,
Spread out in sparsely wooded rolling hills.
After the bombardment the Germans sent
1010 Infantry to clear the way for Panzers.
Surprised, the Americans defended
But were swamped by sheer numbers, and by noon
The Germans had attacked every village
In the Gap. The Americans began
1015 To retreat with columns of vehicles.
German tanks rolled through the Gap, and more came
South of the Schnee Eifel; a convoy reached

Born by nightfall, where they were only four
Miles from St. Vith. A German link-up would
1020 Surround two American regiments
On high ground. In St. Vith Major-General
Jones asked General Middleton, who was based
In the safety of Bastogne, if he could
Withdraw. Permission was refused. They spoke
1025 Again that night on an open line, and,
Speaking in code lest Germans overheard,
Misunderstood each other: Middleton's
Command to withdraw from the Schnee Eifel
Was interpreted by Jones as "stay put".
1030 Ahead was the largest American
Surrender in the entire Second World War.

Just as in medieval times high up
Above the roofs a sharp-eyed watchman stood
In Forbach's single crenellated tower
1035 And looked for enemies, or fires, across
The town in the heart of Alsace-Lorraine
(Which France and Germany long disputed
And was twice French, German and French again),
Above the bells of the church which strikes each
1040 Quarter of an hour, and if he saw smoke
Sounded a bugle to alert the folk
Who, as they went about each day's business,
Saw from afar the tower above a hill
Of thickly wooded trees, rising above
1045 Each dale and valley of that Lorraine town,
So Christ sat in a watchtower high above
The wooded hills and valleys of the earth,
Like a shepherd watching over his sheep
Above the little life of small mankind,
1050 And if he saw smoke, raised the alarm with
The droves of angels who camped near, guarding
Each man from danger as if their own son;
But, aghast at so many puffs of smoke,
The general fighting in the streets below,
1055 The carnage in the towns of old Europe,
Felt it was futile to sound his warning,
To blow his bugle at heedless mankind.

Along eight routes the Panzers pushed towards
The Meuse, and, their communications knocked
1060 Out, the front-line Americans did not

234

Know what was happening, except in their
Immediate sector. Their commanders
Saw fragments. Hodges thought the offensive
A spoiling attack in reaction to
1065 His thrust at the Ruhr dams, and, having rung
Bradley's HQ in Luxembourg at eight
And secured Bradley's agreement as he
Left to meet Eisenhower, sent 9th Armoured
Division to Bastogne, where Middleton,
1070 Hearing booming twenty miles to the east,
Watching red flashes light the eastern sky,
Seeing truly, ordered his troops to stand
Firm. Bradley did not divert troops from his
Impending attacks. Montgomery heard
1075 From Williams as he played golf with Dai Rees
("Sir, the Germans have attacked Hodges' First
Army in the Ardennes, in force") and said:
"This is no ordinary move. LOs
Must scout." And he flew back to Zonhoven
1080 And told Henderson: "Send a signal to
Eisenhower's deputy Chief of Staff that
We have no reserves to block enemy
Penetration, we have no plan, that our
Attacks are unco-ordinated, that
1085 The Supreme Commander's last directive
Was on the twenty-eighth of October,
Eight weeks ago. Unless he now makes up
His mind and issues orders we will drift
Into difficulties with the Germans."
1090 Eisenhower heard at SHAEF's headquarters in
The Hotel Trianon at Versailles where
(Having attended a staff wedding for
Sgt Mickey McKeogh, one of his
"Family", and Pearlie, with Butcher as
1095 Best man, sitting in a pew in the stone
Chapel of Louis the Fourteenth, wearing
Battledress blouse, shivering next to Kay
And having held a champagne reception
For bride and groom at his Saint-Germain house)
1100 He was about to celebrate his fifth
Star, his promotion by the Senate to
General of the Army, equal in rank
To Marshall, MacArthur, Montgomery.
After lunch at the Ritz Bradley arrived
1105 To complain casualties were not being

Replaced by reserves due to the general
Offensive.
                    Eisenhower ducked out into
The War Room. While they talked Hodges rang Strong
1110   And said: "It's more than a spoiling attack.
A captured German document signed by
Von Rundstedt speaks of a pincer attack
Near Aachen, on which depends the future
Of the German nation. They have achieved
1115   Complete surprise and now outnumber us."
Bradley said, "It is a spoiler to draw
Patton's forces from the Saar offensive."
Strong said, "There's German radio silence,"
And Eisenhower immediately sensed
1120   It was bigger than that. "That's no spoiling
Attack," he said intuitively, "for
The Ardennes's not a worthwhile objective,
Nor is Aachen. They must be after some
Strategic gain. It's no counter-attack
1125   But a counter-offensive. I think you'd
Better send Middleton some help." With Strong
He studied the map and noticed that 7th
And 10th Armoured Divisions were out of
The line, and told Bradley to send them to
1130   Middleton. Bradley hesitated, not
Wanting to upset Hodges and Patton.
Eisenhower impatiently said, "They must
Be sent. A new assessment should be made
Tomorrow morning." He and Bradley played
1135   Five rubbers of bridge with Everett Hughes
And Bedell Smith, watched by Kay and Hansen
(Till he joined Hemingway at the Lido).
While he played cards like Louis the Sixteenth
Or like Drake playing bowls while the Spanish
1140   Armada gathered off shore, Eisenhower
Blamed himself for not reading Hitler's mind,
For not realising he was desperate
And would take a huge risk. His own general
Offensive had weakened Middleton's line.
1145   Deciphered Japanese radio traffic
Said Hitler told Japan's Ambassador
In September he would "open a large
Scale offensive in the west soon after
The beginning of November" – and now,
1150   Seeking to understand the German plan,

Wise Eisenhower had perceived the scale of
The offensive and by sending reserves,
The 7th and 10th Armoured Divisions
To St. Vith and Luxembourg to assist
1155   The hard-pressed Middleton, had got it right.

Euphoric and alert, lively, Hitler
Had stayed awake, his left hand trembling. He
Asked Burgdorf, "The Allies?" Burgdorf replied:
"Taken totally by surprise. Before
1160   Dawn an artillery bombardment rained
Down on the American line so fast
It seemed it hailed mortars and shells. Then tanks
Loomed out of mist over forty miles and
The American First and Ninth Armies
1165   Were driven back." "It's Providence!" Hitler
Cried. He rose at eleven. His daily
Conference was mid-afternoon. He was
Waiting in the room, delighted as if
The battle was as good as won. He took
1170   His dog Blondi for a walk. At five he
Had a nap and then talked and drank tea till
The small hours, exhausting his officers
With hopeful interpretations. Doctor
Morell injected glucose, vitamins
1175   And iron. Rundstedt told Hitler that though
He had achieved total surprise, breakthrough
Had not happened. Hitler brushed aside doubts,
Counting on three days' delay while Allied
Commanders in the field cleared troop movements
1180   With their political leaders back home,
And expecting that German divisions
Would block the Allied movements when they came:
"Everything has changed in the west. Success,
Complete success is now within our grasp!"
1185   Fired up, Hitler talked on with bent back, ash-
White moustache, pale skin and twitching left arm
Which his right hand restrained, and studied maps
Till 4 a.m. Then he drank up his tea
And, satisfied, settled into his bed.

1190   All night Manteuffel's troops infiltrated
Between American positions and
Attacked and overran artillery.
At dawn Panzer tanks attacked the river

Clerf crossings at Clervaux to wrest the town
1195 From barring Americans, while Fuller's
Infantry and light tanks attacked Marnach.
Eleven tanks were hit by guns, but they
Attacked again to hold part of Marnach,
And then retreat. By noon the Fifth Panzer
1200 Army surrounded Hosingen, and now
Panzer Lehr joined the attack against just
Five American tanks. The battle raged
Till evening, when all houses on the ridge
Lay in ruins, and only the baroque
1205 Altar of the church still stood in the quiet
As the defenders were taken prisoner.
Round Clervaux from the heights came German tanks.
Under orders to hold it at all costs
Fuller withdrew into the old castle
1210 In the centre of the walled, wooded well.
Here they held out till at noon the next day
A German tank drove down the wooden doors
And forced the defenders to surrender.
The Americans had held off the advance
1215 Of the Germans towards Bastogne, but the
Hundred and Tenth infantry was wiped out
In keeping Bastogne distant from the war.

That dawn the Germans resumed their attack,
Seeking to break the American front
1220 From Monschau to Losheimergraben. There
In the dense woods near Monschau, a dead end
Town hollowed out of wooded hills above
Houses, château and river, to the south
Infantry pressed, to the north grenadiers
1225 Fought at dawn for high ground near Mützenich
And breached the American defences
Both south and north till artillery fire
Retrieved the Americans' position.
Hodges gave Gerow permission to fight.
1230 Gerow urged Robertson to pull his men
Out of the Heartbreak Crossroads trap and face
The enemy at Rocherath-Krinkelt
And Wirtzfeld. Major-General Robertson
Defended these villages, ignoring
1235 Hodges' order to attack the Ruhr dams.
There was a bitter house-to-house battle.
As waves of screaming German infantry

Stormed the tree-covered rise, firing non-stop,
And were answered by volleys that felled some
1240   Who lay groaning beneath the small-arms fire,
And still advanced beside five Tiger tanks
Which pounded the Americans' foxholes
And knocked out bazookas; out of bullets
The American line broke in panic
1245   But then held when the Germans redeployed
Through the Losheim Gap, and some now pulled back
To Elsenborn ridge. St. Vith was full of
Confusion. No one there knew what German
Forces now lurked east of the Schnee Eifel.
1250   Through the first day Skorzeny's Trojan Horse
Panzer brigade was stuck in traffic jams
And lost surprise. Now they drove by, jaunty
In captured US jeeps, and spread alarm
And rumours of retreat. Many wounded
1255   Lay in the snow, their fate linked to the mood
Of their captors, who, if angry or tired,
Shot them for revenge or convenience.
Robertson urged his men to block Dietrich's
Panzer drive west, which with valour they did.

1260   Model at his divisional command
Post prodded his troops and tried to unblock
A huge traffic jam on the Schönberg road.
Peiper had progressed through the traffic jams
To the Losheim Gap, and that same dawn he
1265   Made his own breakthrough with his SS men,
Spearheading and creating chaos in
The American rear as vehicles with
Black-out lights retreated; followed behind
A column and took Büllingen fuel dump.
1270   There he could have cut off thirty thousand
Americans on Elsenborn ridge, but
Instead he ruthlessly spread terror as
Hitler had requested, and shot prisoners,
First at Büllingen, then near the Belgian
1275   Village Malmédy, where he encountered
At the Baugnez crossroads a small convoy
Of American trucks with his long line
Of large German tanks, which opened fire in
Falling snow and forced a surrender. As
1280   The Americans crawled from under their trucks,
Hands up, a German tank commander called

Out, "First SS Panzers welcome you to
Belgium." They were herded into a snow-
White field near the Café Bodarwe. From
1285   A half-track Peiper called, "It's a long way
To Tipperary, boys." He passed by, his
Column fifteen miles long. SS soldiers
Looted watches and rings, and a captain
Who protested was shot. Then the SS
1290   Shouted "Macht alle kaputt", "Kill them all",
And tank machine-guns raked the huddled throng,
And as the wounded, lying in the snow,
Moaned in pain, SS men approached and shot
Each in the head, laughing, under orders
1295   That stemmed from ruthless Hitler's request for
"A wave of terror and fright", to take no
Prisoners. There were more frenzied bursts of
Killing. Then a few survivors stood and
Ran to the Café. The Germans burned it
1300   And shot the Americans as they came
Out of the flames. A few more reached the woods,
And brought news of the massacre – war crime –
Back to American lines, and the world
Mourned eighty-five unarmed US soldiers,
1305   Their bodies left strewn in a field to show
The enemy the tough foe that they faced.
So the SS fed Wotan, or Odin,
God of war who ruled the Realm of the Dead.

Tiptoeing like a latecomer in church,
1310   Eisenhower left his car outside Versailles
And quietly stood near bare trees and some pines
With pine-cones on the ground. By the hedge were
Shepherd's purse, groundsel and chickweed, and gorse
Was in heady bloom. A wood-pigeon cooed
1315   And on high a buzzard wheeled in blue sky.
He wandered past red clover and holly,
And among hedge-sparrows he saw a wren.
A black beetle trailed in the dust, and on
A nearby oak was mistletoe, caused by
1320   A missel-thrush rubbing berries on bark
And leaving the seed on bacteria.
A squirrel scampered from its drey. Nearby
From a gushing stream he heard the "twit twit"
Of a dipper, and in early twilight.
1325   Saw an owl glide like a bomber, and heard

240

Its "hoo, hoo-hoo-hoo-hoo-oo-oo" and the female
Answer "kee-wick, kee-wick", and turned away,
His eyes misting with tears at what should be.

Peiper pressed westwards on towards the Meuse,
1330 Spraying gunfire and terror as he went.
Hodges was shocked to learn the Germans were
At Malmédy, and within reach of his
Army headquarters and the supply dump
At Liège. With Eisenhower's agreement
1335 He sent troops from north of the white Ardennes
To block the roads before thrusting Peiper,
Who was now heading for the Stavelot bridge.
Some engineers blocked their way in the dark,
And after a skirmish – some rifle shots
1340 And bazooka fire – Peiper's leading tanks
Withdrew and his column halted along
Twenty-five miles of muddy roads, his men
Fatigued, for the night, enabling Hodges
To bring troops from the north to block his way.

1345 Next morning Peiper resumed his advance,
Prowled like a hungry lion that's scented prey,
And crossed the Stavelot bridge when commandos
Cut the demolition wires and headed
For the Trois Ponts river crossing. But now
1350 Engineers blew up two bridges and he
Turned north towards La Gleize, captured a bridge,
But was attacked by fighter-bombers and
Took cover, then, finding the way west blocked,
Withdrew for the night into La Gleize and
1355 Stoumont, his rearward radio contact gone.

Now Satan stood at his saluting base
In a great open field like the flat space
Outside Nuremberg, before a billion
Demons who buzzed like excited hornets.
1360 He looked handsome, seductively sincere.
Now like a baby-faced, gentle pop star,
Quietly spoken with an innocent air,
Shown on video as a huge statue,
A god millions adore, himself; now like
1365 A baby-faced, smiling party leader
With earnest eyes, unfurrowed brow and fixed
Smile on his lips which tell deceiving lies;

Satan stood before the throng, full of youth,
Appealing with false truth to the demons.
1370   "Angels," he said, "dark powers, you who are now
Already gods through knowledge and your search,
Know we have inflicted great defeats on
The enemy, the treacherous Allies
And perfidious Christ. First, we saved our
1375   Ally Hitler from assassination
By a rebel Army officer's bomb
Primed by an agent-spy of dangerous Christ.
Then we lured the Allies into our trap,
Appeared to be surrounded and poured out
1380   And drew the unsuspecting enemies
Across the Seine, so, overconfident,
As a result, when our Hitler launched his
New weapons, undefeatable V-2
Rockets that are soundless, they went too far
1385   And we have annihilated them. Our
Pretended retreat at Falaise lured them
Into a great defeat at Arnhem. And
That is not all. Hitler has made a pact
With us to deliver via death the entire
1390   Jewish race to our kingdom here, and to
The Citadel of Lies, so Jehovah,
Christ's God, will have no Jewish soul on earth
To worship him, and what is left of man
Will worship me as their God. He has stepped
1395   Up his transports of Jews, and many from
Hungary have been sent to excellent Death,
And each day Jehovah's power is crumbling,
His influence on earth a little less.
And that's not all, with brilliant deception,
1400   Pretending to defend to attack, our
Own Hitler has struck a surprise blow at
The Allies that has panicked Christ, who is
Rushing about trying to stop a huge
German offensive that outnumbers all
1405   The Allies' defensive forces. Angels,
We are advancing, victory is assured.
And while Hitler advances, so should we.
Heaven is distracted, just as I planned,
And it is now time for us to invade,
1410   Take them by surprise. We support Hitler
As long as he gives us victories over
Our enemies and as long as he makes

Progress towards an atomic bomb, which,
Used, can return earth to chaos. I have
1415 Already lined up Stalin, and as I
Forecast, he is set to join us. As soon
As the outcome of Hitler's offensive
Through the Ardennes is known, I'll implement
Our switch to Stalin to detach one of
1420 The three Allies and sow confusion, to
Deceive the Allied headquarters of SHAEF.
I have already planned to magnify
The disagreements between Eisenhower
And vain Montgomery, and the Allied
1425 Command crisis which Hitler's thrust will cause.
Angels, the great need now is to convert
All humankind to our cause, to exhort
And encourage both our moderates and
Our extremists, our far Left: moderate
1430 Luciferians, who believe they are
Doing good, and extremist Satanists
Who know they are doing evil. Evil,
Angels, is what we seek to bring about,
The triumph of evil's darkness across
1435 The earth and therefore the universe, as
The earth is its only inhabited
Corner. Then I will be Overlord, Lord
Of the Universe. Not for us the way
Of Christ and obedience to a God we've
1440 Never seen. Ours is the way of knowledge,
Of rational inquiry and occult power.
We experience everything, discover
Ourselves, and, through our self-transformation,
We become gods. Gods! I say to you, by
1445 Developing through the knowledge of good
And evil, and doing my will whether
You think you're doing good or know you are
Doing evil, you have, thanks to my help,
Acquired the power of God, each of you has
1450 Become a god! You are gods! That is my
Message. Not slaves. Gods, whose power equals God's.
To be a god is not to see the Light,
As Christ, God's paid agent, wrongly preaches.
To be a god is to know the darkness
1455 And to use its power; for out of darkness
Came Light. Darkness makes all things possible.
Gods! Recognise yourselves for what you are!

Dark gods, prepare now to swarm and storm Heaven,
Following our Hitler's example in
1460   The Ardennes! Heaven is rightfully yours, as
Antwerp is rightfully Hitler's. Dark gods,
Mobilise now to re-enter Heaven."
There was a tremendous buzzing and all
The creatures of Hell rose on their hind legs
1465   And gave Satan a standing ovation
With one accord for telling them they were
Not loathsome insects but divine gods with
A chance – a right – of entering Heaven by force.

In the Adlerhorst bunker, the German
1470   High command drafted their evening report.
Rundstedt, noting Peiper's westward progress,
Called for Wacht am Rhein to end so gains could
Be defended: "We have not made the most
Of our initial surprise. The offensive
1475   Has never gathered speed due to icy
Roads and pockets of resistance, which have
Forced us to resort to full-scale attacks."
Model telephoned Rundstedt and Jodl
And said the offensive had failed. Dietrich's
1480   Army had been rebuffed in the north while
Manteuffel's army in the south was slow.
Rundstedt read his report to grim Hitler,
Who rebuked both Rundstedt and Model for
Being pessimistic: "We must cut off
1485   The rear of the Americans fighting
On both sides of the attack, near Krinkelt
And Echternach, so that they lose supply
Lines and capitulate." But Hitler's will
Could not influence the fuel shortages
1490   On the cold Ardennes battlefield. Next day
The Americans recaptured Stavelot,
Cutting off Peiper from the German lines
And his supplies. They surrounded Peiper.
A few days later, he withdrew on foot
1495   Back to the German force with his unit.
He had failed to carry out Hitler's plan.

Eisenhower, who had been the first to see
The scale of the counter-offensive, saw
That, though taken by surprise and suffering
1500   Painful losses, the Allies could profit.

He held a SHAEF conference with Smith, Whiteley
And Strong, and grasped the German intention
Was to cross the Meuse, splitting Twenty-first
And Twelfth Army Groups, and capture the huge
1505 Allied supply depots at Liège, which
Could refuel tanks for a drive on Antwerp.
As they studied the maps, unaware that
His hand was moved by Christ, Whiteley put his
Finger on Bastogne and said, "These crossroads
1510 Are the key to the battle." Eisenhower
Said: "We'll base our reserves there. For a start
Send 10th Airborne at once. We need some more
To counter-attack the German right flank."

Just as a wheel's hub is the focal point
1515 For the spokes of a seven-spoked cartwheel,
So Bastogne was the hub of seven roads.
Wanting it, the OKW asked
The 26th Volksgrenadiers to seize
The two river crossings at Our and Clerf
1520 For Panzer tanks and then head for Bastogne,
Which the Americans feared must soon fall.
Panic spread through the local populace.
At dawn into Bastogne streamed refugees
From Luxembourg who said the Germans were
1525 Burning villages, and routed troops who
Swore Nazi tanks were approaching the town.
The first shell exploded that afternoon.
Hodges had reinforced the tired VIII Corps,
With which Middleton held the Losheim Gap,
1530 And Eisenhower had sent his last reserves,
The Eighty-Second and Hundred and First
Airborne divisions, the battle-hardened
Veterans of D-Day and Arnhem, All
Americans and Screaming Eagles who
1535 Fought daringly, to block German breakthrough
At Werbomont and hold the Bastogne roads;
Middleton sent his reserve armour, just
Seventeen Sherman tanks and infantry,
To set up two road-blocks on the road from
1540 Clervaux to Bastogne. Sixteen Panzer tanks
Approached, firing, and one roadblock's Shermans
Withdrew, to be ambushed. Panthers attacked
The other roadblock with new infra-red
Night-sights and destroyed Shermans, killing their

1545 Commander. Now Second Panzers could probe
Bastogne unopposed, but near Longvilly
Colonel Lauchert turned north towards the Meuse,
By-passing Bastogne. Panzer Lehr was just
Six miles from Bastogne, but, facing a choice
1550 Of main road with road-blocks or a side road,
On wrong information from a farmer
He led his tanks down a muddy cart path,
And three miles on hearing Americans
Had just passed through, halted for the night, and,
1555 Erring on caution's side, laid a minefield.
German blunders preserved Bastogne until
Colonel Roberts arrived from Eisenhower
With armour to help Middleton, who spoke:
"I am mighty glad to see you right now.
1560 I want you to block three roads leading to
This town." Roberts spoke: "That's no way to use
Armour." Middleton spoke: "Robbie, I may
Not know as much about the employment
Of armour as you, but that's how I must
1565 Use it. Move with the utmost speed, and hold
The positions at all costs." And so two
Groups went east, to Longvilly and Wardin,
And one north-east to Noville. Manteuffel's
Panzers sought to destroy the road-blocks that
1570 Stood between him and Bastogne.
                                                    Brigadier-
General McAuliffe, acting commander
(In the absence of General Taylor in
Washington, his eye on the Pacific)
1575 Of Hundred and First Airborne now arrived,
Unexpected, to confer. He had gone
To see what was happening in Bastogne
On his way to Werbomont, alarmed by
Westward-fleeing traffic. Now Middleton
1580 Told him in front of Roberts: "There has been
A major penetration. Some of my
Units are broken." McAuliffe spoke: "I
Will hold the main road junction with my men."
His expressive, direct and earthy voice
1585 Contradicted his quiet, impassive face.
Four hours later, McAuliffe's deputy,
Colonel Sherburne, en route for Werbomont
Also found the road clogged and detoured to
Bastogne with all Hundred and First units.

1590 So Providence works in its devious way.
Avoiding a clogged road, without a plan,
By "accident" McAuliffe and his men
Found their way "on impulse" to the crisis
Spot and reached Bastogne before Bayerlein.

1595 Next dawn Bayerlein, the commander of
Panzer Lehr, who was Rommel's Chief of Staff
In North Africa, an aggressive man
With a sharp, tough look, advanced on Neffe, east
Of Bastogne, then halted an hour. Hundred
1600 And First Airborne had raced to Bastogne in
Trucks with headlights full on, risking attacks
From the air. McAuliffe conferred again
With Middleton, and sent the first unit
To arrive east, and at Neffe they skirmished
1605 With German tanks, which they thought a roadblock,
And called up howitzers, which now shelled Neffe.
Bayerlein thought it was heavy tank fire
In a counter-attack, and lost his nerve,
Convinced Bastogne could only be taken
1610 By a massive number of Panzer tanks.

Roberts' armour at Longvilly now sought,
Under German anti-tank fire, to flee
Back to Bastogne. One Sherman was ablaze
And two half-tracks ran into it, blocking
1615 The road back to Bastogne. The Longvilly
Roadblock was now destroyed by Luttwitz, who
Fired at the trapped convoy till it burned. He
Told Manteuffel he could capture Bastogne.
Manteuffel told him to continue west
1620 According to the plan, and leave Bastogne
To the infantry, another blunder.
The long column of Longvilly light tanks,
Tank destroyers and armoured cars now lay
Under plumes of black smoke as each vehicle,
1625 Trapped in the queue, was hit. The crews now lined
The ditches, waiting for dark. They had lost
A hundred and seventy-five men and
Thirty-four vehicles, but they had drawn in
A German corps, two Generals and Panzers
1630 From two divisions that should have attacked
Bastogne and not been held up on this road,
And their defeat was victory for Bastogne.

That evening Panzers and their infantry
Clashed with a dozen American trucks
1635 At crossroads near Sprimont, where, under tents
With red crosses, Hundred and First Airborne's
Field hospital stood. The Americans
Fired from the truck turrets but were wiped out.
The vehicles burned and in the flames the red
1640 Crosses were plain to see, but the Germans
Ripped through the tents with machine-gun bursts and
Set them ablaze with tracer shells. Later
In the hospital's charred remains were found
Two dead American parachutists,
1645 Their throats cut by the Germans, who made war
On the sick and wounded without caring.
McAuliffe had lost medical supplies.

St. Vith's road hub was also a target,
And the German planners asked 18th Volks-
1650 Grenadiers to pincer the Schnee Eifel
And take St. Vith, which was undefended.
The 18th was too immobile and slow,
And the Americans counter-attacked
And relieved the defenders on the Schnee
1655 Eifel. American armour arrived
At St. Vith and reinforced the infantry,
Who counter-attacked on the Schnee Eifel
With a tank platoon, and ninety German
Infantry surrendered. But there were no
1660 Supplies for the defenders on the Schnee
Eifel, who were cut off under heavy
Artillery fire which stopped their break-out,
And, not resisting strongly, now gave up.
Seven or eight thousand men surrendered,
1665 With hands in pockets trudged through slush and snow
To Spartan camps, Hitler's prisoners in
The costliest defeat of the war and
After Bataan the greatest surrender
In American history. However,
1670 The Germans had not advanced on St. Vith,
And there were doubts about the success of
The Fifth Army's advance towards the Meuse.

Eisenhower held a conference at Verdun.
He travelled there with Kay, who had become
1675 A WAC in October

And a second lieutenant – Eisenhower
Had pinned on the gold bars in an office
Ceremony – and could no longer drive
Him but now sat beside him in the back.
1680 The Generals met in a cold barracks on
The site of the greatest battle ever
Fought, glumly huddling round an old stove in
Conditions unchanged since the First World War.
It seemed that Peiper had made a breakthrough
1685 And that Germans were pouring through the gap
That was at least thirteen miles wide between
Bastogne and St. Vith. Hiding his concerned
Alarm, Eisenhower spoke first: "Although I
Am very worried about the German
1690 Offensive and have reinforced Bastogne
To hold the line, I now say: the present
Situation is to be regarded
As one of opportunity for us,
Not of disaster. There will only be
1695 Cheerful faces at this conference table."
Boastful, swaggering, yet perceptive, bold,
Patton spoke: "Hell, let's have the guts to let
The sons of bitches go all the way to
Paris. Then we'll really cut 'em up and
1700 Chew 'em up." More cautious, sound Eisenhower
Said: "No, the enemy will never be
Allowed to cross the Meuse. The Germans are
Not going to get away with coming
Out from behind the West Wall line without
1705 Being strongly punished. My plan is: hold
The shoulders of the penetration by
Blocking the Bastogne and St. Vith shoulders
And defending behind the Meuse. This is
First World War textbook doctrine. Hodges can't
1710 Take part – his units have been mauled – and I'm
Tempted to take field command myself. George,
How long would it take you to wheel, to change
The direction of your offensive from
East towards Saar to north towards Bastogne
1715 And counter-attack the German left or
Southern flank? When can you attack?" To which,
Patton replied with cheerful swashbuckling,
With casual nonchalance that seemed flippant,
With ready answer that crowned his career,
1720 Sublime moment that made his deep study

Appear an instant unthought-out response,
"On December the twenty-first, just two
Days' time, with three divisions." Eisenhower
Was annoyed at his casual bravado,
1725 Not knowing Patton had pondered his plan
And pre-arranged coded options with his
Staff. Irritated, contemptuously,
He said: "I doubt if anyone can turn
An army ninety degrees, march through snow
1730 Without full communications and strike
The German flank. There will be a delay
Of twenty-four or forty-eight hours to
Prepare the attack. Cancel your offensive
Towards the Saar, George, change directions and
1735 Counter-attack Bastogne by December
Twenty-third, and I'll have Montgomery
Attack in the north against the German
Right flank. Once this German offensive's been
Blocked Brad's Twelfth Army will mount a single
1740 Offensive to the north." Bradley said, tense:
"That is what Montgomery proposed at
Maastricht and I opposed." Eisenhower said,
"We have to counter-attack, and since then
The situation has changed. All right, George?"
1745 Spoiling for combat, Patton said, "All right,"
Left, and phoned a code to his headquarters,
Triggered the pre-thought-out offensive plan
That would commence on the twenty-second.
Already, by December the nineteenth,
1750 Eisenhower had organised a two-prong
Counter-attack on the German shoulders
That would make the head abruptly recoil
And destroy the Panzers in the Ardennes.

Bradley, warned the previous day he might have
1755 To evacuate his headquarters at
Luxembourg, had retorted: "Never, I
Will never move a headquarters backwards."
Now that evening Hodges sat in his Spa
Headquarters at a table that was laid
1760 For breakfast near a Christmas tree, and talked
About the seriousness of their plight with
His Chief of Staff, General Kean: "Three German
Armies, two of them Panzer armies, are
Approaching us, Panzers are in Stavelot

1765 And heading here, opposed by one roadblock.
It's only a matter of time before
We're overrun. Intelligence wants us
To fly out in the Cub plane that's waiting.
There are four million gallons of petrol
1770 Here, which will fuel the Germans to Antwerp.
We've spoken six times with Bradley today.
We're still not sure if he appreciates
The seriousness of our position. He's
Still talking about Patton's thrust to Saar,
1775 Which has weakened us. Montgomery has
Urged him to cancel that thrust, and so out
Of pride he won't. He wants us to survive
Without weakening Patton. He is not
Interested in coming here. What should
1780 We do?" Kean said, "We've no alternative
But to move HQ." Hodges agreed: "We'll
Burn our secret files and abandon these
Buildings for Chaudfontaine." At 3 a.m.
A German woman saw them leave. They had
1785 Not told anyone of their departure.
That morning Montgomery's Liaison
Officer to Bradley, Tom Bigland, found
The place deserted, breakfast still laid and
The Christmas tree still decorated. It
1790 Was now clear that the Americans had
Completely lost control of the battle.

Montgomery had taken charge on his
Return to Zonhoven. Shaking his head,
He said to Dawnay: "Twenty-eight German
1795 Divisions, and I argued for forty
In my single thrust. I foresaw all this.
I told them so. We are now in danger.
Send three British Divisions – 43rd,
53rd and the Guards Armoured – towards
1800 The Meuse to protect our southern flank and
Signal to General Whiteley at SHAEF that
The Americans are transferring troops
From their northern flank, which will set back by
Months the crossing of the Rhine; and that they
1805 Should draw instead on their southern flank and
Cancel Patton's thrust." After his LO
Found Hodges had evacuated his
Headquarters he telephoned Dempsey: "I

251

Have heard nothing from General Eisenhower,
1810   The Commander-in-Chief in the field, from
Versailles; and Bradley's out of telephone
Communication in Luxembourg. So
I have arranged for you to receive four
Divisions from dawn, to stop the Germans
1815   From crossing the Meuse. My LOs report
No Americans are garrisoning
The Meuse bridges, so under cover of
Darkness I have sent tank patrols fifty
Miles into the American sectors.
1820   I shall tell Mather to find Hodges and
'Order' him to block the Meuse bridges with
Farm-carts. We're ready for Rundstedt, despite
The confusion, lack of information
And faulty command we operate in.
1825   I have told Whiteley at SHAEF, and Brooke, that
I should be in operational charge
Of the northern front. The question is: will
Someone now compel General Eisenhower
To accept, three months too late, what he should
1830   Have accepted at least three months ago?"

Grappling with the German offensive at
SHAEF, Eisenhower was soon urged to accept
That Montgomery should be in charge of
The northern Americans. Alarmed at
1835   Montgomery's reports, Churchill complained
To Brooke in the Cabinet War Room, with
Several lunchtime sherries inside him: "There's
No information coming out of SHAEF.
The War Office, Roosevelt and the Combined
1840   Chiefs of Staff all find the same. The only
Person who knows what is going on is
Monty. I'm using his personal signals
To you to mark this Cabinet map. And
I can see a British counterstroke in
1845   The tradition of my great warrior
Ancestor, Marlborough. I want to order
Monty to hurl Horrocks' 30 Corps at
The Germans." Brooke explained tactfully, "Prime
Minister, only General Eisenhower
1850   Can order Monty, no one in London
Can tell a Field Marshal in the Ardennes
How he should act." Churchill said, "Oh well, what

Can I do to help?" Brooke said, "Telephone
Eisenhower or SHAEF and say the northern
1855   Front should be under the command of one
General: Monty."
                              And so, after his call,
The two British SHAEF Generals Whiteley and
Strong woke up Bedell Smith at SHAEF HQ
1860   At three next morning, and said that German
Forces were round Bastogne and near the Meuse,
And had made it difficult for Bradley
To communicate with Hodges' HQ,
Which had been out of contact for two days.
1865   Strong said: "A report suggests confusion
And disorganisation. We feel that
Monty should now command all troops within
The Allies' northern sector." Bedell Smith
Immediately telephoned Bradley in
1870   Luxembourg: "Sorry to wake you, sir. I
Have Generals Strong and Whiteley here, they say
The Germans are on the Meuse and you've lost
Contact with Hodges. They suggest Monty
Takes over the whole of your front north of
1875   Bastogne. Would you object?" Bradley, annoyed
At being woken, sure Montgomery
Was somehow behind the call, said: "I doubt
The situation's serious enough to
Warrant such a fundamental change of
1880   Command, especially considering
The effect it might have on opinion
In America." Smith then turned on Strong
And Whiteley: "You limey sons of bitches,
You have put me in the position of
1885   Questioning General Bradley's competence,
You're sacked. Because of the view you've taken
Of the situation, neither of you
Can any longer be accepted as
Staff officers to General Eisenhower.
1890   Instructions will be issued relieving
You of your appointments and you will be
Returned to the United Kingdom." But
Next morning Smith went into Eisenhower's
Office with a new report that sixty
1895   German paratroops disguised in Allied
Uniform and led by feared Skorzeny,
The liberator of Mussolini,

253

Were now on their way to kill Eisenhower,
Bradley and other Allied commanders.
1900 Smith said, "Sir, your senior staff members feel
You should stay in your office and not go
Home at all to Saint-Germain." Eisenhower
Asked, "Are you sure it's necessary?" Smith
Said, "Quite sure, you should not go out at all,
1905 No conferences, no visits to any
Generals or to the front." Eisenhower thought.
There was his personal safety, but, much more
Important, the continuity of
Allied command, experienced strategy.
1910 He had a duty not to be killed till
Victory was assured. "Very well," he said.
"I'll remain here in the Trianon. Tell
Kay we're living here now."
                                    Next morning Strong
1915 And Whiteley briefed SHAEF, and Strong ended: "I
Agree with Colonel Lash. The two German
Armoured thrusts may now have joined up, and now
Panzer divisions are being pulled back
From Italy and Russia to assist
1920 The offensive, and they have captured fuel."
Strong said he and Whiteley were going to
See Eisenhower. Smith followed them and said,
"I've been thinking, I'll put your proposal
As my own. I will recommend putting
1925 Montgomery in charge of the north, but
You must keep silent. It's better coming
From an American." Smith went into
Eisenhower's room and said: "I am concerned
At the situation in the Ardennes.
1930 General Strong and General Whiteley report
The Germans are on the Meuse with many
Divisions, two thrusts may have linked up, and
General Bradley's lost contact with Hodges,
Who seems to have left his headquarters. Now,
1935 Montgomery is on the spot. Bearing
In mind you can't go out with paratroops
About, I reluctantly recommend
That he is given command of the northern
Forces, two of Bradley's three armies, First
1940 And Ninth, leaving Brad with Third." Eisenhower,
Astonished, said: "I can't go along with
That. The American press would never

Accept it. It's what Montgomery has
Been pressing for all along and I have
1945   Been refusing. Why, it would look as if
The Americans had to turn to him,
To the British to get them out of this
Crisis." Smith said, "The press don't know just how
Serious the Ardennes situation is.
1950   And there is wartime censorship. And I
Say again, you and General Bradley are
Targets for Skorzeny's assassins. If
Montgomery takes over, they'll switch to
Him." Eisenhower frowned and said, "I'm shocked. I
1955   Need to question Generals Strong and Whiteley
About the latest picture, and these new
Intelligence and operational
Reports." Questioning the two, Eisenhower
Learned of Churchill's concern and swiftly grasped
1960   That the Allied cause required him to take
A course of action he himself opposed
As a sop to British interests. He said
To Smith, "I suppose I will have to go
Along with it. I don't like it, but I've
1965   No alternative." He asked Smith to ring
Bradley, who, on hearing the change, said, "It
Is not necessary." Smith said, "It seems
The logical thing to do. Monty can
Take care of everything north of the Bulge,
1970   And you will have everything south." Bradley
Protested that the change would discredit
The American command. Smith told him
Of the threat from Skorzeny's commando
Paratroops but Bradley was adamant.
1975   Now Eisenhower rang Bradley, who shouted,
"By God, Ike, I can't be responsible
To the American people if you
Do this. I resign." Eisenhower, shocked and
Angry, stood his ground: "Brad, I, not you, am
1980   Responsible to the American
People. Your resignation therefore means
Absolutely nothing." There was a pause.
Bradley still protested. Eisenhower said,
"Well, Brad, those are my orders. Now I want
1985   George to counter-attack in the greatest
Possible strength." Sad to have hurt Bradley,
As if Agamemnon begged Achilles

To leave his tent and turn back the Trojans,
Eisenhower rang Montgomery, who was
1990   In Zonhoven.
                        The line was bad, and cool
Montgomery said: "You're speaking very
Fast and it's difficult to understand
What you're talking about." To Dawnay, he
1995   Said, "I don't know what he's saying, he is
Very excited." Then he grasped the drift:
"It seems we now have two fronts? And I am
To assume command of the northern front?"
He shouted, "I can't hear you properly.
2000   I shall take command straightaway." He put
Down the phone and said to Dawnay, "He's still
Talking wildly about other things. I
Want the largest Union Jack that will go
On the car bonnet and find eight motor-
2005   Cycle outriders." Dawnay quietly said,
"Congratulations, sir." Montgomery
Felt triumphant but said, "Field commanders
Are least important to governments when
They sense victory, most when they smell defeat."

2010   The Wheel of Fortune turned a half-circle,
Moved him from the bottom back to the top,
And plunged Bradley back down. Eisenhower sat
At his desk in a sombre mood. He knew
Montgomery had wanted to divide
2015   The battlefield. Now he had two leaders
Of equal rank, who hated each other.
He rang Patton and cut through his protests:
"No, listen. The Germans are now between
First and Third Armies, and have imperilled
2020   Bradley's communications with the First
Army. He must retreat to protect them.
Montgomery's command will bring British
Reinforcements to the front. Hodges and
You will make a pincer counter-attack."
2025   Like a good Commander, Eisenhower had
Not let his personal feelings colour his
View of Allied needs in the battlefield.

The universe is moral, and when one
Man is too high he is pulled down and one
2030   Who was laid low, has borne tribulation

With dignity, is then raised up, having
Served his term – stretch or sentence – of public
Humiliation and shame, and is then
Rehabilitated, and if he has
2035 Learned what caused his downfall in the first place,
Then operates at the correct level.
Woe betide all whose posture is too high,
Who think they are better than all others.
In Heaven's eyes all talents balance out, and
2040 Every human has a talent of sorts.
The universe is also generous.
Heaven smiles on all who have been cast down and
Have been raised to responsibility,
Inner harmony and serenity
2045 Which the universe would teach us who are
Unruly hooligans in a playschool.
We make our miseries by our mistakes
And our fortune by frequent corrections.
But reinstatement assumes amendment.

2050 The Americans defended St. Vith
And Vielsalm, and the Elsenborn ridge, and
Forced the Sixth Panzer Army to shift south
In its drive towards the Meuse. Though Peiper
Moved between American positions,
2055 An army required a road, and the one
The Germans held was full of traffic jams
Caused by the mud that bogged down light staff cars
Let alone Panzer tanks and trucks for troops.
All other roads led through St. Vith, and now
2060 Model and Manteuffel left their clogged cars
And walked to reach the strategic meeting.
(The German Generals toured close to the front,
Unlike Hodges and Bradley.) There Model
Spoke: "It seems you are lagging round St. Vith."
2065 To which Manteuffel spoke: "Yes, but we'll take
It tomorrow." Model said, "So that you
Will take it quickly tomorrow you can
Use the Führer Escort Brigade." It did
Not want to be diverted from the Meuse;
2070 It was loyal to Hitler and his plan.
Its commander was Colonel Remer, who
Had thwarted Stauffenberg's coup in Berlin.
But now the German Generals hoped the troops
Who had conquered the Americans on

The Schnee Eifel would capture St. Vith. They
Ordered horse-drawn artillery to move
Along the muddy forest paths and point
At St. Vith within range, and surround it.

A hundred planes had droned through windy skies
2080 In a stormy early morning; only
Fifteen had found the drop area, and,
While hundreds fell throughout the Ardennes woods,
Many being killed on their first night jump,
Just a hundred men landed near Krinkelt.
2085 Two days passed while all assembled, and then
A battle was fought as exhausted men
Forded the icy waist-high River Helle
East of the Eupen-Malmédy road, and
The Germans fled back to Monschau where von
2090 Der Heydte, a Baron and veteran
Of the German airborne conquest of Crete
Three years back, knocked on a door. In the warm
Kitchen he wrote a note of surrender,
Which a child took to the Americans.
2095 So ended in the snow the last German
Paratroop operation of the war.

The units were in place for the defence
Of Bastogne. Hundred and First Airborne had
Nearly twelve thousand men formed in a square
2100 Of four infantry regiments, who had
Howitzer and artillery support,
Tanks and tank destroyers. McAuliffe placed
His men all round Bastogne, and visited
Middleton in Neufchâteau that night, and
2105 Said: "My men can hold out forty-eight hours
If they are surrounded." Middleton told
Him four Panzer divisions would attack.
McAuliffe said: "I think we can take care
Of them." He returned to Bastogne. Thirty
2110 Minutes later, German armour moved in,
Being committed to surround the town
After the rebuffs at Neffe and Marvie,
And cut the road behind him and cut off
Bastogne, which was now encircled, marooned.

2115 Next day Remer disobeyed Manteuffel's
Orders and headed for the Meuse, leaving

St. Vith to be attacked by a whole corps
Of German Volksgrenadiers, who began
A deafening artillery barrage
On Prumerberg ridge that afternoon, when
Shells blew trees apart, raining splinters on
American foxholes in a din that
Lasted forty-five minutes and sent men
Into deep shock. Veterans said it was
The worst bombardment they had ever known.
At dusk German infantry attacked, and
Colonel Fuller's few hundred men and just
Eleven tanks, though very outnumbered,
Broke up their advance with artillery.
Some German infantry stole through the gaps
In the American line and now held
The rear. In the dark six SS Tigers
Rolled up the slope towards the ridge and fired
Flares that blinded the crews of five Shermans
Waiting to fire when the Tigers appeared,
And silhouetted the Shermans, which were
Destroyed. Flames leapt in the dark, thick smoke climbed.
The Tigers now fired at the foxhole line,
And the Americans fled to the rear
To be shot at by the infiltrators
As they blundered through woods. Fuller panicked,
Handed his command to an engineer
And fled back to St. Vith "to make new plans".
The Tigers and Volksgrenadiers pursued.
In St. Vith German and American
Vehicles and men mingled as a snowstorm
Began, whirling huge snowflakes from the dark
On the confusion. An American
Radioed for orders and was told "Go west,
Go west." St. Vith's commander, Clarke, now led
A withdrawal to a new line just out
Of the town, while, converging from all sides,
The Germans traffic-jammed St. Vith's streets and
Looted American supplies, sought warmth
And shelter from the driving snow. The roads
To St. Vith were clogged with vehicles; Model
Again had to abandon his staff car
And walk through the blizzard. The Americans
Had over three thousand casualties and
Had lost a hundred vehicles, but had stopped
An entire German corps; delayed for days

The western movement of its troops, guns and
Tanks in congested streets, and choked its main
Lines of communication and supply.

2165   Montgomery had temporary control
Of Allied forces north of the Ardennes
In the Bulge's north sector, including
Hodges' First Army and Simpson's Ninth. He
Addressed the British and Canadian
2170   Commanders at Zonhoven scathingly:
"While the Supreme Commander cowers in
His Hotel and Bradley is in hiding,
Afraid, having moved out of his bedroom,
Fearing attack from Skorzeny's German
2175   Assassination squad, I have a large
Union flag on my car, and drive around
Quite openly to boost the morale and
Self-confidence of the American
Commanders in the field. My strategy
2180   Is not to attack the Germans – the thick
Ardennes forests and hills are easy to
Defend, hard to attack – but to outflank
The Germans and take the Ruhr. We should hold
The Germans with American troops, give
2185   American ground if necessary,
And then thrust to the Ruhr with British and
Canadians." Montgomery issued
A press statement, claiming his new command
As a personal vindication, and next
2190   Day drove to Verviers, a Union Jack on
The bonnet of his Rolls Royce defying
German aircraft, expressing confidence
In Allied air cover, which heartened troops
He passed who cheered and waved; and strode into
2195   Hodges' headquarters "like" (Henderson said)
"Christ come to cleanse the temple". Hodges and
Simpson were waiting to greet him. Hodges
Said: "We're sure glad to see you, Commander.
We've not seen Bradley or any of his
2200   Staff since this battle began. We just want
Someone to give us some firm orders now."
"We'll soon have a properly organised
Set-up for command," Montgomery said.
"The battle will soon be under control.
2205   We're going to win and push the Germans back

Where they came from." He rudely refused lunch,
Ignored their operations map for his,
And put the Americans' backs up by
Saying: "There is a definite lack of
2210 Grip and control. No one now seems to have
A clear picture of the situation."
He ordered that the front should be "tidied",
That Simpson should be responsible for
The sector north of Monschau and command
2215 Divisions "now in it". Hodges, with some
"Sorting out" could hold the line: Elsenborn
Through Malmédy, Stavelot, Durbuy, Hotton
To Marshe. He ordered that 82nd
Airborne should withdraw north to a better
2220 Position.
        The Americans, irate,
Said they would not retreat. But military
Science prevailed. Montgomery studied
Maps, and, seeing five Panzer divisions
2225 On the Bulge's western and northern edge,
Was sure the Germans were about to make
Their greatest assault yet, and decided
To absorb a terrific blow before
He counter-attacked, convinced the setback
2230 For the Americans was a defeat,
Wanting to magnify the great retreat
Before he turned it round with a triumph.
He wanted "Lightning Joe" Collins, the most
Aggressive corps commander in Europe,
2235 To stay out of battle till counterstroke,
And now sought Hodges' support for this view.
At first, his back still up, Hodges refused,
But Montgomery insisted: "No, you
Must withdraw, don't think what Bradley will say.
2240 Bradley and Patton talk counter-attack,
But there are now twice as many German
Troops in the Ardennes as we landed back
On D-Day – three hundred and thirty-five
Thousand – and more than nine hundred tanks in
2245 The ice and snow, and Bradley, cooped up in
His Luxembourg Hotel, and Eisenhower,
Locked and shuttered in his Versailles prison,
And Patton, talk of counter-offensives
And do not know the picture I have from
2250 My Liaison Officers. They wage their

War by telephone, I mine by scouts who
Each day visit the entire front line and
Bring back sightings of enemy movements.
Bradley underestimates German strength,
2255 And so, in Versailles, Eisenhower does too,
And optimistically thinks that Patton
Is about to finish off the Germans
Completely. Bradley draws lines on maps with
Brown crayon which indicate advances
2260 To be made, but does not know where the men
Are who will make them, whereas I honour
The fighting men. I say 'Hodges' troops' are
Tired, they have fought with honour and have been
Under strain and should withdraw and become
2265 Reserves, which will be most useful. No more
American lives should be lost than is
Necessary." Hodges said: "I agree
To be overruled and I will order
The withdrawal." Montgomery now smirked,
2270 Elated at imposing his will on
The northern Americans who would now
Retreat, while British and Canadians
Would counter-attack and thrust to the Ruhr.

The Germans' shortest route to the Meuse had
2275 Been blocked on Elsenborn ridge, and now their
Next best route, from Bastogne to Liège, had
Been blocked as the delay around St. Vith
Had allowed the Americans the time
To strengthen their defence south of Liège,
2280 Where Eighty-Second Airborne defended
A fifteen-mile long sector to be breached.
The Germans now had to push through the gap,
At least thirteen miles wide, between St. Vith
And Bastogne, link up with Peiper's spearhead,
2285 Defeat the American bent flank from
St. Vith to Malmédy and then Manhay,
And then press on quickly towards the Meuse.

As a great wave breaks foaming up a beach,
Breaching sandcastle walls left by children,
2290 So Peiper reached high-water mark. Behind
Him, laid waste, lay the ruined ramparts of
The Allies' centre, though their shoulders held
On either side of his penetration.

262

Eisenhower's brave Order of the Day called
2295   On the Allies to "rise to new heights of
Courage, resolution and effort" for:
"We cannot be content with mere repulse.
By rushing out from his fixed defences
The enemy may give the chance to turn
2300   His great gamble into his worst defeat.
Let everyone hold before him one thought,
To destroy the enemy on the ground
And in the air, everywhere – destroy him."
Now Patton began his offensive from
2305   The south in a swirling snowstorm. His plan
Was to relieve Bastogne and race up to
Houffalize and cut off the German probe.

As jaunty as a medieval king
Under siege in a fortified castle,
2310   In surrounded Bastogne McAuliffe grouped
His armour and paratroops, undaunted.
Sent by General von Lüttwitz as a bluff,
Without the approval of Manteuffel
Or Kokott, the implementer of threats,
2315   Five Germans approached the American
Lines, carrying a large white flag along
The Arlon road near Remoifoisse, and paused
In front of the foxholes, at Kessler Farm.
The two officers Wagner and Henke
2320   Were blindfolded and driven via the platoon
And company posts to the battalion
Command post at Marvie, where their message
Was relayed to McAuliffe's headquarters:
A foul, damp cellar under Bastogne's old
2325   Military barracks. There it was translated:
"To the American commander of
The encircled town of Bastogne. There is
Now only one way to save your troops from
Complete annihilation: honourable
2330   Surrender." The ultimatum now reached
McAuliffe, who asked, "What does it say, Ned?"
Jones told him, "They want us to surrender."
McAuliffe laughed out loud and said, "You mean,
American surrender? Aw, nuts! We
2335   Are giving them one hell of a beating."
He felt their demand was ridiculous
And inappropriate. He sat to draft

A reply, but could not think what to say.
He asked his staff. One said: "That first remark
2340 Of yours would be hard to beat." So he wrote:
"To the German commander. Nuts!" But this
The German negotiators could not
Understand. Henke asked, "Is the reply
Affirmative, or negative?" Colonel
2345 Harper, while removing their white blindfolds,
Told them: "If you don't understand what 'Nuts'
Means, in plain English it's the same as 'Go
To hell'. And I will tell you something else.
If you continue to attack we will
2350 Kill every goddam German that tries to
Break into this city." The five Germans
Left with the reply, an affront to von
Lüttwitz, who had misunderstood the town's
Determination, and now McAuliffe
2355 Restricted artillery fire to save
Ammunition, allowing the Germans
To move openly all round Bastogne till
Relief came. And through the snow it came as
Patton's Third Army advanced on a front
2360 Between Echternach and Martelange,
And Hugh Gaffey of 4th Armoured, assigned
The mission of relieving Bastogne, sent
McAuliffe a radio message: "Hugh
Is coming." Many of his tanks had crossed
2365 France, having broken out in Normandy,
And were mechanically unsound with new
Crews. Hugh's progress was slow, and the Germans
Attacked Bastogne with tanks and infantry
Repeatedly and wore the defenders
2370 Down. The next day dawned bright, and bombers swam
Like shoals of silver minnows in the bright
Winter sun, hunting for vehicle tracks in
The snow and following them till they found
Their quarry with rockets, bombs and napalm.
2375 Transport aircraft dropped pathfinders and then
Supplies, and, despite anti-aircraft fire,
Aimed accurately and preserved Bastogne.

Manteuffel's advance guards captured a bridge
Over the Ourthe, and were now forty miles
2380 From the Meuse, the farthermost limit of
The Bulge, but he could not move quickly for

Parts of his forces were still at Bastogne,
His units were weary after fighting
Six days and fuel supplies had not got through.
2385 Model hoped he would force the Americans
Back against the Meuse and destroy them there,
And he now sought to broaden his spearhead.
The east-west roads were clogged with traffic, and
As troops took a long time to reach the front
2390 Model ordered Manteuffel's advance guard
To proceed to the Meuse on foot quickly.

Model had made Manteuffel's Fifth Panzers
The main effort now. Dietrich's Sixth Panzers,
Its thrust blocked on Elsenborn ridge, was now
2395 Relegated to protecting his flank.
The Second SS Panzer Division,
The best in the army, moved to attack
Baraque de Fraiture on the main road from
Bastogne to Liège, their object, between
2400 Houffalize and Manhay. American
Patrols captured an SS officer,
Who told of the plan to seize the crossroads.
Gavin, commander of 82nd,
Fearing the Germans could trap his men and
2405 Troops leaving St. Vith against the rivers
Amblève and Salm, sent infantry reserves,
A glider regiment with snow-sledges.
That night there was a heavy fall of snow.
At dawn SS Panzergrenadiers moved
2410 Against Baraque de Fraiture, a snow-white
Enclave within tall firs, and caught the troops
Eating breakfast. The reserves countered through
German mortar and artillery shells,
And called for help. Five Shermans from Manhay
2415 With infantry and paratroops arrived
At the crossroads, exhausted survivors
From the rout at St. Vith. Second Panzers
Attacked after artillery fire and,
With eight Panzers and two Panthers, they now
2420 Overran the crossroads and captured troops,
Took Baraque de Fraiture, opened the road
To Liège, which Gavin now tried to block,
But then hid in the woods as clearing skies
Allowed American fighter-bombers
2425 To hunt for tracks and rocket and napalm.

Model ordered units forward but feared
The Panzers could not hold out till relieved.

Skorzeny's "Americans" (or Steilau's
English-speaking commandos) in US
2430 Jeeps and US uniforms had MPs
Stopping each other at road-blocks, asking
Each to name three baseball teams or to sing
The American national anthem. A lone
Sherman with three relaxed "Americans"
2435 Was stopped at Aywaille twelve miles from the Meuse
Bridge at Engis. The men could not repeat
The password, and were found to have German
Military pay-books. They were tried as spies,
And sentenced to death. In the small village
2440 Of Henri-Chapelle the three impostors
Were tied to posts before a whitewashed wall
While a twelve-man firing-squad waited in
The rutted mud of a wide vehicle track.
One of the three, Wilhelm Schmidt, had told his
2445 Interrogators that Operation
Greif's real mission was to reach Paris,
Rendezvous in the Café de Paris,
Stalk SHAEF's headquarters and assassinate
Eisenhower. Disruptive to the last, Schmidt
2450 Played on Skorzeny's past exploits – he had
Rescued Mussolini from his Allied
Captors and had the reputation of
The most dangerous man in all Europe –
And stuck to his hoax in the face of death
2455 So Eisenhower was confined to his room
In his headquarters, Versailles' Trianon
Palace Hotel, and a double called Smith
Drove round Paris in a staff car to lure
Skorzeny's killers into an attack.
2460 Now Schmidt, Pernass and Billing stood alone
And upright at three posts, hands tied behind
Backs. Billing, bespectacled, called shrilly
In German, "Long live our Führer." Two rows,
One kneeling, one standing, aimed rifles at
2465 Round targets on the men's hearts, which were filled
With patriotic fervour. All cracked in
Unison, puffs of dust rose behind each
Man as he slumped, as if his spirit left
His executed body and hung its

2470 Cloudy substance before journeying to
Its new abode in a more subtle place.

Sitting in the ancient chapel of the
Pescatore Foundation, Luxembourg
City, as if radioing headquarters,
2475 Patton prayed for improving weather: "Sir,
This is Patton talking. The last fourteen
Days have been straight hell – rain, snow, more rain, more
Snow – and I'm beginning to wonder what's
Going on in Your headquarters. Whose side
2480 Are you on anyway? For three years my
Chaplains have been explaining that this is
A religious war, the Crusades again,
Except we're riding tanks, not chargers. They
Insist we are here to annihilate
2485 Godless Hitler and the German Army
So that religious freedom may return
To Europe. Till now I have gone along
With them. You have given us Your unreserved
Co-operation: clear skies and calm sea
2490 In Africa, Sicily. You supplied
Excellent weather for our armoured dash
Across France, the greatest military
Victory you have thus far allowed me.
You have often given me excellent
2495 Guidance in difficult decisions and
You have led German units into traps
That made their elimination simple.
But now, You have changed horses in midstream.
You seem to have given von Rundstedt breaks
2500 And frankly, he's been beating the hell out
Of us. My army is neither trained nor
Equipped for winter warfare. This weather
Is more suitable for Eskimos than
For southern cavalrymen. But now, sir,
2505 I can't help but feel that I've offended
You in some way, that suddenly you've lost
All sympathy for our cause, that You are
Throwing in with von Rundstedt and his god,
His paper-hanging god. You know without
2510 Me telling you our situation is
Desperate. Sure, I can tell my staff that
Everything's going according to plan,
But there is no use telling You that my

Hundred and First Airborne's holding against
2515 Tremendous odds in Bastogne, and that this
Continual storm means we cannot supply
Them from the air. I've sent Hugh Gaffey, one
Of my ablest Generals, north to relieve
The encircled garrison and he's finding
2520 Your weather more difficult than he is
The Krauts. I don't like to complain but my
Soldiers from the Meuse to Echternach are
Suffering tortures of the damned. Today
I visited several hospitals, all
2525 Full of frostbite cases; the wounded die
In the fields because they cannot be brought
Back for medical care. But this is not
The worst of the situation. Lack of
Visibility, continued rains have
2530 Grounded my air force. My battle technique
Calls for fighter-bomber support, and if
My planes can't fly, how can I use them as
Aerial artillery? But, worse yet,
My reconnaissance planes have been grounded
2535 For fourteen days, I haven't the faintest
Idea of what is going on behind
The German lines. Damn it, sir, I can't fight
A shadow. Without Your co-operation
From a weather standpoint I am deprived
2540 Of accurate disposition of these
German armies and how in hell can I
Be intelligent in my attack? All
Of this probably sounds unreasonable
To You, but I have lost all patience with
2545 Your chaplains who insist that this is a
Typical Ardennes winter, and that I
Must have faith. Faith and patience be damned. You
Have just got to make up Your mind whose side
You're on. You must come to my assistance,
2550 So that I may dispatch the entire German
Army as a birthday present to Your
Prince of Peace. Sir, I have never been an
Unreasonable man, I'm not going
To ask You for the impossible. I
2555 Don't even insist on a miracle.
All I request is four days' clear weather
So that my planes can fly, fighter-bombers
Bomb and strafe, my reconnaissance pick out

268

Targets for my artillery. Give me
2560 Four days of sunshine to dry this blasted
Mud, so my tanks roll, so ammunition
And rations may be sent to my hungry,
Ill-equipped infantry. I need these four
Days to send von Rundstedt and his godless
2565 Army to their Valhalla. I am sick
Of this unnecessary butchery
Of American youth, and in exchange
For four days of fighting weather, I will
Deliver You enough Krauts to keep Your
2570 Bookkeepers months behind in their work." He
Finished, as if squaring up, with "Amen"
And sat on in belligerent silence.
Christ, standing near, looked at his clouded heart,
Noted the lack of Light in his aura,
2575 Sadly saw the possibility that
He would be killed and buried in this town,
An event not certain, depending on
The rashness or caution of his outlook.
Understanding and sympathising with
2580 The justice of his altruistic plea,
Now realising that Satan had sent fog
To help the forces of evil advance,
Christ took his prayer into the cosmic Light,
Which carried it into the Ardennes clouds
2585 And dispersed them as salt disperses snow.

The weather changed! A cold dry wind cleared skies,
The sun rose on a frosty landscape, there
Was a clear blue sky over the Ardennes,
Which was soon filled with planes and swirling clouds
2590 Of smoke like Christmas paper chains and bells.
On Christmas Eve at the Adlerhorst word
Arrived that Second Panzers were just three
Miles from the Meuse – without fuel. Hitler
Stood outside the Adlerhorst bunker and
2595 Watched as above a thousand enemy
Bombers glistened in the pale winter sky
Like a shoal gliding in a limpid stream.
Christa Schroeder, his secretary, looking,
Said, "We've lost the war, haven't we?" Hitler
2600 Said, "No." Later Manteuffel rang Jodl
And said he would assault Bastogne, but he
Could not also reach the Meuse and Antwerp.

Hitler said, "Antwerp must be taken. I
Have made sacrifices, for five years I
2605   Have not been to a play, concert or film.
I devote my life to the simple task
Of running the war. If there's no iron
Will behind it the battle can't be won."

When Montgomery ordered that Collins'
2610   Three-division tactical reserve corps
Should stay out of battle till counterstroke,
The Americans disagreed, sensing
Victory; and the German attack through
Baraque de Fraiture had drawn in Collins'
2615   Corps. Major-General Harmon rang Collins'
HQ and asked permission to attack
Second Panzers' spearhead east of Dinant
As they had no fuel. In Collins' absence
A deputy rang headquarters. Harmon
2620   Believed they had agreed to his attack.
On his return Collins, interpreting
Montgomery's orders loosely, allowed
The attack to proceed on Christmas Day.

McAuliffe's headquarters was sombre, men
2625   Embraced on Christmas night, sure they would die
Next day. McAuliffe went up for air and,
Walking among the brick barracks buildings,
Heard the German prisoners sing "Stille Nacht"
In hushed tones in their cell windows. He stopped,
2630   Breathless under the stars which swam like swans
As tears of peace streamed down his radiant cheeks.
The tune and words were from his own culture,
There was a oneness in the universe
That twinkled through the many different stars.
2635   He went into the prisoners and was stunned
As one said, "We'll soon be freed. It's you who'll
Be a prisoner, you'll like it here, General,
It's cosy. We'll be in Antwerp next month."
He said, "I'm here to wish you a merry
2640   Christmas." Loving his enemies in spite
Of himself, ecstatic in his full heart,
McAuliffe drove out of Bastogne by jeep,
To Savy. In the battery command
Post he attended midnight mass, dry-eyed
645   Now he was back among his companions.

At 3 a.m. on Christmas Day Bastogne,
Which was to be Hitler's Christmas present,
Was attacked by Panzergrenadiers and
Eighteen tanks. The waning moon lit the snow-
2650 Covered fields. A fresh division had not
Arrived, and the German commander there,
Colonel Kokott, a shy, bespectacled,
Erudite man who did not raise his voice
And had respect, had not been given time
2655 To plan or reconnoitre. Model said,
"The Fifth Army must seize Bastogne at once,
And lance this boil," using surprise for it
Was Christmas. The assault began at Champs
As camouflaged infantry came through woods
2660 And grenadiers advanced to the crossroads,
Leaving reserves to clear Americans
In house-to-house combat behind their path.
Then came the German main attack: painted
White in the moonlight on the snow, followed
2665 By foot-soldiers in white, a ghostly troop,
Advancing in eerie silence, eighteen
Panzers rolled over the foxhole line – men
Ducked in dread as treads rolled over heads – and,
Spurting great jets of fire from flame-throwers,
2670 Brushed aside tank destroyers, and then split,
Half towards Rolle, to be caught in crossfire,
And half towards Hemroulle, which their leader
Mistook for Bastogne. As he radioed
That he had reached the objective, fire from
2675 Two Shermans, howitzers, bazookas and
Tank destroyers knocked out all Panzer tanks,
And their crews were captured. The fields were strewn
With sixty grenadiers cut to pieces
By crossfire from three sides. The plan called for
2680 The attackers to be in Bastogne by
Eight a.m., when US fighter-bombers
Would first appear. By ten Kokott asked for
Permission to withdraw, knowing the plan
Could not be fulfilled, but he was refused.
2685 Half-heartedly Kokott fought on. Having
Reached within a mile of Bastogne, Kokott's
Attack had petered out, run out of thrust.
Christmas was now observed. In a clearing
In woods, an American chaplain now
2690 Performed Mass – from the back of a parked jeep,

Troops kneeling in surrender in a line.

Harmon advanced from Ciney, and, with troops
Collins had assembled for him, after
An artillery barrage and thunderous
2695   Fighter-bombers, which strafed the fuelless tanks,
Destroyed Second Panzers' reconnaissance
At the farthest point of penetration
And encircled the German force round Celles,
Killing a thousand, capturing more and
2700   Destroying or taking some eighty tanks,
Eighty artillery pieces and five
Hundred vehicles. It was a great German
Defeat, and seized the initiative from
The Germans, though Hitler did not see this.

2705   Pale Hitler slept at four a.m. and woke
At noon. Like Odin, god of battle, in
Valhalla, he greeted his Christmas Day
Callers with a limp handshake, more senile
Than seized by the Prince of Darkness's power.
2710   He drank a glass of wine and all sat round
A candlelit Christmas tree, ate goose, and
Keitel made a short speech while Hitler beamed.

At Zonhoven Montgomery received
Bradley, who, having been out of touch for
2715   Three weeks, had come out of his Hotel, "Braved
The assassins", wearing an old combat
Jacket, looking tired, having had only
An apple and a pear for Christmas lunch.
Montgomery did not send a car to
2720   The airfield. Bradley used a staff car sent
By Hodges. Montgomery greeted him
In well-creased battledress with ribbons and
Shining leather shoes: "I haven't seen you
Since Maastricht, when I proposed we should have
2725   One unified command, when you preferred
To command the American army."
He led him past hanging Christmas cards to
His study, saying, "I'll brief you. I know
What's going on in the American
2730   Sector." While Bradley sat uncomfortably,
Montgomery reviewed the battle. He
Concluded: "So the Germans have given

The Americans a bloody nose, and
The Americans deserve this counter-
2735 Attack, it's entirely their own fault for
Trying two thrusts at the same time, neither
Being strong enough. If there'd been a strong
Single thrust, none of this would have happened.
Now we are in a muddle. I always
2740 Advised against the right going so far.
You advised in favour of it and then
General Eisenhower took your advice. So
We must withdraw. If Patton's" (he had not
Heard the news from Bastogne) "counter-attack
2745 Is not strong enough then I'll have to deal
Unaided with the Fifth and Sixth Panzer
Armies, in which case General Eisenhower
Will have to give me more American
Troops. Do you agree with my summary?"
2750 Bradley said uncomfortably, "I do."
Montgomery asked, "Then what does General
Eisenhower propose to do? He has not
Spoken to me since giving me command
Of the main battle in the Ardennes. It's
2755 True, the Supreme Commander has given
No orders. So I ask you, what does he
Propose to do?" Bradley said, "I don't know."
Montgomery screeched, "Don't know? You don't know?
A commander has to know." Bradley squirmed:
2760 "I have not seen Eisenhower recently."
"But you and he agreed a better way,"
Montgomery said, "than a unified
Command at Maastricht. Surely he has been
In touch?" Bradley said, "Skorzeny and his
2765 Paratroops in Allied uniform are
Trying to kill us both." Montgomery
Said scornfully, "And I have been riding
Round the front line with a large Union Jack
On my Rolls Royce, and I haven't seen them."
2770 Bradley said, "The security problem
Has hindered communication, and my
Telephone lines were cut." Montgomery
Scolded, "Because you went too far and in
Too weak a second thrust." Bradley sat in
2775 Silence, smouldering, humiliated,
Shamed as if a Headmaster had just shamed
A naughty boy, vowing to get even

273

With Montgomery, demand that First and
Ninth Armies should return to his command.

2780   Soon after 6 p.m. in the mess at
Ewell's command post on the Neffe road, near
An unexploded bomb, McAuliffe and
Eight officers, sitting on chairs, all ate
Christmas dinner round a table and tree
2785   Decorated with bits of tin cans and
Silver paper planes used to jam radar.
After sardines and biscuits, Sergeant Smith
Produced lemon meringue to loud applause.
Terrific explosions shook the building.
2790   All rushed down to the cellar, and when they
Returned, the dessert was covered with white
Plaster and quite uneatable. Great was
The men's disappointment that cold evening.

On icy Boxing Day to the south-west
2795   Through thick snow, and a cold so biting that
Men with frost-bitten hands stamped their feet in
Their half-tracks, Patton's relieving force, slowed
Down by broken bridges and cratered roads,
Crawled and slithered, making little headway,
2800   And, watching hundreds of cargo planes fly
Low like geese in a line towards Bastogne,
Colonel Abrams telephoned Gaffey, who
Asked Patton to authorise a short-cut
That followed the cargo planes' direction.
2805   Patton said, "I sure as hell will." Risking
A German attack on his flank, Colonel
Abrams, cigar in mouth, told his twenty
Shermans, "We're going in now. Let 'er roll."
Tracks squealing, guns firing to left and right,
2810   After an artillery bombardment
Abrams entered Assenois, infantry
Leapt from his tanks and, after house-to-house
Fighting, cleared the village. Private Hendrix
Shot and clubbed Germans in foxholes, then charged
2815   Two large guns and took prisoner their amazed
Crews, then snatched a man from a burning half-
Track. The Cobra King Sherman tanks rolled on
And machine-gunned white silhouettes, who fell
Like ducks caught in a woodland shoot between
2820   The pine trees. They left the woods for open

Country, snow-white fields covered with cargo
Parachutes like red, yellow and blue flowers,
And at Bastogne broke through the German ring
To Hundred and First Airborne's lines, where they
2825 Were greeted by McAuliffe, who stood on
Top of a snow-white hillock: "Gee, I am
Mighty glad to see you." Bastogne was safe.
Bold Patton, who had modelled himself on
His idol Napoleon's dash and sense of
2830 Destiny, had broken the snow-deep siege
And relieved the slow strangling of Bastogne,
Which he called in a letter to his wife,
"The outstanding achievement of this war."

The next day at noon proud Hitler awoke
2835 To learn that Patton had lifted the siege
Of Bastogne and put the Seventh Army
To flight. Undeterred, undismayed, tranquil,
Confident, Hitler said, "The side that lasts
The longer wins. We can outlast the US
2840 As Frederick the Great did the alliance.
Bastogne must be taken. At present it's
Like having a fish bone caught in my throat."
The Second Panzers were out of fuel and
Were being attacked. Now Jodl said, "Mein
2845 Führer, we must face facts. We cannot force
The Meuse." Hitler disagreed: "We have had
Unexpected setbacks because my plan
Was not followed to the letter, but all
Is not lost for the war can't last as long
2850 Again as it's lasted. The question is,
Which side will crack first? I say the side that
Lasts longer will do so only if it
Stands to lose everything. We stand to lose
Everything. If the Americans say,
2855 'Stop, no more boys to Europe,' it won't hurt
Them. But if we say, 'We have had enough,
We're packing up,' then Germany will cease
To exist." So he deluded himself
With such vain hopes – he, the great deluder.
2860 Krebs spoke: "A certain culminating point
Has been reached today." Hitler said nothing.
Near the end of the day Göring arrived
And discussed the battle on two fronts and
Promptly declared: "The war is lost, we shall

275

Seek a truce." Angrily Hitler rejoined:
"I forbid you to take any steps in
This matter. And if you go against my
Orders I will have you shot!" Göring paled.

The German offensive now disappeared
Like thawing snow: each day it was less seen.
Hodges' barrier held from Dinant to
Elsenborn, and now Bastogne was relieved
The Americans wanted to attack
The shoulders of the Bulge, citing Harmon's
Success. Montgomery disagreed, for
That was too "risky" a strategy, and
The rift threatened to fracture the Allies'
Unity, just as Hitler had forecast
So shrewdly. Cautious, Eisenhower resolved
To compromise and forfeit a swift rout,
Forfeit the hot pursuit Patton wanted,
To attack the demoralised Germans
Further west in a northern counterstroke. .

Four days of clear weather, as Patton asked,
Had allowed the Allied air force to smash
German transporters, wreck bridges, bomb tanks,
Forcing the Germans to take cover, halt.
The Allies' artillery, tanks, planes and
Infantry were poised. Enraged by Patton's
Relief of Bastogne, Hitler now decreed
That "Bastogne be cleared": the Americans
Destroyed. The German forces, everywhere
On the defensive, regrouped round Bastogne
And bombed the town at midnight and at dawn.
American reinforcements, 11th
Armoured, headed for the town on that clear,
Cold night under a brilliantly bright moon.
Next day the weather became overcast.
The dead lay frozen stiff; loading corpses
In trucks was like picking up large pine logs.
Clouds formed and Arctic winds brought blizzards and
Freezing temperatures. General Taylor drove
Into Bastogne by jeep and was received
By his joyful staff and McAuliffe, who
Gave back his command. A blinding snowstorm
Ended the Allies' air attacks, stopped tanks,
Forcing infantry to wade through snow-drifts,

Slowing the Allied counter-attack to
Erase the Bulge. Hampered by driving snow,
2910 The Germans fitfully attacked Bastogne
And Elsenborn ridge, but were soon repulsed.

The German command acknowledged failure:
Model said Antwerp "must be shelved", and that
The Germans should destroy the Allies east
2915 Of the Meuse. Von Rundstedt agreed: "The long
Range objective of the plan can't be reached
With the forces at hand." He feared pincers
At Houffalize, to cut off the western
Portion of the German army. Hitler
2920 Told Thomale, Motor Transport Inspector:
"Although, unfortunately, the offensive
Has not resulted in the decisive
Success which might have been expected, there
Has been a tremendous easing of the
2925 Situation. The enemy has had
To abandon all his plans for attack,
Regroup, throw in units that were fatigued.
The enemy is criticised at home,
And has admitted that the war will not
2930 Be decided before August. This means
That there has been a transformation in
The situation such as nobody
Would have believed two weeks ago." He blamed
"Horrendously bad roads" and said: "Because
2935 Of traffic congestion a great part of
Our Panzer divisions have not even
Been committed. Only the first wave of
Tanks was in action. Behind, a convoy,
Jammed so solid no petrol could get through.
2940 The tanks' engines were idling and were run
All night to keep men warm, and when they moved
Could only move in first gear on those roads."
He disparaged Hundred and First Airborne
And said, "We must have Bastogne. Nordwind, my
2945 New offensive, begins on New Year's Day
South of the Ardennes and will encircle
Patton's entire army there. Then we'll see
What happens. There will be a further blow:
A whirlwind attack on Metz in Lorraine."

2950 As Eisenhower pressed for his counterstroke

To start in the north, a command crisis
Again involving Montgomery blew
Up like a snowstorm, and the deepening drift,
Like snow settling on a frozen washing-
2955 Line, stiff clothes propped up by a long forked pole,
Threatened to weigh down and snap the Allies'
Unity just as Hitler had forecast
Presciently. Eisenhower had denied
Montgomery's demand for more troops and
2960 Bradley's for First and Ninth Armies to pass
Back to his command. He was in complete
Control of the battle, and considered
It had vindicated his decisions
To rush reserves to Bastogne, change Patton's
2965 Direction and hand the northern flank to
Montgomery. He told Devers he must
Withdraw to a line near Strasbourg and now
Worried that the Allied counter-attack
Would be late as at Kasserine, and he
2970 Was irritated that Montgomery
Would not move forward till all conditions
Were at their best. Tedder said at a SHAEF
Meeting the good weather would not last and
The Germans should be bombed while planes could fly.
2975 Eisenhower said, "The German divisions
Are understrength and pummelled, their supply
Lines are poor. I want to hit them quickly."
A message came through from Montgomery
That he had a new plan of attack that
2980 Used two corps, 7th US and 30th
British, and Eisenhower exclaimed, "Praise God
From whom all blessings flow."
                                        Montgomery
Hesitated, complaining to his staff
2985 He did not know where Eisenhower was and
Nor did Bradley, that Smith said he was "locked
Up", that Eisenhower was more interested
In the Russian offensive – about to send
Tedder and Bull to Stalin – than the Ardennes.
2990 Now he thought up a new strategic plan,
Which he explained to Dawnay: "Ultra shows
The Germans will make one last attack on
The northern shoulder of the Bulge. We must
Lure them onto our positions, receive
2995 The attack. Collins will feint and we'll strike

At the Ruhr."
　　　　　　　The following afternoon
Eisenhower visited Montgomery
To hurry him up. Eisenhower's train drew
3000　Into Hasselt station, Belgium, and as
Machine-gunners leapt out to guard his suite
Eisenhower greeted Montgomery, who
Had been waiting on the platform with de
Guingand and Williams, and, observing his
3005　Security, said caustically as he
Stepped aboard the carriage, "Having arrived
In a mere armoured car I feel naked
Before assassins." Eisenhower replied
Uncomfortably, "In due course there will be
3010　An enquiry on the need for all this."
Montgomery said, "Ike, I want to have
This meeting without any staff present.
You have not brought Smith or Tedder; Williams
And de Guingand can wait outside in this
3015　Corridor." Obliging, Eisenhower led
Him to his study in the carriage and
Came straight to the point: "I've heard your northern
Counter-attack will employ two corps in
An offensive role. Bradley travelled to
3020　Versailles yesterday afternoon, and is
Strengthening the southern flank and will then
Attack. I want to hit the Germans hard.
How soon can you attack?" Montgomery
Said, "I cannot discuss timing. You must
3025　Understand, we're fighting a defensive
Operation in the Ardennes. You can't
Attack in thick forests and hills. Ultra
Has the Germans making one last attack
On the northern shoulder of the Bulge. We
3030　Must receive their attack, and then counter
At the tip of the Bulge, drive the Germans
Back to the West Wall." Eisenhower, dismayed,
Cried: "The tip? We need to attack their flank
And cut them off. We can't wait or Rundstedt
3035　Will withdraw from the Bulge or put up new
Infantry divisions and pull his tanks
Back in reserve. You must attack quickly."
Montgomery, thinking of the Ultra
Intercepts, said obstinately, "But first
3040　We must receive and stop the big German

Attack." Eisenhower said, "There will be no
German attack. What if there's no German
Attack today or tomorrow? Would you
Counter-attack on January the first?"
3045   Montgomery said, "I suppose I'd have
To," which Eisenhower took as agreement.
"But once we've held the Germans here, we can
Invade Germany, take the Ruhr. I have
A master plan for the future conduct
3050   Of the war. It is vital to decide
On this so present actions can accord
With the future plan. It means allotting
All offensive power to the northern front
Under one man's command. Bradley has made
3055   A mess of the situation." Annoyed,
Eisenhower said, "Bradley, Patton, Devers
All wanted the Frankfurt thrust, and I gave
Way to them. There are difficulties with
Unified command. I've explained about
3060   American public opinion." Bold
Montgomery said: "I think you'll find it
Difficult to explain the true reason
For the bloody nose you have just received
From the Germans was your division of
3065   The unified command." Irritated,
Eisenhower said, "You still don't understand
That Americans can't be commanded
By British as they are supplying three-
Quarters of all troops." Montgomery spoke:
3070   "I'll say it again, I will serve under
Bradley if that will see a unified
Command." The meeting broke up. Eisenhower
Believed Montgomery had agreed to
Counter-attack.
3075   But two days later de
Guingand arrived at SHAEF HQ, Versailles,
And said, "Montgomery will not attack
Until January the fourth." Eisenhower
Exploded: "The fourth? He told me the first."
3080   "You must have misunderstood," de Guingand
Said. "He would not have said that." Bedell Smith
Said, "What makes me so mad is that Monty
Won't talk in anyone else's presence."
Exasperated, Eisenhower complained,
3085   "Damn it, he agreed. He's lied to me, he's

Trying to lead me by the nose. We have
A great opportunity in the Ardennes
Which he's squandering by slowness, wanting
Perfect conditions for attack. The time
3090 Has come to break with Montgomery." Smith
Said, "We're all in rebellion at how he's
Carried on. You should dictate a letter
To him." Eisenhower said, "Tell him that if
He doesn't live up to his promises,
3095 He will be sacked." A letter was typed out
And shown to de Guingand, who pleaded with
Them not to send it till he had talked with
Montgomery and "straightened things out", and,
Hopeful that de Guingand could secure his
3100 Attack with affable charm, Eisenhower
Agreed. De Guingand saw Montgomery
On New Year's Eve and flew back to Versailles
And reported to a SHAEF meeting there:
"He confirms that the proper strategy
3105 Is to let the Germans exhaust themselves
With one final attack before we go
On the offensive." Angry, Eisenhower
Screeched, "But he definitely promised to
Attack on January the first, which is
3110 Tomorrow." De Guingand said, "You must have
Misunderstood." Eisenhower said, "Bradley
Is already attacking, believing
Montgomery will attack tomorrow.
The Germans have already begun to
3115 Move Panzer divisions from the north to
The south. We want an attack now. This shows
Montgomery's timing in military
Operations is seriously flawed.
He's unable to see things from SHAEF's side.
3120 He's welshed." De Guingand said awkwardly, "He's
Written you a personal letter." Grimly
Eisenhower read and, shocked, announced: "He says
The Allies have suffered a tremendous
Defeat – he calls our victory a shameful
3125 Defeat – and that my policies are wrong.
He demands control of the land battle.
There must be one commander for all land
Operations in North-West Europe – him.
He says that there must be a single thrust
3130 To seize the Ruhr, with Patton's flank restrained,

Or else the Allies will fail, and he sends
A directive on those lines for me to
Sign." There was general indignation and
Outrage, a gasp of "O-o-h". Tedder said, "He's
3135 Insubordinate. It makes me seethe. Sack
Him." Montgomery had gone too far and,
Knowing his own credibility as
Supreme Commander was at stake, grimly
Eisenhower said, "Bedell, cable General
3140 Marshall and the Combined Chiefs of Staff and
Say it's Monty or me. And if it's me,
Then I want Alexander." Just then Smith
Had a message: "It's from General Marshall,
Chairman of the Combined Chiefs of Staff. It
3145 Says you have their complete confidence, that
You're doing a grand job, and aren't to pay
Attention to British press calls for a
British Deputy Commander, Monty,
To lighten your task as back home this would
3150 Be resented." Alarmed, de Guingand begged
Eisenhower, "Please don't send your cable for
A few hours, till I've spoken with Monty
At Zonhoven." Relenting, reasonable
Even under extreme provocation
3155 Eisenhower said decisively: "All right.
But I'm now issuing my directive
Which flatly contradicts Montgomery's
On every point. First Army's back under
Bradley's control, there must be a double
3160 Thrust into Germany, and we must seize
The initiative at once, we must act
Quickly with speed and energy before
The Germans move in more Panzers. Now draft
A covering letter. Say that I do
3165 Not agree there should be a single ground
Commander. I don't want to hear any
More about putting Bradley under his
Command. I have planned a broad-front advance
To the Rhine, will no longer tolerate
3170 Any debate. Say I don't want to take
Our differences to the CCS, but
If necessary I will, even though
It damages goodwill between Allies."

Like a weary rambler in a rucksack

Reaching a Youth Hostel with tired limbs,
          De Guingand returned to Zonhoven in
          Thick fog and drank tea with Montgomery
          In "A" mess. They then went upstairs to his
          Study. De Guingand said, "Feeling against
3180   You in SHAEF is very strong. Eisenhower's
          Drafted a message to Marshall saying
          It's him or you. He is set to resign.
          Marshall has cabled the CCS's
          Support. Smith's very worried. They think you'll
3185   Have to go." Montgomery said: "It can't
          Be that serious?" De Guingand, handing him
          Eisenhower's letter and directive, said:
          "If the CCS sack you, there's little
          Churchill can do now the Americans
3190   Have three-quarters of the whole war effort."
          Montgomery asked, "Who would replace me?"
          De Guingand said, "Alexander's name is
          In the draft to the CCS." "He is,"
          Montgomery said scornfully, "a weak
3195   Commander who knows nothing about field
          Operations and is quite unable
          To give firm and clear decisions. He is
          Ineffective in Italy, he'd be
          A disaster. What a team: Eisenhower,
3200   Bradley and Alexander. The Germans
          Would push them back to Normandy." He stared
          At Alexander's name and, realising
          He faced the sack, his vanity crumbled.
          He whimpered, "What shall I do, Freddie? What
3205   Shall I do?" From his battledress pocket
          De Guingand pulled a note he had drafted
          And said, "Sign this, it's an apology
          To Eisenhower. It says you know there are
          Many factors he has to consider
3210   'Beyond anything I realise' and he
          Can rely on you 'one hundred per cent',
          And you are 'very distressed' your letter
          Demanding sole command upset him, and
          He should tear it up." Montgomery signed
3215   The note. Ruthless in that same room, he had
          Humiliated Bradley, and he had
          Put down Eisenhower on his train, but now
          He had to swallow his pride, eat humble
          Pie to keep his job. He said, "I shall start

My attack twenty-four hours early, at
Dawn on the third." It would actually be
Forty-eight hours late, but de Guingand said,
"I'll take this straight back to SHAEF," and left. He
Thought Montgomery looked nonplussed, lonely,
Aware he had lost. Montgomery sat
And brooded. It had hurt his principles
To recant. The single thrust and the sole
Command were right. Marshall, and Roosevelt, had
Removed his command of First Army just
When he had defeated the Germans in
The finest defensive Allied battle
Of the war, just as four months before they
Had taken away his land command just
When he had defeated the Germans in
The finest offensive Allied battle
Of the war. And so Eisenhower had forced
The counter-attack, which would last a month
As the Germans retreated fighting hard
Just as they had done on the eastern front.
Eisenhower had wanted the attack to
Be greater but it did its job and took
The Allies through the snow and the West Wall.

Two days before, after thrusts and retreats
Left lines static, General Guderian
Called on Hitler. He said that the Soviet
Winter offensive would soon begin and
The Germans should withdraw from the Ardennes
So "everything could be thrown to the east".
Hitler refused. Rundstedt asked for fresh troops
To take Bastogne, but Hitler said they were
Earmarked for other tasks, and that he must
Make do as best he could with tired fighters.

The next day the Germans attacked Bastogne
With an artillery barrage. Then tanks
Clanked from the east, half turned to Villers-la-
Bonne-Eau, half to Lutrebois, but were then stopped
Before Bastogne. American tanks pushed
South-west and near Lavaselle lost seven
Shermans to German tanks, and many men;
They pushed west towards St. Hubert but were
Forced back by Panzer Lehr and lost ten tanks,
Which billowed smoke above the frozen snow.

Misty weather had returned, in the gloom
Fewer Allied planes flew, but seventy-
3265   Three German planes bombed Bastogne. All that night
Fires raged out of control, many were killed.
An eerie silence fell, snow muffled noise.
Now the American and German thrusts
Collided round Bastogne. Volksgrenadiers
3270   Took back Villers-la-Bonne-Eau and captured
The American forces there. US troops
Seized Remagne, but 11th Armoured lost
More men that sunny day near Pinsamont
And Chenogne than on any other day.
3275   General Patton arrived by jeep and drove
Contemptuously through these combats. He
Toured with McAuliffe, sitting on a red
Leather seat, legs wrapped in blankets, looking
Through binoculars, two Colts with handles
3280   Of ivory hanging from his belt, which
He wore outside a fur-lined air jacket.
Back in Bastogne he talked with Taylor and
Then pinned the Distinguished Service Cross on
McAuliffe's chest and issued free brandy
3285   So all the troops could welcome the New Year.
To the Bulge's north Collins prepared to
Attack Houffalize down the highway and
Link up with Patton's north thrust from Bastogne.
On New Year's Day Patton ordered rapid
3290   Fire from every gun in the Third Army.
Though Germans could be heard screaming in woods,
Fighting was inconclusive. Under grey
Sky, gusts of wind blew up snow. The German
Operation Nordwind blew through Alsace,
3295   While a thousand German planes bombed Allied
Airfields in Holland and Belgium, and caught
Montgomery's Dakota on the ground.

The Germans threw all into a final
Attack near Bastogne, urged on by Model.
3300   American planes strafed, artillery
Fired, as American infantry took
Gerimont and Bonnerue, while armour seized
Mande St. Etienne. Model now regrouped
And with Hitler's approval made attacks
3305   From the north-east. Manteuffel knew it was
Time to retreat from the Ardennes. Model

285

Refused permission, knowing Hitler's rule
Of "no retreat". East of Bastogne, US
Armour reached Wardin, where they met Panzers
3310 And lost fifteen Shermans. Now from the north
American tanks, foot soldiers riding,
In a twenty-five mile front pushed down through
Waist-high snow and minefields, through hilly woods,
Only achieving a few miles a day.
3315 Seeing their intention, to pinch the Bulge,
The Germans felled trees for road-blocks and fired
Anti-tank guns or laid mines. Riflemen
Waded through deep snow to by-pass German
Positions, and were fired on or shelled. Each
3320 American advance was slow, in scenes
Of deep winter and frozen limbs, yet soon
Beffe, Trinal, Magoster, Malempré and
Trois Ponts had fallen. The British attacked
The tip of the Bulge in a great snowstorm
3325 And crawled for days as scout cars, trucks and tanks
Slid back down hills and bumped those following
Or skidded or slithered on icy roads.
Hitler saw the original goals were
Now out of reach, and focused on Bastogne,
3330 Where Model now proposed an assault from
The north and north-east, not the defended
South-east, and fifty-six small tanks arrived.
Volksgrenadiers broke through American
Lines and retook Michamps and Oubourcy,
3335 And briefly entered Longchamps till they were
Repulsed by Hundred and First Airborne. Great
Was each side's troops' admiration for their
Foes, who, though cold and hungry, fought hard. Fierce
Battles took place round Bastogne. No foxholes
3340 Were dug in the frozen ground. Pockets of
Americans were surrounded in woods
Near St. Hubert. Next day a blizzard stopped
Montgomery's attack in the north, yet
Lamorménil, Jevigne and Lansival
3345 Were taken, and by nightfall Odrimont.
The Germans counter-attacked; Pinsamont,
Rechrival and Hubermont saw grim war
As tanks crawled through and then returned, Patton
Observing, "We can still lose this war." Now,
3350 Entrenched in his bunker, the Adlerhorst,
Hitler was optimistic, calling for

The destruction of the enemy where
He was, and for northern Alsace to be
Cut off. North-east of Bastogne German tanks
3355   Advanced in the blizzard, artillery
Fire round them, took Magaret and Wardin,
But retreated under a bombardment.
Now Panzergrenadiers were put to flight
By Hundred and First Airborne, the Screaming
3360   Eagles, in the bloodiest and the most
Costly fighting of the Ardennes war. South-
East of Bastogne the Americans took
Lutrebois. Now von Rundstedt and Model urged
Cross Hitler to evacuate Bastogne,
3365   And next day Hitler sent SS Panzers
North and withdrew the Hitler Youth. The last
Offensive of Wacht am Rhein had thus failed.

Like a street urchin thumbing his nose with
Spread fingers in insufferable contempt,
3370   Montgomery managed to cock a snook
At the American Generals, who were
Annoyed he still commanded the US
Ninth Army. Churchill came to Zonhoven
With Brooke after travelling on Eisenhower's
3375   Train, the Alive (a taunt at Skorzeny).
Churchill said in the study, of the new
Counter-attack, "Your battle seems to be
Going well." Montgomery said, "In three
Feet of snow in places, which makes it hard
3380   For tanks to advance, and the Germans won't
Withdraw. Collins is fighting hard, but we
May not have the strength to push the Germans
Out of the penetration area.
We are fighting a defensive battle,
3385   Not an offensive battle, no matter
How they present it in SHAEF." Brooke said, "And
The business with Eisenhower was sorted
Out?" Still recalling Brooke's lack of support
After Arnhem, Montgomery replied
3390   Slightly defiantly: "Ike's abandoned
The American advance to Frankfurt
Via the Saar, and the main effort is to
Be north of the Ruhr, with the US Ninth
Army under my command, in Twenty-
3395   First Army Group. I've 'power of decision'

287

To plan for the Ruhr, and Bradley has to
Move his headquarters to be nearer mine.
I have most of what I asked for, and Ike
Has given me a new Dakota as

3400   Mine was destroyed in the New Year's Day raid
On Brussels' Zaventem. He'd ordered it
For himself, it had just arrived, brand-new."
Churchill said, "But Bradley's not pleased. He has
Driven to Etain airfield to protest

3405   To Ike." Brooke said, "On the switch to the north."
Montgomery said, "Bradley wants the Ninth
Army back, but Ike knows he's been the cause
Of an American defeat." Brooke said,
"The American public will soon know

3410   As SHAEF have held a press conference today.
For the first time, Americans will know
You have fought the battle of the Ardennes,
Not Bradley." Churchill asked doubtfully, "Is
The Anglo-American alliance

3415   Still strong?" Montgomery said, "Yes, I am
Giving Hodges two hundred British tanks.
We're closely knit. The German breakthrough would
Have been most serious but for the Anglo-
American Army's unity. But

3420   We need more fighting troops if we are to
Advance." Helpfully Churchill volunteered,
"I'll cable President Roosevelt tonight.
There is a campaign in the British press
To cast doubt on Eisenhower's fitness to

3425   Command the Allied Armies in Europe.
Eisenhower has had difficulties with
De Gaulle. He's had to help the French defend
Strasbourg with troops who should be reserves for
The Ardennes. I am concerned to preserve

3430   Allied solidarity." Still smouldering
At the forced recanting, Montgomery
Saw his opportunity and now asked
Innocently, "Could I help Eisenhower
And set things straight by talking frankly to

3435   The press? I would recount the story of
The battle of the Ardennes, explain how
We stopped the Germans in a joint effort,
Stress the great friendship between me and Ike,
Call for more Allied solidarity

3440   And team spirit." Churchill said, "That would be

Invaluable."
                    And so, two days later,
Montgomery held a press conference,
Wearing a red Airborne Corps beret with
3445   Two badges. Jauntily, Montgomery
Told the story of the battle: "As soon
As I saw what was happening, I took
Certain steps myself to ensure that if
The Germans reached the Meuse they'd certainly
3450   Not get over it. And I carried out
Certain movements to meet the danger that
Threatened, i.e. I was thinking ahead.
General Eisenhower put me in command
Of the northern flank. I brought the British
3455   Into the fight and saved the Americans,
And the Germans never reached the Meuse or
Antwerp. You have the picture of British
Troops fighting on both sides of the US
Forces who had suffered a hard blow. This
3460   Is a fine Allied picture. It has been
A very interesting battle, rather
Like El Alamein. Indeed, I think it's
Possibly one of the most interesting
And tricky battles I've ever handled.
3465   GIs make great fighting men when they are
Given proper leadership." Sitting by
Montgomery, Williams was appalled. It
Was coming across as if he'd rescued
The Americans, as if the British
3470   Had won the Battle of the Bulge, whereas
The Americans had stopped the Germans
Before Montgomery came on the scene.
The Americans were enraged because
Hardly any British forces took part
3475   In the battle, and Montgomery had
Not directed the victory but got in
The Americans' way and delayed SHAEF's
Counter-attack. Patton gave an angry
Press interview, saying Montgomery
3480   Had botched the attack: "Had it not been for
Montgomery, we could have bagged the whole
German army. I wish Ike were more of
A gambler, but he's a lion compared
To Montgomery, and Bradley's better
3485   Than Ike as far as nerve's concerned. Monty

Is just a tired little fart. War requires
The taking of risks and he won't take them."
Bradley was under a direct order
From SHAEF not to make an unauthorised
3490 Statement to the press, but Hansen, his aide,
Urged him to ignore SHAEF: "The staff's morale's
Breaking. Montgomery is the symbol
Of the British, you of the American
Effort. Ike has to straddle the two, it's
3495 For you to speak to correct the British
Press and the BBC who are saying
There was an increase in Montgomery's
Command." Bradley agreed to speak, and told
Hansen: "Although I am pleased my Ardennes
3500 Plans are passed, Ike still pursues the northern
Thrust to the Ruhr and I am still upset
That Ninth Army stays with Montgomery.
At bottom he is a British General
Whose plans have one aim: to further his own
3505 Aggrandizement." Like a mischievous boy
Who's lobbed a stone, Montgomery was pleased
He had stirred the Americans up, and
Put his own case. Eisenhower had remained
Above it all; the true victor did not
3510 Stoop to claim the credit that was his due.

The Allied offensive spun on sheet ice,
Halted in fog, froze in waist-deep snow-drifts.
A clear day allowed air support, and now
The Americans took part of Odeigne
3515 And La Vaux. Volksgrenadiers reinforced
The Germans from near Monschau. In thick snow
The Americans took the crossroads at
Baraque de Fraiture, and Wanne and Spineux;
And to the north Dochamps and Morcouray,
3520 Regne, Verleumont and Sart, Guvonne, Farniers
And Mont. South-west of Bastogne Patton rushed
Rechrival and Flamierge, but then withdrew
That night. East of Bastogne German assaults
Were repulsed with artillery fire, and
3525 An American advance was blocked. Now
Manteuffel urged that Fifth Panzer Army
Should be pulled back to Houffalize. Hitler,
Fearing another Falaise pocket, moved
It back between Dochamps and Longchamps. Now

3530　　The Germans were already retreating
　　　　Before Allied pressure on the Bulge north
　　　　Of La Roche and along the Salm. But round
　　　　Bastogne SS armour remained. Next day
　　　　Patton attacked northwards through snow two feet
3535　　Deep in a temperature of minus six
　　　　Fahrenheit, and next day retook Villers-
　　　　La-Bonne-Eau and Harlange and could surround
　　　　The Germans, who now counter-attacked, till
　　　　Many dead lay in the snow. Tillet fell
3540　　To the Americans, Hundred and First
　　　　Airborne advanced towards Noville. Patton
　　　　Pressed towards Houffalize, but then halted,
　　　　For SHAEF feared a German attempt to take
　　　　Luxembourg City. Collins pressed down on
3545　　The Bulge from the north and fought for Bihain,
　　　　Petit Langlir and Samrée. Both sides took
　　　　Exhausted troops into their reserves. Now
　　　　The German offensive at Bastogne was
　　　　Over. Some Germans left for Alsace and
3550　　Then the Americans took Bonnerue, St.
　　　　Hubert, Pironpré, Amberloup, Sprimont,
　　　　Mande St. Etienne, Flamizoulle and Wardin.
　　　　East of Bastogne, infantry took Doncols
　　　　And Bray and encircled a thousand men,
3555　　German paratroopers. SS Panzers
　　　　Tried to reach the trapped men, who were destroyed
　　　　In fierce tank battles. To the north General
　　　　Bolling now cleared La Roche, a deep ravine
　　　　In the Ourthe valley. Americans took
3560　　Langlir and Chabrehez, and at Stavelot
　　　　Took the crossing across the Amblève which
　　　　Peiper had seized nearly a month before.

　　　　The Soviet winter offensive began.
　　　　Hitler sent the Sixth Panzer Army east
3565　　And withdrew other tanks to Houffalize.
　　　　The Americans pressed towards St. Vith.
　　　　Ridgway pincered Volksgrenadiers, and when
　　　　They escaped, replaced a commander. VII
　　　　Corps saw Patton's guns flash in the south sky
3570　　Like distant summer lightning on the snow,
　　　　Beyond the horizon. Patton's forces
　　　　Surrounded Bertogne and took Compogne, while
　　　　Hundred and First Airborne briefly took Foy,

Then took Bertogne and Noville. Round Stavelot,
3575 La Roche and Bastogne the Americans
Attacked while the British were made reserves.
The Americans crossed the Ourthe, taking
Nadrin, Wibrin and Berismenil, and
Harmon's tanks, clanking through hamlets, headed
3580 For Houffalize. The River Salm was crossed,
But the Germans counter-attacked. Now at
Houffalize, US First and Third Armies
Pincered, Hodges' and Patton's men, and were
Reunited under Bradley's command.

3585 The battle ebbed and flowed in the white snow.
Attack followed counter-attack, hamlets
Changed hands and back. Hundred and First Airborne
Finally took Bourcy and Hardigny,
And Patton attacked the base of the Bulge
3590 Across the Sûre, round Diekirch and the Sauer
To Echternach. The Americans took
Courtil, Petit Thier, Vielsalm and
Burtonville. Volksgrenadiers defended
Recht and Poteau, and Model reinforced
3595 Deidenberg, which controlled roads to St. Vith.
Fearing the Germans would escape the Bulge
Patton crossed the icy Sauer before
Dawn in snow, took Erpeldange, and by-passed
Bettendorf and Diekirch, which were secured.
3600 In snowstorms and snow-drifts the Germans fought
From the Meuse to the Moselle, and fell back
To the West Wall. In a blizzard the Ourthe
Was reached, and, next day, Deidenberg. Model
Sent reserves to block the Americans
3605 North of the Sauer; they fought for Fouhren and
Gave up Lipperscheid, Bourscheid and Kehmen.
The Americans headed for Hoscheid, which
Lay on a hill. German reserves held it.
Now Hitler transferred Sepp Dietrich's SS
3610 Army and Führer troops to the eastern
Front, and ordered a stand by the West Wall.
Out of fuel and spare parts, Germans left their
Vehicles on snow-blocked roads, and fled on foot.

Clear weather came and from the cloudless sky
3615 The US pilots saw a queue of stalled
German vehicles across the Our valley,

Which they bombed. Now the retreat was a rout.
Soldiers on foot took cover as fighter-
Planes swooped and bombed and strafed. As fish dart in
3620 A stream small men veered off. And now General
Clarke led 7th Armoured back to St. Vith
And after a delay at new road-blocks,
Entered the ruins and threw out the same
Volksgrenadiers who had ejected him
3625 A month before. Patton cleared eastwards of
The River Our, and threatened Gemünd while
North-east the Americans fought west of
The Our and took villages. The Germans
Were retreating from the Ardennes back to
3630 The West Wall and towards Hungary, yielding
Moderscheid, Büllingen and Wallerode.
In the south the Americans at last
Captured Hoscheid, Heinerscheid, Grindhausen,
Wilwerwiltz, Merscheid and Clervaux, close to
3635 The Germans' starting-point. In the north they
Took Heppenbach, Herresbach, Hepscheid, and,
Along the Our, Weiler, Wahlhausen and
Holzthum; then Drauffelt, Hosingen and Pintsch,
And fierce fighting took place around Putscheid
3640 While Seventh Army fled across the Our.
Eighty-second Airborne flushed out Germans,
Like pheasants, from the snow-thick forests near
Holzheim, Losheim, Lanzerath. Wirtzfeld and
Rocherath-Krinkelt fell to the US.
3645 The Americans crossed the Our into
Germany. Now Belgium and Luxembourg
Were liberated, and all German troops
Were inside their own frontier. Again
The Allies occupied the lines they held
3650 On December the sixteenth, and Hitler's
Ardennes offensive had at last ended
In defeat, not one tank across the Meuse.

The Americans lost ten thousand killed,
Nearly fifty thousand wounded and more
3655 Than twenty thousand missing while they fought
The Battle of the Bulge, and the Germans'
Losses were more, and they could not replace
The hundreds of Panzers lost in the snow;
Though Wacht am Rhein nearly split the Allied
3660 Command, Eisenhower, who had sought to be

293

Even-handed between the Americans
And British, knew he should have followed his
Subordinates' advice – cut the Germans
Off at the base of the Bulge as Bradley,
3665 Patton and Hodges wished – and not preferred
Montgomery's cautious advance against
The Germans at the Bulge's tip. Hitler
Knew he should have backed Fifth Panzers' success,
Not reinforced Sixth Panzers' failure; and
3670 That, once Antwerp was unattainable,
He should have surrounded the Americans
Round St. Vith and the high Elsenborn ridge
And destroyed them against the River Meuse.
He knew he should have attacked Bastogne in
3675 One all-out massive onslaught, not piecemeal.
He knew he should have sent his reserves east
As soon as it was clear the west had held.
Hitler had weakened the Americans
And had protected the Ruhr for a while.

3680 As in an earthquake Europe was shattered;
Many towns and villages were destroyed –
Malmédy, St. Vith, Houffalize, La Roche,
Wiltz, Clervaux, Vianden and Echternach –
As the traditional European
3685 Culture, with its medieval spires and
Beauty, fractured before a cruel present.
Hitler's fissure had riven the continent.
So ended the greatest American
Battle of the war and hardest victory,
3690 Which, by drawing German divisions out
Of hiding, destroying and leaving them
Too short of strength and undermanned to block
The Soviet offensive, shortened the war.
As a matador sticks darts in a bull
3695 And weakens to a sway its token charge
So it is open to a thrusting sword
Between the horns into its neck as it
Watches bemused the bullfighter's red cape,
So Eisenhower had weakened Germany,
3700 Which was at the mercy of Stalin's sword.